Atheism or Theism?

Atheism or Theism?

The Perspective of Saïd Nursi

Hakan Gök

WIPF & STOCK · Eugene, Oregon

ATHEISM OR THEISM?
The Perspective of Saïd Nursi

Wipf and Stock Publishers
199 W. 8th Ave., Suite 3
Eugene, OR 97401

www.wipfandstock.com

PAPERBACK ISBN: 978-1-5326-4679-9
HARDCOVER ISBN: 978-1-5326-4680-5
EBOOK ISBN: 978-1-5326-4681-2

Cataloguing-in-Publication data:

Names: Gök, Hakan, author.

Title: Atheism or theism? : the perspective of Saïd Nursi / Hakan Gök.

Description: Eugene, OR: Wipf & Stock Publishers, 2018 | Includes bibliographical references and index.

Identifiers: ISBN 978-1-5326-4679-9 (paperback) | ISBN 978-1-5326-4680-5 (hardcover) | ISBN 978-1-5326-4681-2 (ebook)

Subjects: LCSH: Nursi, Said, 1873–1960 | God—Proof, Cosmological | Islamic philosophy | Islam and science | Religion and ethics

Classification: BP253.Z8 2018 (print) | BP253.Z8 (ebook)

Manufactured in the U.S.A. 08/21/18

To Ariane Stoll

Contents

Acknowledgements | ix
Note on transliteration and Sources | xi
Introduction | xiii

1. Thesim and Atheism: Historical Background | 1
2. A Brief Biography of Saïd Nursi | 43
3. The Teleological Argument | 64
4. Prophethood (*Nubuwwah*) | 98
5. Revelations [*Waḥy*] | 131
6. Morality and Conscience | 164
7. Analysis and Conclusion | 200

Appendices
Appendix 1: Chronology and Diagram of the *Risale-i Nur* Collection | 213
Appendix 2: Names and Attributes of God in Islam | 215
Appendix 3: Elements in the Human Body | 220
Appendix 4: Marriages of the Prophet Muḥammad (571-632) in Chronological Order | 221
Appendix 5: The Names and Characteristics of the Prophets Mentioned in the Qur'ān | 223
Appendix 6: Major Sins (*Al-Kaba'ir*) in Islam Deduced from the Qur'an and the *Hadīth* | 225
Appendix 7: Nursi's Exposition of The Qur'an's Miraculousness | 228
Appendix 8: Chronology of the Prophet Muḥammad's Life | 230

Acknowledgements

DURING THE WRITING OF this book many people have helped me with their knowledge and expertise. It is my duty to express my gratitude to these immensely supportive colleagues and friends.

First and foremost, I would like to thank my inspirer and chief motivator Colin Turner for his invaluable support. I would like to thank fellow colleagues Hasan Horkuç, Ömer Kuru, and Dusmamat Karimov for their academic and technical support.

I would like to express my gratitude to Abdullah Aymaz for his scholarly input.

Last but not least, my gratitude goes to Durham University, Mevlana University and Leeds Beckett University where this book came into being.

Acknowledgments

Note on Transliteration

Saïd Nursi lived during the last years of the Ottoman Empire and the first decades of modern Turkey. In these two periods, two different alphabets were used. During the Ottoman Empire era, the Arabic alphabet was used and terminology was dominantly influenced by the Arabic language, whereas the post-1923 era (i.e., the Turkish Republic era) sees the introduction of the Latin alphabet and the uses of relatively more non-Arabic terminology. Therefore, Nursi's *magnum opus* The Epistles of Light (*Risale-i Nur)* contains Ottoman Turkish, Arabic and modern Turkish terminologies.

In this book, I try to use the transliteration of Arabic and Ottoman Turkish terms and names: al-Fārābī, not Alfarabi, Qur'an, not Koran, Muḥammad, not Muhammad for example. I generally followed the transliteration system used in the United States *Library of Congress.*

Note on sources

The *Risale-i Nur* Collection has been translated into English and published by several publishers. Throughout this book, I use Nesil Publication's twin-volume *Risale-i Nur Külliyatı* published in 2004 in Turkish.[1] English translations are cited from eRisale.com using the actual page numbers from Nesil's hard-copy books. Therefore, the page numbers cited in this book might differ from those given on the eRisale.com websites.

The citations of the Qur'an are taken directly from the Ali Ünal's "*The Qur'an with Annotated Interpretation in Modern English*"

1. See Saïd Nursi, *Risale-i Nur Külliyati 1* (Istanbul: Nesil, 1994) and *Risale-i Nur Külliyati 2* (Istanbul: Nesil, 2004).

Introduction

THE RECORDED HISTORY OF philosophy goes as far back as the fourth century BC, the era of great ancient Greek philosophers such as Socrates (470–399 BC), Plato (428–347 BC), and Aristotle (384–322 BC). These philosophers all tried to answer the famous age-old question: "Is there a God?"

Perhaps the unrecorded predecessors of these philosophers had been preoccupied with the same question. Let us assume the starting point of philosophy as the fourth century BC and travel through time. Along the way, we come across many more philosophers who also tackled the same issue of the existence or non-existence of God.

St Anselm (1033–1109), Roger Bacon (1220–92), and St Thomas Aquinas (1224–74) are some of the medieval philosophers of the European Christian tradition who dealt with the same matter. It is commonly accepted among academics that modern philosophy was born with the work of René Descartes (1596–1650). In his famous work *Meditations*, he introduced the idea of the necessity of God's existence. In the same century and the next, John Locke (1632–1704), Gottfried Leibniz (1646–1716), George Berkeley (1685–1753), and Voltairc (1694 1778) took part in the debate.

When we reach eighteenth-century Europe, we find the criticism of the theistic argument presented by David Hume (1711–76). Also, the great German philosopher Emmanuel Kant (1724–1804) appeared with his *Critique of Pure Reason.*

Bertrand Russell (1872–1970) and Ludwig Wittgenstein (1899–1951) were two of the thinkers who contributed to the argument in the nineteenth and twentieth century. The debate never cooled down in the twentieth century as A. J. Ayer (1910–89), J. L. Mackie (1917–81), and Richard Swinburne (1934–) are some of the philosophers who have worked in the field.

Atheism and theism are the main topics of this book. J. L. Mackie defines theism as:

> . . . the doctrine that there is god, and in particular a god conceived in the central tradition of the main monotheistic religions, including Judaism, Christianity and Islam.[2]

Throughout this book, when I refer to God, I shall adopt Swinburne's definition of the God of monotheism, which is commonly agreed upon by all as follows:

> God is a person without a body (i.e., Spirit), present everywhere (i.e., Omnipresent), the creator and the sustainer of the universe, a free agent, able to do everything (i.e., Omnipotent), knowing all things (i.e., Omniscient), perfectly good, a source of moral obligation, immutable, eternal, a necessary being, holy, and worthy of worship.[3]

Since the atheism-theism debate is at the center of all three Abrahamic religions, it deserves to be studied from a wider perspective than the mainstream Western Christian one. To give it a fair hearing, I shall also examine the Jewish and Muslim philosophical worlds.

Although there are a lot of conflicts among these Abrahamic religions, all three have in common the concept of monotheism, the belief in the existence of one God, with different names but almost the same qualities in all three religions. All these faith groups agree that there is a god who created man and the universe.

Two of the most famous Jewish philosophers we mention in this study are Saadia (882–942) and Maimonides (1135–1204), who made their own contribution to theistic philosophy, especially to the cosmological argument.

When we examine the Islamic tradition, we find five remarkable philosophers and/or *mutakallimūn* who massively influenced and shaped the Muslim world. They are al-Kindī (801–43), al-Fārābī (872–950), Ibn Sina, also known as Avicenna (980–1037), al-Ghazzālī (1058–1111), and Ibn Rushd (1126–98), also known as Averroes. These Muslim theologians and philosophers are remarkable in the sense that they are the forefathers of the *kalām* cosmological argument, which is the version of the cosmological argument recently reintroduced in modern philosophy by William L. Craig.[4]

Saïd Nursi said that he had dedicated his life to prove that there is God, the Creator and the Sustainer of the universe, and that nothing can come

2. Mackie, *The Miracle of Theism*, 1.

3. Swinburne, *The Coherence of Theism*, 2.

4. William L. Craig is widely accepted as the modern philosopher who rediscovered this unique version of the cosmological argument. See Craig, *The Kalam Cosmological Argument*.

into existence by pure chance.[5] He tackles the atheist views on the meaning of life and the origin of the universe by using several theistic arguments, such as the teleological arguments, the moral arguments, the arguments from miracles, and the arguments from religious experience.

Aims and objectives of this book

The overall aim of this study is to explore how the existence of God is argued for and against in general, and how Saïd Nursi contributes to these arguments.

The key objectives of the study are to identify the arguments for the existence of God since the times of the ancient Greeks, including Jewish, Christian, and Muslim scholars and philosophers, to determine what kind of counterarguments have been developed to refute these theistic arguments, to review *Risale-i Nur* in order to find out about Saïd Nursi's theistic arguments, to identify Nursian defence against the atheists' and skeptics' claims, to locate Nursi among other philosophers and theologians, and to identify novel inputs of Nursi to the debate between theism and atheism.

Outline of the book

This book consists of six chapters, an introduction and a conclusion.

Chapter 1 is the general historical overview of literature from the ancients to modern-day philosophers. Here, I try to establish how the arguments concerning atheism-theism have developed from pagan communities like that of ancient Greece to the Jewish, Christian and Muslim communities. The main theistic arguments explained in this chapter are the ontological arguments, cosmological arguments, the teleological arguments, and arguments from miracles, from morality, and from religious experience. Chapter 1 also highlights the criticisms of these theistic arguments with special reference to the problem of evil and suffering, the problem of hell, and theological non-cognitivism. This chapter forms the bedrock of the study in terms of laying out what is already out there. The arguments and counterarguments set out here are re-examined in the following chapters from Nursian point of view.

Chapter 2 examines Saïd Nursi's life, which spread over the end of the Islam-ruled Ottoman Empire era to the first decades of the secular Republic

5. *Risâle-i Nur Külliyatı müellifi Bediüzzaman Saïd Nursî: Tarihçe-i Hayat* in Nursi, *Risale-i Nur Külliyati* 2, 2109–242.

of Turkey. His method of struggle against disbelief (*jihād*) is also examined here. Certain original terminology developed by Nursi is explored here. Concepts such as 'the book of universe' (*kitāb-ı kāināt*), the self or the human 'I' (*anā*), the 'self-referential' and the 'other-indicative' (*ma'nà-i ismī,* and *ma'nà-i ḥarfī)* are looked at.

Chapter 3's focus is on Saïd Nursi's first and most frequently used argument for the existence of God, which is essentially the design argument, even though Nursi calls it 'the great book of the universe' argument (*kitāb-ı kabīr-i kāināt*). Here, we examine Nursi's attempt to refute the three atheistic assumptions of how things might have come into existence. These are: nature as creator (*iqtaẓathu al-ṭabīʿah)*, self-creation (*tashakkala bi nafsihi)*, and causes as creator (*aʿwjadathu al-asbāb*). We also examine Nursi's answers to the Darwinian explanation of existence.

Chapter 4 examines Nursi's arguments for the existence of God through prophethood (*nubuwwah*). Here, the criticisms to the arguments from religious experience are discussed and Nursi's approach to the problems is analyzed.

In Chapter 5, we study Nursi's third argument, the argument from scriptures (*waḥy*). Nursi's arguments to support the idea that the Qur'an is the genuine revelation of God and, hence, the proof for His existence, are examined.

And finally, Chapter 6 explores the Nursian and the atheist arguments of morality and conscience (*wijdān* or *fiṭrat-ı bashar)* and how they could be or could not be the proof for the existence of a deity.

This book is not about establishing whether theism or atheism has a stronger case. Instead, it attempts to understand the Nursian philosophy and determine whether it contains any originality.

1

Theism and Atheism

Historical Background

Introduction

In the philosophy of religion, five theistic arguments among many stand out as defending the existence of God. Before focusing on Saïd Nursi's philosophy, we begin by setting out the existing basis of theism and atheism. Although there is no evidence that monotheism existed in ancient Greece, and we are mainly concerned with the God of monotheism, the thoughts of the ancient Greek philosophers are still considered, owing to their philosophical significance for and influence upon later monotheism. The theistic arguments to be examined in this chapter are: the ontological arguments; the cosmological arguments; the teleological arguments; the arguments from morality and conscience; and the arguments from miracles and religious experience. The main criticisms that may be leveled at each of these arguments are also examined.

Concept of God

The ontological meaning of the concept of God—the creator and ruler of the universe and source of all moral authority; the Supreme Being with regard to knowledge (omniscience), power (omnipotence), and extension (omnipresence)—seems to be accepted by all Abrahamic religions. The concepts of God in philosophy and in religion are interwoven. Although the existence of a Supreme Being is widely accepted in philosophy and religion, there are certainly different versions of God throughout history and across religions.

The Ancient Greeks

The ancient Greeks dealt with the concept of God at an early stage of their known history. Plato and Aristotle both consider God to be the crafter of the universe and of uncreated matter. Plato does not subscribe to the idea of monotheism, that is, one Supreme Being. He observes the planetary movements and concludes that there must be supreme powers behind all these celestial events. There is clear evidence that Plato believed in the existence of gods (*hoi theoi*) rather than of God (*ho theos*). To him, different gods are responsible for different events. This is also evident in ancient Greek literature, where there are mentions of gods such as Zeus, Prometheus, Aphrodite, and Athene.

Aristotle's description of God as unmoved mover is different from that of Plato. To Aristotle, God's divine existence is apparent through perfection and change in the universe. Aristotle perceives God as the detached transcendent demiurge, the highest being, the apex of knowledge and uncreated matter—but not necessarily as loving.

Plotinus also accepts the existence of God with different qualities. He claims that God is the source of the universe: that is, the universe comes out of God (*ex deo*) in a timeless process. He rejects creation, since this would imply consciousness and will, which limits God. For Plotinus, God is Most Virtuous and Most Truthful.

Ashqar makes the criticism that the gods of the ancient Greeks are like normal people. They have gender (e.g., Zeus is male and Aphrodite female), they have weaknesses, and they have emotions. He writes:

> Zeus was the chief of their gods. . . . Their image of him was closer to the image of devil than of a god. He was filled with hatred and enmity, preoccupied with his desires for food and love. He cared nothing for the affairs of gods or men, unless they could help him to maintain his hold on power and persist in his tyranny.[1]

Ashqar, therefore, concludes that the ancient Greek concept of God is fundamentally in contradiction with that of monotheism, especially Islam.

The Jews

The concept of God in Judaism is very similar to that of Islam. Maimonides' thirteen principles of faith describe the Jewish God openly. The essential

1. Ashqar and Khattab, *Belief in Allah*, 430.

qualities of the Jewish God, according to Maimonides, are as follows. God exists; God is one; God is incorporeal; He has no body; He is non-physical; God is eternal, that is, He has no beginning or no end; He transcends time; God is omnipresent, omniscient, and omnipotent; God will reward good and punish evil.[2] Ashqar argues that the Jews deviated from the true *tawḥīd* (Oneness of God), and descended to the level of idolatrous concepts like that of the ancient Greeks.[3]

The West

Western concepts of God have developed around Greek and Islamic philosophy. Like the ancient Greeks, the Christian West has divided opinions about God. Early Christians such as Tertullian (160–220) rejected Greek philosophy on the basis that it professed a number of unworthy views, whereas American Lutheran Christian scholar Martin E. Marty (1928–) believed that Christianity is compatible with the highest in Greek thought.

Augustine of Hippo (354–430) developed a theme similar to that of Plato, Socrates, and Zeno. His definition of God is: "something than which nothing more excellent or sublime exists." He lives in the highest sense, and is the most powerful, most righteous, most beautiful, most good, most blessed. According to Augustine, God did not have to create, but did so as an act of love. However, Augustine disagrees with Socrates as regards whether the greatest being (i.e., God) must be aware only of himself. Augustine says that God created men and all creatures, and incarnated in Christ in order to be revealed to them.[4]

St Anselm (1033–1109) employed the concept of "perfect being," making it the foundation of his ontological argument.[5] To Anselm, God is the highest being, under which there are lesser and lesser beings.

Thomas Aquinas (1225–74) believed that the knowledge of God could be obtained through reason and revelations. In this respect, he seems to be in agreement with Aristotle and many other Christians of his day. Although he accepts the gradation of form and matter, he claims that God is non-material, but has pure intelligence and activity. Aquinas's God is a God of Love, and providential.

2. For a lengthy discussion of the concept, see Birnbaum, *A Book of Jewish Concepts*.
3. Ashqar and Khattab, *Belief in Allah*, 432.
4. See Augustine, *On the Trinity. Books 8–15*.
5. See Chapter 1 for St Anselm's ontological argument.

During the Enlightenment, deism, which regards reason as the only source of knowledge, emerged as a new form of theism.[6] Physicists such as Kepler, Boyle, and Newton explained the mechanics of the universe within the laws of physics. Newton maintained that "there is no room for an outside cause in the universe"; hence he rejected the existence of a First Cause.[7] Deists based their argument for natural religion on Newton's claims.

The attribute of "benevolence" has been introduced into the concept of God by René Descartes (1596–1650). Descartes believed that God is benevolent, therefore He cannot mislead us. Descartes claimed that God is the uncaused cause, but He is his own cause. John Locke (1632–1704) believed that God could not be known by reason alone. Revelation helps us to understand God. Revelations do not violate reason; otherwise they cannot be accepted as revelation. Hence, reason must judge the truthfulness of revelation. In agreement with Descartes, Spinoza suggested that God is the source of causality. George Berkeley (1685–1753), the empiricist, argued that God is the source of perception. Hume accepted Berkeley's empiricism, but held the skeptical view that the concept of God must be rooted in the emotions and not reason alone.

With Kant (1724–1804), the objective concept of God became subjective. Kant argued that knowledge acquired through reason does not offer a way of knowing God. God can neither be demonstrated nor disproved. Ultimate reality is unknowable and unattainable. According to Kant, God has a regulative value, and is a source of morality. While Nietzsche (1844–1900) completely rejected God as a weak and untenable concept, Freud (1856–1939) regarded God as a projection of mind, and a product of wishful thinking.[8]

God in Islam and in the *Risale-i Nur*

Islam is unique in the sense that it uses the term "*Allāh*" in reference to God. Linguistically, *Allāh* cannot be male, female, or plural, although the attributes given to *Allāh* are generally masculine. The term "*Allāh*" comes from Aramaic,[9] the language of Jesus. The term "*Allāh*" can only be used

6. See Encyclopaedia Britannica at http://www.britannica.com/EBchecked/topic/156154/Deism

7. For Newton's views on God, see Newton, *Newton's Philosophy of Nature: Selections from His Writings.*

8. Morley, *Western Concepts of God*, IEP (2005) at http://www.iep.utm.edu/god-west/

9. The Aramaic language was the international trade language of the ancient Middle East. Originating in what is modern-day Syria between 1000 and 600 B CE, it became

to denote the God of Islam. By contrast, the term "God" did not mean a specific being for the ancient Greeks. Similarly, the Christian definition of God might be confusing, since the doctrine of the Trinity is a very common teaching in the church. The doctrine of the Trinity,[10] formulated in the fourth century AD, essentially attributes deity to the three persons: the Father, the Son, and the Holy Spirit. Christian theologians still struggle to justify this doctrine, since Christianity is a monotheistic religion, insisting on the unity of the one God.

Although some Islamic philosophers, such as Al-Fārābī, Ibn Sina, Al-Ghazzālī and Ibn Rushd, gave philosophical explanations for God's nature, the solid description of God is always derived from the Qur'an. In *Sūrat al-'Ikhlās* (The Sincerity), the Qur'an says: "He is *Allāh*, [who is] One, the Eternal Refuge. He neither begets nor is born, nor is there to Him any equivalent." Throughout the Qur'an, *tawḥīd* (the oneness of God) is always the main emphasis. This is due to the context applying at the time of the revelation, when the concept of God had been corrupted by inventions such as the doctrine of the Trinity, and the idolatrous culture of the Arabs. Before Islam, Arabs had the religion of the prophets Abraham and Ishmael, who taught *tawḥīd* (the Oneness of God). However, they later deviated from *tawḥīd* and started worshipping stone idols. They had many idols, which were kept inside *al-Ka'bah* (the Sacred House in Mecca), and worshipped them. The practice of the prophet Abraham's *Hajj* changed, from worshipping God to worshipping idols. Arabs travelled to Mecca and circumambulated the *Ka'bah*. The pre-Islamic period (*jāhiliyyah*) in the Arabian Peninsula saw a great many strange religious practices. People used to carry stones to worship; when they had found a better-looking stone, they would throw away the stone they were worshipping and begin worshipping the new stone. People used to carry four stones on their travels. Three of these were used to rest their cooking pot on, and one of them was worshipped. Among the many idols of the pagan Arabs, three were particularly famous and are mentioned in the Qur'an. These were *Manāt*, *Al-Lāt* and *al-Uzzā*. On the day of the conquest of Mecca, the prophet Muḥammad was reported to have found

---

extremely widespread, spoken from the Mediterranean coast to the borders of India.

10. The concept of the Trinity was formulated at three councils. At the Council of Nicaea in 325 AD it was claimed that Jesus was of the same substance as God the Father, and therefore he was declared divine. At the Council of Constantinople I in 38 AD, they confirmed the teachings of the council of Nicaea and expanded: the Holy Spirit is also fully divine; thus the Trinity has one divine 'nature,' but three distinct 'persons.' It was in 451 AD, at the Council of Chalcedon, that the Trinity was declared authoritative. Debates on the matter were no longer tolerated; to speak out against the Trinity was now considered blasphemy.

three hundred and sixty idols in different shapes and sizes in Ka'bah and to have destroyed them.[11]

In fighting for the re-establishment of *tawḥīd*, the Qur'an frequently mentions the Oneness of God and his attributes.[12] *Sūrat al-Ḥashr* (The Gathering) describes the God of Islam (Allāh). Verses 59:22–24 read:

> He is Allāh, other than whom there is no deity, knower of the unseen and the witnessed. He is the entirely merciful, the especially merciful. He is Allāh, other than whom there is no deity, the sovereign, the pure, the perfection, the bestower of faith, the overseer, the exalted in might, the compeller, the superior. Exalted is Allāh above whatever they associate with him. He is Allāh, the creator, the inventor, the fashioner; to him belong the best names. Whatever is in the heavens and earth is exalting him. And he is the exalted in might, the wise.[13]

The Qur'an also addresses the people of the book (Christians and Jews), correcting their false beliefs in God. *Sūrat al-Nisā* (The Women) 4:171 explains:

> O People of the Scripture, do not commit excess in your religion or say about Allāh except the truth. The Messiah, Jesus, the son of Mary, was but a messenger of Allāh and his word which he directed to Mary and a soul [created at a command] from him. So believe in Allāh and his messengers. And do not say, "Three"; desist—it is better for you. Indeed, Allāh is but one God. Exalted is He above having a son. To him belongs whatever is in the heavens and whatever is on the earth. And sufficient is Allāh as Disposer of affairs.[14]

The Qur'an discusses the position of Christians and Jews in various chapters. It announces that those who adhere to the Oneness of God will be saved; however, those who deviate from *tawḥīd* will be punished. In *Sūrat al-Mā'idah* (The Table Spread) 5:73, the Qur'an says:

> They have certainly disbelieved who say, "Allāh is the third of three." And there is no god except one God. And if they do not

11. For a detailed description of the pre-Islamic era in the Arabian Peninsula see Ashqar and Khattab, *Belief in Allah*, 443–54.

12. See Appendix 2: The Names and Attributes of God in Islam.

13. Qur'an, 59:22–24.

14. Qur'an, 4:171.

> desist from what they are saying, there will surely afflict the disbelievers among them a painful punishment.[15]

Nursi, in his *Risale-i Nur*, considers the Qur'an to be the only source of knowledge. It aims, he says, to explain four important concepts of Islam. These are *tawḥīd* (Oneness of God), *nubuwwah* (prophethood), *ḥashr* (resurrection), and *'adalah* (justice). Nursi systematically explores God's attributes throughout his work. Instead of using the term "*Allāh*," which is mentioned in the Qur'an 2,806 times, Nursi prefers to use the names and attributes of God which are apparent in a particular context. For instance, when he explains order in nature, where there is apparent cooperation between creatures in terms of supporting each other's life, Nursi tells us that this is the work of *Razzāq al-Karīm* (The Generous Sustainer). When he mentions the beautiful work of God in nature, he calls God *Ṣāni al-Raḥmān* (The Compassionate Artist). Some of Nursi's descriptive phrases for God are: *Fāṭir-i Ḥakīm* (The All-Powerful Creator), *'Ādil al-Muṭlaq* (The Absolute Just), *Wājib al-Wujūd* (The Necessarily Existent), *Wāḥid al-Aḥad* (The Single One of Unity), *Qādir al-Zuljalāl* (The All-Powerful One of Glory), *Khāliq-i kulli shay* (The Creator of All Things), *Mudabbir-al Ḥakīm* (The Lowing Career), *Qahhār-i zul-Jalāl* (The Compelling One of Glory).[16] These are the attributes regarding God's power and wisdom that the human mind can comprehend. However, some characteristics of God are said to be incomprehensible, such as his Hand, his Face, and him sitting on his Throne,[17] since these are in no way within the framework of human intelligence. Nursi criticizes philosophers such as al-Fārābī and Ibn-i Sina on the basis that they try to attain knowledge mainly through reason. He seems to be in alliance with Al-Ghazzālī, who rejects joining theology with philosophy since mind and senses are subject to error. To Al-Ghazzālī, truth must come from Divine Grace, not mind and senses. In this sense, Al-Fārābī, Ibn-i Sina and their like could only attain the faith-level of an ordinary Muslim, despite their great level of intelligence.[18]

15. Qur'an, 5:73.

16. Nursi, *The Rays*, 865–72.

17. The verses such as Qur'an 55:27, "And there will remain the Face of your Lord, Owner of Majesty and Honor" and Qur'an 38:75, "Allāh said, O *Iblīs* (Devil), what prevented you from prostrating to that which I created with My hands? Were you arrogant then, or were you already among the haughty?" and Qur'an 2:225, ". . . his throne included the heavens and the earth, and He is never weary of preserving them . . ." have always been controversial among scholars in terms of explaining God's hand, face or throne.

18. Nursi, *The Words*, 245.

Ontological Arguments

Originally mentioned implicitly by Plato and formulated by Ibn Sina (Avicenna) in the eleventh century, the ontological argument was introduced into Western philosophy for the first time by St Anselm (*c.*1033–1109), the Archbishop of Canterbury.

After staying dormant for some three hundred years, it was revived by René Descartes (1596–1650) in the seventeenth century. In the twentieth century, Alvin Plantinga (1932–), Norman Malcolm (1911–1990), and Charles Hartshorne (1897–2000) all developed new interpretations of the argument.

Each of these theist philosophers had to face certain kinds of opposition. For instance, Monk Gaunilo, a contemporary of St Anselm, Thomas Aquinas (1224–74), and David Hume (1711–1776) tried to refute St Anselm's version of the argument. Immanuel Kant (1724–1804) produced some serious criticisms of Descartes and Cartesian philosophy. Bertrand Russell (1872–1970), Anthony Flew (1923–2010), and Nicholas Everitt have been the leading modern critics of the ontological arguments.

The ontological arguments may be represented in terms of three different versions, and these are discussed in turn.

St Anselm's Version

The original and the most basic form of the ontological argument came from St Anselm, Archbishop of Canterbury in 1078. St Anselm explained that if we talk about or think about a being than which nothing greater could be conceived, this being must exist not only in mind but also in reality. He calls this being "God."[19] In his *Proslogion*, St Anselm argues that denial of the existence of God is absurd since, by definition, God is a being than which nothing greater could be conceived. Inspired by a psalm,[20] St Anselm names his imaginary atheist friend "the fool." The fool says "There is no god." St Anselm asks him to think about a being than which nothing greater can be imagined. The fool understands this and accepts the existence of this being in his mind; however, he denies his existence in reality. The case is similar to that of a painting which exists in the artist's mind but not in reality. Here, St Anselm remarks that the fool is contradicting himself. If the being existed only in the fool's mind, he could not be the being than which

19. Anselm, *Proslogion*, Chapter 4.

20. Psalms, 53:1: The fool has said in his heart: There is no God. Corrupt are they, and have done abominable iniquity: there is none that does good.

nothing greater could be conceived. Surely, the being which exists only in the mind is not the greatest being, as it lacks the ultimate quality of existing in reality. Therefore, in his own words, St Anselm concludes:

> . . . there is absolutely no doubt that something than-which-nothing-greater-could-be-thought exists both in mind and in reality.[21]

St Anselm received his first criticism from his contemporary, Monk Gaunilo of Marmoutiers, another man of God. Gaunilo argued that if Anselm's theory proves the existence of God, it also proves the existence of his imaginary "lost island," which is full of every conceivable delight.[22] Gaunilo explains that "the lost island" could exist in minds but not necessarily in reality. Since both cases are highly parallel, Gaunilo believes that Anselm's ontological argument fails to prove the existence of God.

However, Plantinga, the twentieth-century ally of St Anselm, disagrees with Gaunilo. Plantinga argues that there is no such thing as a "perfect island." The concept of a perfect island is impossibilistic.[23] Whichever way such an island might be described, there could be one better in terms of size, shape, climate, etc., whereas there are no contradictions in St Anselm's definition of the ultimate being.

During a conference, when challenged by a member of the audience, Craig responded similarly, that the perfect conceivable being is possible and is understood in the same way by every mind; however, "Perfect Island" could have an infinite number of different descriptions.[24]

Hume, without mentioning St Anselm's name or his ontological argument, offered a comment on existence which was another blow against St Anselm. According to Hume, when we think of something we think of it as existent. This, however, does not automatically prove its existence: that is, anyone can think of a unicorn, but this is not proof of the existence of the unicorn.

Two centuries after the first appearance of St Anselm's version, Aquinas put his objection forward. Despite being a theist himself and a powerful advocate of the cosmological argument, Aquinas claimed that the existence of God could not be proven by defining God. He explained that the self-evidence of something is related to the natural knowledge of that thing within individuals. Since we do not know the essence of God, the proposition is

21. Anselm, *Proslogion*, 87–88.

22. Everitt, *The Non-Existence of God*, 34.

23. Ibid.

24. William Lane Craig's lectures on the Existence of God lectures can be found in many popular video-sharing sites.

not self-evident to us, but needs to be demonstrated by things that are better known to us.[25]

Norman Malcolm and Charles Hartshorne both agree that there are two versions of St Anselm's ontological argument. The first assumption is that existence in reality is greater than existence in mind alone. One of the properties of the greatest being is existence. Since Kant proved that existence is not a property, Malcolm and Hartshorne agree that this first version fails. Taking his cue from St Anselm's reply to Gaunilo, Malcolm points out that, in the second version of St Anselm's argument, the concept of existence is treated differently. Existence-as-a-matter-of-necessity is perfection. A being that exists in some possible worlds has only contingent existence, whereas a being that exists in every possible world has existence-as-a-matter-of-necessity (i.e., necessary existence).

René Descartes' Version

The second version of the ontological argument arose some six hundred years after St Anselm. René Descartes' ontological argument is a mathematics/geometry-based piece of reasoning. Descartes believed that the existence of God could be proved mathematically. He argued that if the addition of three inner angles gives one hundred and eighty degrees, the shape such angles form can only be that of a triangle. Similarly, the holder of all great qualities must have the quality of existence, since this completes the greatness. Since God has all the great qualities. He is all-wise, all-knowing, all-good. He also must have the quality of existence. Existence belongs to the nature of God. Hence, he exists.[26] Descartes says that though he might be wrong in everything in his *Meditations* he is absolutely sure of one thing, which is the existence of God.

Everitt attempts to discredit Descartes' argument outright, since he considers it ludicrous and worthless. Everitt goes on to make a reverse argument concerning a being called a "shunicorn" which is a supreme unicorn that possesses perfection of existence. This argument seems fairly plausible since, to the atheistic mind, both unicorn and god are invented beings.

One of the sternest critiques of Descartes is that of Immanuel Kant. Kant constructs a fourfold counter-argument. In his first criticism, Kant chooses to deny both subject and predicate in Descartes' statement "God is omnipotent." It is like positing a triangle but rejecting it having three angles. If we reject only the predicate of omnipotence, we might be seen to posit the

25. Hick, *The Existence of God*, 32.

26. Everitt, *The Non-Existence of God*, 37.

concept of God, which is a contradiction. However, if we reject both subject and predicate, there is no contradiction.

In his second criticism, Kant explains that it is unfair to ask someone to enquire open-mindedly whether God exists or not, while describing God as a being possessing all good qualities, including the quality of existence.

Kant's third criticism derives from the distinction between "analytic" and "synthetic" judgments. He asserts that all existential propositions are synthetic. He believes that we cannot make any analytic judgments about existential propositions because they are synthetic assumptions.

In his fourth and final criticism, Kant argues that "being" is not a real predicate. In "God is omnipotent," the subject is "God" and "omnipotent" is the predicate. The word "is" plays a linking role. This appears to be a linguistic issue, rather than a real philosophical contribution to the debate.[27]

Alvin Plantinga's Version

A fresh contribution to the ontological argument was made in the twentieth century by Alvin Plantinga. Unlike Anselm and Descartes, Plantinga's argument draws its premises from two new terms, namely: "maximal excellence" and "possible worlds." Plantinga begins his argument by introducing the idea of excellence. A being is excellent to the extent to which he is knowledgeable, powerful and morally good[28] (God is maximally excellent in omnipotence, omniscience and moral perfection). This excellent being could exist in our world but not necessarily in other possible worlds. Plantinga proceeds to strengthen his argument by talking about a being A, who is excellent in this world, and a being B who is excellent in all other possible worlds. He implies that B is greater than A as its excellence covers wider worlds. Plantinga challenges us to prove the impossibility of the following:

Premise 1: It is possible that something is maximally great.

Premise 2: In this world there exists a being who is omnipotent, omniscient and morally perfect.

This, therefore, implies that God exists.

Plantinga's argument could be challenged on the grounds that the excellent being must have necessary existence, having both moral and intellectual qualities. The first quality of existence could be met by abstract entities such as numbers, concepts, propositions, whereas the second group

27. For Kant's full discussion, see Kant and Smith, *Critique of Pure Reason*, 500–507.

28. Everitt, *The Non-Existence of God*, 42.

of qualities could be met only by people. Everitt claims that Plantinga's argument suffers from a question-begging premise of doubtful intelligibility.[29]

The ontological arguments are arguably the weakest of the theistic arguments in the sense that reverse arguments could easily be developed using this line of thinking. They have been criticized brutally and have been ridiculed by reverse analogies such as pink unicorns, perfect islands, etc. Anselm made a genuine attempt to explain to "the fool" what God is and how he can believe that God really exists without holding any strong philosophical ground. His argument still stands as one of the pillars of theism today.

Cosmological Arguments in the West

The cosmological argument, as the name implies, examines the observable world and the cosmos in order to find the First Cause. Thus, it refers to the contingency of the world. Craig describes the cosmological argument as a *posteriori*[30] argument for a cause or reason for the cosmos.[31] The cosmological arguments are always based on existentialist premises. If something exists, there should be a reason and a cause for its existence. Therefore, the argument is mainly concerned with causality.

Cosmological arguments are among the oldest of the six arguments (i.e., ontological, cosmological, including *kalām*, teleological, moral, arguments from miracles, and argument from religious experience) with which we are concerned. First the pagans of ancient Greece, then from the ninth century AD onwards Muslims, and then Christians (both Catholic and Protestant), Jews, and even pantheists have contributed to them.[32]

The cosmological argument is one of the most durable arguments, owing to the fact that it has received many eloquent testimonies from some of the greatest philosophers of all time. Plato is considered to be the

29. Ibid.

30. Here it might be useful to give the dictionary definition, quoted from IAP: "The terms '*a priori*' and '*a posteriori*' are used primarily to denote the foundations upon which a proposition is known. A given proposition is knowable *a priori* if it can be known independently of any experience other than the experience of learning the language in which the proposition is expressed, whereas a proposition that is knowable *a posteriori* is known on the basis of experience. For example, the proposition that all bachelors are unmarried is *a priori*, and the proposition that it is raining outside now is *a posteriori*."

31. Craig, *The Cosmological Argument from Plato to Leibniz*, x.

32. Ibid., xi.

founding father of this argument. Later, Aristotle was also an advocate of this argument.

The argument remained dormant for around eleven centuries, until the second Islamic empire of the Abbasids started promoting science and *falsafa* through the great translation movement of the Abbasid caliph in the eighth century.[33] It has been reported that the caliph offered gold matching the weight of any book translated into the Abbasid State language of Arabic. This era saw the greatest leap of Islamic science and philosophy. Before the Abbasid era, Arabs were writing only poetry, mainly for political purposes.[34] The first decades of Islam, during the Prophet Muḥammad's life and afterwards under the four righteous caliphs' rule, saw the establishment and spread of Islam. After this, the Umayyads formed what is considered to have been the first Islamic state (661–750 AD). Since it was the first Arab-Islamic state, the Umayyads were mainly concerned with setting up the organs of their state system while spreading Islam further afield. Hence, little or no philosophical progress was made during their eighty-nine-year rule. The Abbasids ended the Umayyads' reign in 750 AD. They then moved the capital city of the new Islamic State from Damascus to Baghdad. The new Islamic State of the Abbasids enjoyed the benefits of translation stemming from the Umayyad era. Now, the new Islamic State was strong, rich and well established. Majid Fakhry suggests that this was why the Abbasids suddenly shifted their attention to science and philosophy.[35]

The Abbasids came into very close contact with the Greeks as their empire expanded. This brought inevitable interaction with Greek culture. Al-Kindī, Ibn Sina, Al-Fārābī and Al-Ghazzālī were chief among the fine philosophers (*mutakallimūn*) this era produced. Ibn Rushd and Ibn Tufayl represent the Western Islamic trend of Muslim Spain, which came to life as a rival principality to that of the Abbasids. During the bloody end of Umayyad rule in Damascus around 750 AD, the Abbasids killed most members of the Umayyad dynasty. The surviving prince of the Umayyads crossed Gibraltar into the Iberian Peninsula, where he set up the Al-Andalus Umayyad State. The new al-Andalus Umayyads, also, benefited from the previous state's experience. They were quick to develop fantastic Andalus cities; hence, scholars quickly flourished under the ruler's protection. The Muslim theologians made a massive contribution to the *kalām* cosmological argument.

33. See Fakhry, *A History of Islamic Philosophy*, 1–33. Chapter 1, The Legacy of Greece, Alexandria, and the Orient, gives very detailed information about this period of Islam.

34. Ibid.

35. Ibid., xxi.

In time, the Greco-Muslim tradition of philosophy passed to Jews such as Saadia and Maimonides, as well as to many Western philosophers such as Anselm, Bonaventura, Aquinas, Duns Scotus, Suarez, Descartes, Spinoza, Berkeley, Locke, and Leibniz.

Saïd Nursi (1877–1960) was the modern-day scholar who used a version of the cosmological argument in his writings, although he heavily criticized some early Muslim philosophers such as Ibn Sina and Fārābī owing to the *Mu'tazilah* influence on their thinking.[36]

Plato

Plato (428–348 BC), in introducing natural theology into the subject matter of Western philosophy, has rightly been called the creator of philosophical theism.[37] In Book X of the *Laws*, Plato established the basis of both the cosmological and the teleological arguments.[38] According to Plato, there are eight different motions: motion round an axis, movement from place to place, movement both from place to place and round an axis (i.e., planetary motion), retardation, acceleration, growth, decay, and destruction.

At first, this looks like a subject for physics. But then, Plato immediately begins analyzing these motions. The interaction between the forces is rather clear and easy to explain, until it reaches the point of the First Mover or Unmoved Mover. Plato concludes that the ultimate cause of the universe in motion must be a living soul, and one of a higher order than the human soul. This is the first quality of what is later named "God."[39]

Aristotle

One of Plato's students, Aristotle of Stagira (384–322 BC), studied physics, metaphysics, poetry, drama, music, logic, rhetoric, politics, government, ethics, biology and zoology. At first, Aristotle ascribes intelligence to the cosmic objects: he thinks they generate their own movement voluntarily.[40] Later, he concludes, like Plato, that everything in motion must be moved by something. If something is not self-moved, it is moved by something else. And nothing can be self-moved. This rebuts his earlier argument of the

36. See footnote 43 for the schools of theology in Islam.
37. Plato, *The Laws*, 99.
38. Hick, *The Existence of God*, 71.
39. Plato, *The Laws*, 490.
40. Cicero and Pease, *De Natura Deorum*, 2.15.42.

intelligence of heavenly objects. Rather inaccurate and yet brilliant for its time, Aristotle's cosmology is described by Ross as follows:

> The universe consists of series of concentric spheres. The earth is a sphere of no great relative size, at rest at the center of the universe. The outer shell of the universe—the first heaven—is a finite sphere containing what we now call the fixed stars. These stars have no motion of their own but are carried around by the uniform rotation of the first heaven once in 24 hours. With regard to the more complex movements of the sun, the moon, and the planet Aristotle adopts with a modification the theory of Eudoxus as it had been developed by his own friend Callippus. Aristotle thought the movement of the first heaven was due to the action of God, operating as the object of love and desire. Yet the movement of the sun, the moon and planets is explained by the action not of God but separate moving agent of each sphere.[41]

Owing to the great translation movement during the Umayyad era, Socrates, Plato and Aristotle had a major impact on Islamic philosophy.

The Kalām Cosmological Argument

Probably no chapter in the history of the cosmological argument is as significant—and as universally ignored—as that of the Arabic (Muslim) theologians and philosophers.[42] Influenced by the ancient Greeks, early Muslim philosophers were the first to establish the cosmological argument in medieval (and modern) Western philosophy. These Muslim philosophers brought forward the two important versions of cosmological argument, namely *temporal regress* and the *argument from contingency*. "*Kalām*" and "*falsafa*" are the two Arabic terms that will be used in the following chapters. *Falsafa* is the Arabic word used to denote philosophy, in the sense of Arabic Aristotelian and Neo-Platonic philosophy, while *kalām* simply means "speech" in Arabic, and is the philosophy of Islamic doctrinal theology. A scholastic theologian or practitioner of *kalām* is called *mutakallim* (plural *mutakallimūn*). Initially, one might think that all Muslim *mutakallimūn* are in total agreement regarding the philosophical issues surrounding God's existence and his qualities. However, in reality this has never been the case. There have been serious disputes and arguments, which have resulted in extreme accusations, the parties calling each other *kāfir* (infidel). In order to

41. Ross, *Aristotle*, 181.

42. Craig, *The Cosmological Argument from Plato to Leibniz*, 48.

understand Islamic philosophy better, one needs to examine the traditions and schools of Islam.

The first division is between Western and Eastern philosophical traditions. The former stem from Ibn Rushd (Averroes), Muḥyiddin ibn Ārābī, Ibn Bajja and Ibn Tufayl from Muslim Spain, and the latter from Al-Fārābī, Ibn Sina (Avicenna), Al-Ghazzālī from the Eastern tradition. This division has had less effect, however, on Islamic philosophy than has the division of schools.[43]

43. There are five very distinct schools of theology in the Islamic philosophical tradition. These are [1] Sunni, within which are [1.a] Ash'ari, [1.b] Athari (Salafi), and [1.c] Maturidi; [2] Shia, with the sub-schools of [2.a] Imami and [2.b] Ismaili; [3] Khariji; [4] Mu'tazili; and [5] Murjiah.

[1]. Sunni schools: The Sunni school is one of the largest branches of the Islamic faith. The word *Sunni* originates from *sunnah*, which means the tradition of Islam's Prophet Muḥammad. There are four Sunni schools of law (*madhhab*), which are Hanafi, Shafi'i, Hambali and Maliki. All four schools of law take their creed (*ʿaqīdah*) from the three schools of theology, Ash'ari, Athari and Māturidī.

[2]. Shiʿa school: It is the second largest Islamic school after the *Sunni* school. In ʿaqīdah they are based on the Imami and Ismaili schools. Among other differences, the main one we are concerned with is the interpretation of Islam's Holy book the Quran, hence the faith itself. Shias believe that the true interpreters of Islam are the direct descendants of the Prophet Muḥammad's daughter Fatima and son-in-law Ali, who was also the fourth righteous caliph. These descendants are called *imāms* and they are the only ones to follow. Whereas the Sunni school believes that *sunnah* is narrated by the Companions and that there is no need to have a direct blood link with Fatima and Ali in order to interpret Islam.

[3]. Khariji: Khariji literally means *those who went out. Kharijites* believed that the act of sinning is analogous to *kufr* (disbelief) and that every grave sinner was regarded as *kafir* (a disbeliever) unless he repented. They considered the Qur'an to be the source of Islamic Jurisprudence (*fiqh*), but regarding the other two sources (*hadīth* and *ijmā*) their concepts were different from ordinary Muslims.'

[4]. Mu'tazili: This school of Islamic theology came into being through controversies involving the interpretation (*ta'wil*) of the Qur'an in its anthropomorphic description of God and the denial of free will. The *Mu'tazilites* denied literal interpretation of the Qur'anic passages and affirmed man's free will, while the orthodox traditionalists adhered to literalism and determinism. They believe that people are the creators of their own acts, not God. They also deny the Divine Destiny (*qadar*).

[5]. Murji'ah: As opposed to the Kharijites, Murjites advocated the idea of deferred judgement of people's beliefs. The Murjite doctrine held that only God has the authority to judge who is a true Muslim and who is not, and that Muslims should consider all other Muslims as part of the community. In another contrast to the Kharijites, who believed that committing a grave sin would render a person non-Muslim, Murjites considered genuine belief in and submission to God to be more important than acts of piety and good deeds. They believed that Muslims committing grave sins would remain Muslim and be eligible for Paradise if they remained faithful.

Al-Kindī

The first systematic writer, philosopher and theologian in Islam is Abu Yusuf Ya'qub b. Ishaq al-Kindī (*c.*801–*c.*873), who is also the promoter and the patron of the translation movement and a champion of the introduction of Greek and Indian writings into the Muslim world.[44] Taking his theological stance in the *Mu'tazilah* tradition, Al-Kindī proceeds to develop a philosophy that can best be characterized as "neo-platonized Aristotelian." Al-Kindī stands historically as the bridge between *kalām* and *falsafa*, and it was his conviction that revelation and philosophy attain to identical truths, albeit in different ways.[45] Al-Kindī argued that God's existence may be demonstrated by proving that the universe was created in time.[46] Indeed, the most important argument for God's existence in the philosophy of al-Kindī is his argument for creation, and he stands apart as the only Muslim peripatetic philosopher not believing in the eternity of the universe and matter.[47] Despite the influence of Aristotle and Plotinus on his thought, he consistently upheld creation *ex nihilo*: God creates the universe out of nothing (*al-mubdī*), and al-Kindī uses the word "*ibda*" to specifically denote God's action as creation in time out of nothing.[48] He reasons that, if it may be proved that the universe began to exist a finite number of years ago, the existence of a Creator may legitimately be inferred.[49]

In his book *On First Philosophy*, al-Kindī utilizes three arguments for the creation of the universe: an argument from space, time, and motion; an argument from composition; and another argument from time.[50] The upshot of al-Kindī's lengthy first argument is that body implies motion and motion implies time; therefore, if time had beginning, then motion and a body must have had a beginning as well, for it is impossible for body or motion to exist without time. Al-Kindī argues that time must be finite. Therefore, the beginning of the universe must be finite as well.[51]

Al-Kindī's second argument may be summarized as follows. Composition involves change, since it is a joining and organizing of things. Bodies are composed in two ways: (1) they are composed of substance, which is

44. Fakhry, *A History of Islamic Philosophy*, 67.

45. El-Ehwany, *'Al Kindī' in A History of Muslim Philosophy*, 175.

46. Craig, *The Cosmological Argument from Plato to Leibniz*, 61.

47. Atiyeh, *Al-Kindi: The Philosopher of the Arabs*, 49.

48. Ibid., 52.

49. Craig, *The Cosmological Argument from Plato to Leibniz*, 61.

50. Kindi and Ivry, *Al-Kindi's Metaphysics a Transl. Of Ya`Qub Ibn-Ishaq Al-Kindi's Treatise "on First Philosophy" (Fi Al-Falsafah Al-Ula)*, 67.

51. Craig, *The Cosmological Argument from Plato to Leibniz*, 63.

their genus and their three dimensions, which make them all differ from one another; and (2) they are composed of matter and form. Composition involves motion from a prior composed state. Thus, if there were no motion, there could be no composition, and if there were no composition, there could be no bodies. Now time is the duration counted by motion. Body, motion, and time thus occur simultaneously in being. Therefore, since time is finite, motion is finite; and since motion is finite, composition is finite; and since composition is finite, bodies are finite, too.[52]

The third argument is that it must be the case that before every temporal segment there is another segment of time until we reach the beginning of time, that is, a temporal segment before which there is no segmented duration. So, past time is finite. Since future time consists of adding consecutive, finite times to the time already elapsed, it is finite too. We ought to agree that two things quantitatively finite added together produce a finite thing. Thus, future time never reaches the actually infinite.[53]

Al-Kindī's position as the first self-described philosopher of the Islamic world makes him a transitional figure in several respects. His philosophy is continuous with the ancient tradition, even as it begins to respond to a very different intellectual milieu. To some extent, al-Kindī's reception of Greek philosophy set the agenda for *falsafa* in the generations to come; for instance, his treatment of the intellect and the theory of creation resonate throughout Islamic philosophy. Above all, the attempt to assimilate Greek thought in al-Kindī's circle proves the wider points that translation is always interpretation, and that philosophers can be at their most creative when they take up the task of understanding their predecessors.[54]

Al-Fārābī

Muḥammad b. Muḥammad b. Tarkhan Al-Fārābī (d. 950), better known in classical sources and among the Latins of the Middle Ages as Abū Naṣr (Latin: Abunaser),[55] or Alpharabius was the founder of Arab Neoplatonism and the first major figure in the history of that philosophical movement since Procolus.[56] To him one may credit the first exposition of the modern

52. Kindi and Ivry, *Al-Kindi's Metaphysics a Transl. Of Ya`Qub Ibn-Ishaq Al-Kindi's Treatise "on First Philosophy" (Fi Al-Falsafah Al-Ula)*, 73–74.

53. Ibid., 74–75.

54. Adamson and Taylor, *The Cambridge Companion to Arabic Philosophy*, 48–49.

55. Fakhry, *A History of Islamic Philosophy*, 111.

56. Ibid., 132.

cosmological argument from contingency. Al-Fārābī's distinctive contribution to the cosmological argument is as follows:

> Contingent beings . . . have had a beginning. Now that which begins to exist must owe its existence to the action of a cause. This cause, in turn, either is or is not contingent. If it is contingent, it also must have received its existence by the action of another cause, and so on. But a series of contingent beings, which would produce one another, cannot proceed to infinity or move in a circle. Therefore, the series of causes and effects must arrive at a cause that holds its existence from itself, and this is the first cause (*ens primum*).[57]

Al-Fārābī presents six "principles" (*mabādi*) of being in a system: (1) the First Cause, (2) the Second Cause (i.e., incorporeal intellects), (3) the Active Intellect governing the sub-lunar world, (4) Soul, (5) Form and (6) Matter. The First Cause, Al-Fārābī says, "one should believe that it is God," is the incorporeal First Mover, in that the celestial spheres move out of desire for It.[58] It is worth concentrating on a few of Al-Fārābī's arguments concerning the First Cause (*al-sabab al-awwal*), since they provide us with an interesting insight into the manner in which metaphysics and epistemology come to be combined in his thought. In the *Principles of the Opinions*, Al-Fārābī tells us:

> The First Cause cannot be divided in speech into the things which would constitute Its substance. For it is impossible that each part of the statement that would explain the meaning of the First could denote each of the parts by which the substance of the first is so constituted. If this were the case, the parts which constitutes Its substance would be causes of Its existence, in the way that meaning denoted by parts of the definition of a thing are causes of the existence of the things defined, e.g., in the way that matter and form are causes of existence of things composed of them. But this is impossible with regard to the First, since It is the First and Its existence has no cause whatsoever.[59]

In short, the contingency argument of Al-Fārābī posits that God exists since everything including the universe that exists contingently has a reason for its existence, and the reason of the existence of the universe is, therefore, has to be God.

57. Hammond, *The Philosophy of Alfarabi and Its Influence on Medieval Thought*, 21.
58. Adamson and Taylor, *The Cambridge Companion to Arabic Philosophy*, 56–57.
59. Farabi and Walzer, *On the Perfect State*, 67.

Ibn Sina

Abū Ali al-Husain ibn Sina (980–1037), known in the West as Avicenna, brought Fārābī's Neoplatonism to full bloom, and from that point on "Ibn Sina" was synonymous with *falsafa* and became an open target of the *mutakallimūn*, who readily discerned the unorthodox nature of his philosophy. His debt to Al-Fārābī is great, as it is evident even in his remark that he had read the *Metaphysics* of Aristotle forty times and had never understood it until he came upon Al-Fārābī's commentary.[60]

Before Avicenna, *falsafa* (Arabic Aristotelian and Neoplatonic philosophy) and *kalām* (Islamic doctrinal theology) were distinct strands of thought, even though there was a good deal of cross-fertilization between them. After Avicenna, by contrast, the two strands fused together, and post-Avicennan *kalām* emerged as the truly Islamic philosophy, a synthesis of Avicenna's metaphysics and Muslim doctrine.[61]

Like Al-Fārābī, ibn Sina employed the *essence/existence distinction* and the *necessary/possible distinction* in his proof of God's existence.[62] He writes:

> Everything except the One who is by His essence One and Existent acquires existence from something else. . . . In itself it deserves absolute non-existence. Now it is not its matter which deserves non-existence but totality (of matter and form).[63]

The term "Necessary Being" (*al-wājib al-wujūd)* was ibn Sina's main addition to Islamic philosophy. It depends on reasoning similar to that behind Al-Fārābī's First Cause (*al-sabab al-awwal*). Both philosophers argued that for every movement or matter there has to be a reason. In modern times, the example of a train is, although it is not totally satisfactory, mentioned frequently. In the train example, a bystander asks what pulls the last car. The answer is clearly visible—that it is being pulled by the car in front. When the locomotive is reached there is seemingly nothing pulling it. Hence it may be concluded that the locomotive is self-powered. In the universe the locomotive is what Al-Fārābī calls the First Cause and what Ibn-i Sina calls the Necessary Being, which is God.

60. Fakhry, *A History of Islamic Philosophy*, 147.

61. Adamson and Taylor, *The Cambridge Companion to Arabic Philosophy*, 92–93.

62. Nasr, *An Introduction to Islamic Cosmological Doctrines; Conceptions of Nature and Methods Used for Its Study by the Ikhwan Al-Safa, Al-Biruni, and Ibn Sina*, 198.

63. Morewedge and Avicenna, *The Metaphysica of Avicenna (Ibn Sìna); a Critical Translation-Commentary and Analysis of the Fundamental Arguments in Avicenna's Metaphysica in the Danish Nama-I `Alai (the Book of Scientific Knowledge)*, 8.5.

Al-Ghazzālī

Abu Hāmed Muhammad ibn Muhammad Al-Ghazzālī was born in 1058, in Khurasan. He was a jurist, a theologian, and, above all, a mystic. He met Al Juwayry, one of the leading *Ash'arite* scholars of the time. *Ash'arite* theology was designed in opposition to the *Mu'tazilah*. Al-Ghazzālī was a teacher at the Nizām al-Mulk Madrasah of Baghdad, which was the medieval equivalent of a modern-day university. These *madāris* (single *madrasah*) were set up by the Turkish Seljuk vizier of Nizām al-Mulk. Since the Seljuk state adapted orthodox (*sunni*) Islam, they were in disagreement with the Shi'ite Fatimid in Cairo.[64] Hence, one of the purposes of these *madāris* was to counteract the Fatimid (*Shi'ite*) doctrine. From Al-Ghazzālī's time onwards we see the increased influence of *Ash'arite* doctrine on the Islamic world.[65]

Al-Ghazzālī excelled in philosophy and in hitting back against the Neo-Platonic philosophers, such as Al-Fārābī and Ibn Sina, with their own weapon. The aim of his *kalām* was to attack heretics in defense of orthodox Islam. In this sense, Al-Ghazzālī was the first true *mutakallim*, whereas his predecessors, Al-Fārābī and Ibn Sina, were just philosophers like Plato and Aristotle. One of Al-Ghazzālī's most important works of philosophy was "The Intentions of Philosophers" (*al Maqāṣid al-falāsifa*). The Criterion (the standard measure) of Science (*Mi'yār al-ʿilm*) and The Collapse of the Philosopher (*Tahāfut*) complete his philosophical trilogy.

It is important to note that, in his criticisms, Al-Ghazzālī does not usually give names, but just refers to both Al-Fārābī and Ibn Sina as "the philosopher."[66] According to Al-Ghazzālī, the Neo-Platonists have failed to prove the existence of God. In their argument, the Neo-Platonists could regress to the First Cause or Necessary Being. This proof, according to Al-Ghazzālī, is invalid since their distinction between the necessary-in-itself and the necessary-through-a-cause, upon which their proof rests, is unfounded.[67] Al-Ghazzālī accuses the Neo-Platonists of denying the divine attributes altogether. Such attributes, according to them, are accidents of the essence and, as such, involve plurality and contingency in the subject.[68]

After reviewing Al-Fārābī's and Ibn Sina's work, Al-Ghazzālī concludes that sixteen metaphysical and four physical propositions are totally

64. Adamson and Taylor, *The Cambridge Companion to Arabic Philosophy*, 138.

65. For instance, the majority of Sunni Muslims in modern Turkey follow the *Maturidi*, which is along the same lines as the *Ash'arite*.

66. Adamson and Taylor, *The Cambridge Companion to Arabic Philosophy*, 144.

67. Al-Ghazali and Kamali, *Al-Ghazali's Tahafut Al-Falasifah: (Incoherence of the Philosophers)*, 176.

68. Ibid.

unacceptable according to orthodox Islamic norms, and the unguarded public should be warned about them. Al-Ghazzālī condemns most of these propositions as heresy (*bid'ah*) and three of them as irreligion (*kufr*),[69] and castigates individuals holding these beliefs as deserving to be declared renegades (*murtad*)[70] and to be punished accordingly.

According to Al-Ghazzālī, these propositions are: [1] the eternity of the world a *parte ante*, [2] God's knowledge of universals only, and [3] the denial of the resurrection of the body.[71]

Craig has summarized Al-Ghazzālī's *kalām* cosmological argument as follows:

> There are temporal phenomena in the world which are caused by other temporal phenomena. The series of temporal phenomena cannot regress to infinity. Therefore, the series must stop at eternal. The series of temporal phenomena must have a beginning. Therefore, according to the principle of determination, an agent must exist who creates the world.[72]

It is important to note that this particular philosophical argument resembles that of Al-Fārābi's and Ibn Sina's. However, Al-Ghazzālī advocates with the Qur'anic and Prophetic teachings to clarify that the principal agent is Allāh.

Ibn Rushd

Born in 1126 in Cordoba in Spain, Abū 'l-Walīd Muḥammad ibn Aḥmad ibn Rushd, also called Averroes, is one of the few Western Islamic philosophers well-known in the West.

Thus far, Islamic philosophy had seen two important stages. The first was the Abbasid movement for the translation of Greek literature, which resulted in the creation of Neo-Platonism in the Islamic world by al-Kindī, Al-Fārābī and Ibn Sina. In the second stage, there was witnessed the victory of *kalām* over *falsafa* thanks to Imām Al-Ghazzālī, who attacked Neo-Platonic Islamic philosophy relentlessly. Now, Ibn Rushd came onto the stage of history to revitalize Neo Platonism through commenting on Aristotle. Ibn Rushd supported the philosophers in arguing for the eternity of the world.[73]

69. Ibid., 376.
70. Ibid.
71. Ibid.
72. Craig, *The Cosmological Argument from Plato to Leibniz*, 101.
73. Hourani, '*The Dialogue between Al-Ghazzālī and the Philosophers on the Origin*

Unlike Al-Fārābī and Ibn Sina, who used "contingency" as proof of the existence of God, Ibn Rushd used the Qur'anic proofs, which are proofs from [1] providence (*taqdir Ilāhi*) and [2] the wonders of creation (i.e., the teleological argument).[74]

Although he used the "prime mover" argument for the motion of spheres[75] in his *Incoherence of Incoherence*, Ibn Rushd based his argument on Ibn Sina's redefined "contingency" theory, but his argument does not rely on the distinction between essence and existence. He writes:

> If one wanted to give demonstrative form of the argument used by Ibn-i Sina one should say: Possible existents must of necessity have causes which precede them, and if these causes again are possible it follows that they have causes and that there is an infinite regress; and if there is an infinite regress there is no cause; and the possible will exist without a cause, and this is impossible. Therefore, the series must end in a necessary cause or without a cause, and if through a cause, this cause must have a cause and so on infinitely; and if we have an infinite regress here, it follows that what was assumed to have a cause has no cause, and this is impossible. Therefore, the series must end in a cause necessary without a cause, i.e., necessary by itself, and this necessarily is the necessary existent. And, when these distinctions are indicated the proof becomes valid.[76]

Appointed as religious judge (*qāḍī*) of Seville, Ibn Rushd produced commentary on Aristotle's works, the *Republic* of Plato and *Isogage of Prophecy*. It is important to note that Ibn Rushd has no recorded disciples or successors. Nevertheless, he influenced the Jewish philosopher Maimonides and the medieval European philosopher St Thomas Aquinas, whom will be discussed in the following chapters.

Ibn Rushd disagreed with Aristotle regarding the cosmological argument and Ibn-i Sina's (as well as the *Ash'arite*) thesis of "contingency." He claimed that the best proof is the argument from invention (creation) and the argument from providence or design (*dalīl al-'ināyah*). The basis of his argument, as well as of all philosophical arguments for God's unity, is the Qur'anic verses 21:22, 23:91, and 17:44.[77]

---

of the World,' in Muslim World 48, 183–91.

74. Nirenstein, *The Problem of the Existence of God in Maimonides Alanus and Averroes*, 46.

75. Averroes, *Tahafut*, 1:34, 237–38.

76. Averroes, *Tahafut*, 1:165.

77. Qur'an, 21:22: Had there been within the heavens and earth gods besides Allāh, they both would have been ruined. So exalted is Allāh, Lord of the Throne, above what

With the death of Fakr al-din al-Rāzī in 1209, the so-called "Golden Age" of Islamic philosophy ended. However, thanks to close contacts with the Abbasid and Islamic Spain, Greek and Islamic philosophy continued its influence in the coming centuries on Jewish and Christian theology.

Four leading figures of the Muslim world mentioned above form the foundations of the *kalām* cosmological arguments which is illustrated in Appendix 10 at the end of this study. Although Al-Ghazzālī differs from the other three in terms of overall philosophy, their cosmological arguments display very similar characteristics. All four base their arguments on the assumption that infinite regress is not possible, and a beginning of creation is required for the existence of the universe.

A Critical Comparison of the Islamic Tradition

The Islamic philosophy emerged owing to the translation of Greek literature in the seventh century. Prior to "the translation movement" there seems to be virtually no Islamic, or Arabic for that matter, material available. Islam's emergence in the seventh century successfully established a monotheistic belief system. The already existing concept of God was strengthened by the Qur'an which argued for God's existence from the cosmos.

In this section, Nursi's theology is compared to that of the four most prominent scholars of Islamic tradition.

Al-Kindī is the first leading figure which introduced Aristotelian philosophy into Islamic world. He claims that Greek philosophy is to be welcomed as it might assist people to attain the knowledge of God. The trend set by al-Kindī continuous with Al-Fārābī and Ibn Sina. As indicated in Appendix 10, al-Kindī, start off with premises that time is a finite entity. That is, creation occurs in time, and time is not infinitive. It has to have a beginning. Similarly, Al-Fārābī and Ibn Sina theorize around the contingency principle. That is, every contingent being has to have an explanation for their existence. As the regress cannot go to infinity it has to have a beginning. To Al Fārābī, that is "The First Cause," to Ibn Sina, that is "Necessary Being." Ibn Rushd, though takes the Qur'anic arguments as the primary

---

they describe.

Qur'an, 23:91: No son did Allāh beget, nor is there any god along with him: (if there were many gods), behold, each god would have taken away what he had created, and some would have lorded it over others! Glory to Allāh. (He is free) from the (sort of) things they attribute to him!

Qur'an, 17:44: "The seven heavens and the earth, and all beings therein, declare his glory: there is not a thing but celebrates his praise; and yet ye understand not how they declare his glory! Verily he is oft-forbear, most forgiving!"

proof, develops a version of the contingency argument of his predecessors. He analyses the movement and concludes that the source of all movements is the Prime Mover. There is quite a parallel between Nursi and Ibn Rushd as both scholars used the Qur'anic arguments. Nursi, though not use the cosmological arguments as in the sense of his predecessors, builds his theism around the teleological argument like Ibn Rushd who argues from the "wonder of creation" and "providence." Nursi, however, differs from Ibn Rushd with regards to his argument from the miraculousness of the Qur'an. Though he imitates Qur'anic arguments, his argument from revelation revolves around the assumption that the Qur'an is not a product of human intelligence; it is the work of the divine, which is an automatic proof of the existence of the Divine.

Meanwhile, Al-Ghazzālī, though criticized the philosophers of the Mu'tazili tradition, utilizes similar arguments. He explains that everything that exists requires a cause for its origin, highlighting the temporal character of the universe. He does not believe the efficacy of secondary cause. Since the universe is temporal, it requires a creator upon which all possible things have their ground. Al-Ghazzālī's other argument is the teleological argument. In this respect, Al-Ghazzālī and Nursi seem to be on the same page.

Although Islamic theism has developed around the *kalām* version of the cosmological argument, Nursi does not appear to follow the trend of his predecessors. There is clear evidence that he has a credible knowledge of philosophy and his methods resembles that of a philosophy.

The rivalry among Islamic scholars is a well-documented fact. Especially Al-Ghazzālī's attack on Mu'tazili affiliated Al-Fārābī and Ibn Sina in *Incoherence of the Philosophers*, and Ibn Rushd defense of the pair in *The Incoherence of Incoherence is* well known matters. However, one might argue that these differences are not due to the disagreement on the theism or the ways to arguing for it. The conflict appears to be risen from the technical disputes on other issues such as causality, predestination, and free will. Nursi, being in Ash'ari school like Al-Ghazzālī, heavily criticizes Mu'tazili tradition on the aforementioned issues not on their cosmology. In fact, there are traces of Mu'tazili cosmology in various pieces of Nursi's writings. Al-Ghazzālī and Nursi agree on the shortcomings of the *kalām* cosmological arguments. The *kalām* cosmological arguments of the Neo-Platonists, unless supported with the Qur'an and Sunnah, falls short of full knowledge of God. They simply demonstrate the impossibility of infinite regress and establish the necessity of an Uncaused Cause.

In short, Nursi's philosophy shows strong hints of "reason and intellect" similar to the ones seen in the Neo-Platonist, yet has clear spiritual elements like that of al-Ghazzālī at the same time.

Jewish Philosophers

Jewish philosophers of religion are the bridge between Islamic philosophy and medieval Western philosophy. Directly influenced by Muslim theologians, they adopted the cosmological argument to prove the existence of God, and hence justify Judaism. Guttman remarks that Jewish philosophy is the offspring of Muslim *kalām*.[78] Unlike their Muslim Neo-Platonist and Aristotelian predecessors, who dealt with a wide range of philosophical issues, Jewish philosophers were mainly concerned with the theological aspect of Islamic philosophy and *kalām*.[79]

Among several theistic arguments, the Jewish philosophers only used the cosmological argument. Wolfson claims that the causality principle is the main argument of the Jewish philosophers.[80]

Perhaps one of the strongest evidences of Muslim–Jewish philosophical interaction is the fact that most Jewish philosophers wrote in Arabic rather than in their native language of Hebrew,[81] although most of their work was translated into Hebrew sometime after their deaths.

Saadia Ben Joseph

Saadia ben Joseph (882–942) was one of the best-known early Jewish philosophers who used the Islamic *kalām* cosmological argument for proof of the existence of God and the superiority of Judaism.[82] Saadia put forward four arguments for creation. These are: [1] the argument from the finitude of the world, [2] the argument from composition, [3] the argument from the temporality of accidents, and [4] the argument from the finitude of time.[83] He argues that the concept of an *infinite time* is absurd.

Saadia's argument from the finitude of time may be summarized as follows:

> It is impossible to regress mentally to reach the beginning of time, because infinite cannot be traversed and the time is, *ex hypotesi*, infinite. It is impossible for existence to progress through time to reach the present moment, because existence must traverse exactly the same series that our thought traversed. But,

78. Bamberger, *Julius Guttmann, Philosopher of Judaism*, 11.
79. Ibid.
80. Wolfson, *Notes on Proofs of the Existence of God in Jewish Philosophy*, 584.
81. Craig, *The Kalam Cosmological Argument*, 37.
82. Husik, *A History of Mediaeval Jewish Philosophy*, 61.
83. Craig, *The Cosmological Argument from Plato to Leibniz*, 128.

> the traversal of such a series has been shown to be impossible. Therefore, we do not exist, which is absurd. Therefore, the time must be finite, because otherwise existence could never have traversed it and reach the present moment.[84]

Here, we instantly see the similarity between Al-Ghazzālī's finitude of time argument and Saadia's.[85] By reversing the argument, Saadia claims that since the universe and time exist now, they must have come into existence at some point in the past. Since nothing can come into existence by itself, they (both the universe and the time) had to be created by God.[86]

Moses Maimonides

Moses ben Maimon (1135–1204), Ibn Maymūn in Arabic, lived nearly a century after Saadia. While Saadia made his mark on history as "the first philosopher," Maimonides was considered the "most remarkable" of the Jewish philosophers.[87] The chief difference between the two is that Saadia took *kalām* as the starting point of his philosophy, whereas Maimonides took philosophy's standpoint.[88] Strauss claims that although *kalām's* starting point of "arbitrary presuppositions" was an easier one to use to prove the beliefs taught by the laws, Maimonides chose the harder philosophical route, with the nature of things as starting point.[89]

Starting his argument as a true philosopher rather than as a *mutakallim*, Maimonides presented twenty-six propositions.[90] His first argument is

84. Ibid., 129.

85. Saadia died in 942, nearly a century prior to Al-Ghazzālī, who was born in 1058. It could be suggested that Al-Ghazzālī might had been influenced by Saadia as he wrote in Arabic and lived in the Middle East like
Al-Ghazzālī himself.

86. Sa`adia and Rosenblatt, *The Book of Beliefs and Opinions*, 45.

87. Husik, *A History of Mediaeval Jewish Philosophy*, 236.

88. Craig, *The Cosmological Argument from Plato to Leibniz*, 131.

89. Strauss, *Philosophy and Law: Essays toward the Understanding of Maimonides and His Predecessors*, 39.

90. Maimonides' propositions are: [1] An infinite magnitude cannot exist. [2] An infinite number of finite magnitudes cannot coexist. [3] An infinite number of causes and effects cannot exist. [4] Change may be in substance, quantity, quality, or place. [5] Motion implies change and transition from potentiality to actuality. [6] Motion is essential or accidental, the former being due to an external force, the latter to its participation in the motion of another thing. [7] Changeable things are divisible and, hence, corporeal. [8] A thing moved accidentally must come to rest. [9] A thing that moves something else does so by setting itself in motion. [10] Anything in a corporeal body is either an accidental or an essential property. [11] Some properties of corporeal

the argument from motion, which discusses the nature of motion in the universe at great length. He narrows the possible reasons for the motion of the spheres down to four. These are [1] a corporeal object without the sphere, [2] an incorporeal object separate from the sphere, [3] an internal force extended throughout the sphere, and [4] an invisible force within the sphere.[91] After disproving the first, third and the fourth possibilities on logical grounds, he proclaims: "The Prime Motor of the spheres is God, praise be his name."[92] It is easy to see the similarity between Aristotle's *First Cause* argument and Maimonides's *Prime Motor* argument. Maimonides's second proof is also a simpler version of the "argument from motion." Craig summarizes this second argument as follows:

> Given a thing composed of two elements, if one of the elements exists separately, then the other element does so as well. Because the separate existence of one element proves that the two elements are so indissolubly united that they cannot exist separately. There are objects that are in motion and move others, and objects that are in motion but do not move others. Therefore, there must be something that moves other things but is not itself in motion. This is the Prime Mover, God.[93]

Perhaps the third argument, which is a version of the cosmological argument, is the most important one that Maimonides produced. Maimonides gives three possibilities for existence. They are: [1] all things are without beginning or end, [2] all things have a beginning and end, and [3] some things have beginning and end. Refuting the first and second arguments immediately, Maimonides goes on to argue the existence of an eternal, indestructible being whose existence is real, not just possible. This external

---

objects (e.g., color) are divisible; others (e.g., Soul) are not. [12] A force occupying all parts of a corporeal, finite object is finite. [13] Only circular locomotion can be continuous change. [14] Locomotion is the most basic motion. [15] Time and motion are inseparable. [16] Incorporeal beings cannot be numbered, unless they inhabit a corporeal body. [17] Everything in motion is moved by an agent, either internal or external. [18] Everything that passes from potentiality to actuality is caused to do so by an external agent. [19] A caused being is a possible being. [20] A necessary being has no cause. [21] The essence of a composed being does not necessitate existence, since its composition is the cause of its existence. [22] Material bodies are composed of substance and form and are subject to accidents. [23] Every possible being may at some time be without actual essence. [24] Potentiality implies corporeality. [25] Every composed being consists of matter and form and requires a cause for its existence. [26] Time and motion are eternal.

91. Craig, *The Cosmological Argument from Plato to Leibniz*, 132.

92. Maimonides, *Maimonides, the Guide of the Perplexed*, 2.1.

93. Craig, *The Cosmological Argument from Plato to Leibniz*, 141.

force, therefore, is the absolutely necessary being, the source of existence of all things.[94]

According to Husik, Maimonides does not bring any new argument into philosophy. He merely repeats what is originally Aristotle's.[95] Husik also claims that the argument was introduced into Jewish philosophy by Abraham ibn Daud prior to Maimonides.[96]

Despite the dispute over the originality of Maimonides' argument, Riedl suggests that it was Maimonides who was the main source of inspiration for Thomas Aquinas's Five Ways a few decades later.[97]

Both Maimonides and Saadia act as a bridge between Islamic philosophy and the Medieval European philosophy.

Thomas Aquinas: The Five Ways

Thomas Aquinas (1224–74) is one of the first Western Christian philosophers of religion. Aquinas, like many other Christian philosophers, was influenced by early Christian theologian, Saint Augustine (354–430). Considered to be a saint, he is the patron saint of the Roman Catholic Church.[98] Aquinas is one of the first and most prolific defenders of the cosmological argument in Christian theology. After his death, the philosophers and thinkers who followed his cosmological tradition were called "Thomists."

Although Aquinas was a Christian man of God, he used his philosophical arguments only to prove the existence of God, rather than going into the more controversial "Trinity" debate.[99] Aquinas believed that the existence of God could be proven philosophically by the natural power of reasoning.[100] He started off his endeavor from an Aristotelian position, as he acknowledged later in his writings. Aquinas formulated five theories for the existence of God in his *Summa Theologiæ*, which are widely known as "the Five Ways of Thomas Aquinas."

Aquinas's Five Ways are [1] the argument from motion, [2] the argument from the nature of efficient cause, [3] the argument from possibility

94. Ibid., 143.
95. Husik, *A History of Mediaeval Jewish Philosophy*, 218.
96. Ibid.
97. Riedl, *Maimonides and Scholasticism*, 27–28.
98. Hick, *The Existence of God*, 80.
99. Craig, *The Cosmological Argument from Plato to Leibniz*, 159.
100. Hick, *The Existence of God*, 80.

and necessity, [4] the argument from gradation, and [5] the argument from the governance of the world.[101]

It has commonly been agreed in the world of philosophy that the first three ways are truly cosmological arguments, and these will be examined in the present chapter. The fourth way is described by Craig as "the most Platonic of Aquinas's arguments."[102] The fifth way is clearly a teleological argument, and is the subject of Chapter 3 of this book.

The First Way: Like many early Greek, Muslim, and Jewish philosophers, Aquinas forms his first proof from the concept of motion. In his *Summa Theologiæ*, he proceeds to argue that it is obvious from our senses that whatever is moved is moved by something else, for nothing can be moved except if it is in a state of potential vis-à-vis that towards which it is moved, whereas a thing moves inasmuch as it is in action. Motion is a shift from potentiality to actuality. But nothing can be shifted from potentiality to actuality except by something which is already in a state of actuality. For instance, fire is actually hot, and wood is potentially hot; hence fire burns wood and makes it actually hot. In this sense, things cannot be in actuality and potentiality simultaneously. Therefore, things cannot be mover and moved at the same time. As we regress along the mover—moved chain, we reach the first mover, which is in actuality not moved by any other mover. This first mover is understood by everyone to be God.[103]

The Second Way: Aquinas names Aristotle as the source of this proof in the *Summa Contra Gentiles*.[104] The second way is based on the nature of causation. Aquinas argues that there is an order for every cause in the observable universe. It is impossible to have a final cause without an intermediate cause. We never observe anything causing itself. This series of causes must eventually stop at the First Cause, to which everyone gives the name "God."[105]

In order to show the difference between the first way and the second way, Gilson explains that the first way argues from the change in things, while the second way argues from the existence of things.[106] Aquinas goes

101. Aquinas, *Summa Theologiae: Latin Text and English Translation, Introductions, Notes, Appendices, and Glossaries*, 1a.3.

102. Craig, *The Cosmological Argument from Plato to Leibniz*, 160.

103. Aquinas, *Summa Theologiae: Latin Text and English Translation, Introductions, Notes, Appendices, and Glossaries*.

104. Aquinas, *Summa Contra Gentiles*, 1.13.

105. Aquinas, *Summa Theologiae: Latin Text and English Translation, Introductions, Notes, Appendices, and Glossaries*, 1a 2:3.

106. Gilson, *The Christian Philosophy of St. Thomas Aquinas. With a Catalog of St. Thomas's Works*, 67.

on to conclude that while the first way brings us to God as the source of cosmic motion, the second way leads us to him as the cause of the very existence of things; hence the second way is the proof for God as the creative cause of the universe.[107]

The Third Way: The Third Way is the argument from possibility and necessity. Remotely sourced from Al-Fārābī's argument from contingency,[108] Aquinas's argument states that it is possible for everything in nature to *be* or *not to be*, since everything is generated and corrupted. It is impossible for these things to exist at all times. Since things which do not exist come into existence by means of something already existing, there must be a being who necessarily exists in the first place. Therefore, we cannot but admit the existence of some being having of itself its own necessity and not receiving it from another, but rather causing in others their necessity. This being is what all men refer to as God.[109]

Here, a hint of agnosticism can be felt in Aquinas's proofs, since they eliminate reasons leading into a being whose qualities and attributes we do not really know.

In *The Existence of God* Hick writes, "The main weakness of the cosmological argument, considered as an instrument for demonstrating the existence of God to an atheist or an agnostic is that the argument begs the question."[110]

Among many Thomists such as Gilson and Martin, F. C. Copleston (1907–94) wrote a detailed commentary on Aquinas's Five Ways. This he did mainly to clarify it by making a distinction between *in fieri* (pending) causes and *in esse* (essentially) causes[111] valid for the twentieth century. In his book *Aquinas*, Copleston also acknowledges the weakness mentioned by Hick. Copleston admits: "it is not possible even to begin to lead a non-believer to God by means of this reasoning unless they share the cosmological arguer's basic conviction that the fact that there is a world at all is a puzzle which demands an explanation."[112]

Having discussed Aristotle, Al-Fārābī, Ibn Sina and Maimonides in the previous paragraphs, we can clearly see that no new contribution was made to the cosmological argument by Aquinas. According to Copleston,

107. Ibid., 77.

108. Craig, *The Cosmological Argument from Plato to Leibniz*, 182.

109. Aquinas, *Summa Theologiae: Latin Text and English Translation, Introductions, Notes, Appendices, and Glossaries*.

110. Hick, *The Existence of God*, 81.

111. The Latin term *in fieri* means in becoming, *in esse* means in existence.

112. Copleston, *Aquinas*, 134.

Aquinas's denial of the "accidentality of existence" was his only original contribution.[113]

David Hume and the Critique of the Cosmological Argument

David Hume (1711–76) is one of the best-known Scottish philosophers, whose chief argument is his objection to causality. Although he never openly admitted his atheistic position, he is commonly regarded as an atheist. Hume's method of expressing his philosophical opinions came in the form of dialogues between three fictitious characters in his 1779 book, *Dialogues Concerning Natural Religion*. In the *Dialogues*, Demea defends the cosmological argument, Cleanthes represents the experimental theist who uses the argument for design in the universe, and Philo represents the skeptic. According to the common view, Philo is actually Hume himself.[114]

We observe events, Hume argues, following other events. We do not actually observe any causality. That perception is a result of human habits. Passmore explains Hume's theory by means of a practical example of a young child dropping a ball. The child has never experienced a ball drop in his life before; hence he is surprised to observe that the ball bounces off the floor, whereas an adult knew even before the child had dropped the ball that the ball would bounce. This is simply because the adult had seen balls bounce many times prior to this particular event. He simply conjoins the events as a result of habit.[115]

Back in Part IX of the *Dialogues*, we find an exchange between Demea and Cleanthes on the issue of causality. Demea says:

> Whatever exists must have a cause or reason to its existence, it being absolutely impossible for anything to produce itself or to be the cause of its own existence[;] . . . therefore, from effects to cause, we must either go on in tracing an infinite succession, without any ultimate cause at all, or must at last have recourse to some ultimate cause that is *necessarily* existent.[116]

This is a clear, brief theory of causality (i.e., the cosmological argument). Although it is Philo who usually sounds the atheistic argument, on

113. Ibid., 135.

114. For a full analysis of Hume's characters see Mackie, *The Miracle of Theism: Arguments for and against the Existence of God*, 134–35.

115. Passmore, *Hume's Intentions*, 39.

116. From Hume, *Dialogues Concerning Natural Religion*, Part IX.

this occasion Cleanthes jumps in and tells Philo that he will not leave this matter to him. Cleanthes proceeds to argue in an attempt to refute Demea's causality theory. Cleanthes says:

> I shall begin with observing that there is an evident absurdity in pretending to demonstrate a matter of fact, or to prove it by any arguments *a priori*. Nothing is demonstrable unless the contrary implies a contradiction. Nothing that is distinctly conceivable implies a contradiction. Whatever we conceive as existent, we can also conceive as non-existent. There is no being therefore; whose non-existence implies a contradiction. Consequently there is no being whose existence is demonstrable. I propose this argument as entirely decisive, and am willing to rest the whole controversy upon it.[117]

In short, Hume rests his objection to the cosmological argument on the fact that it is *a priori* (from what is before). He considers the design argument to be *a posteriori* (from what is after), yet he raises an objection to it as well.

The Design Argument

One of the most popular theistic arguments is the argument from order or argument from design in the universe. It is also known as the teleological argument, a term derived from the Greek *telos*, which means aim or purpose. Hence, the term "teleological" concerns end-purpose. It is considered to be the oldest argument in natural theology, with roots going back to Plato and Aristotle in ancient Greece. Plato claims that there are two reasons why men have to believe in God: [1] the existence of the soul, and [2] order and motion in the universe, which are essentially the signs that there is an intelligent designer at the starting point of it all. Plato's student Aristotle bolstered the design argument in his *Metaphysics*.[118] Aristotle tells the story of a caveman who lived under ground all his life. He suddenly comes to the surface as a result of an earthquake or something similar. Aristotle asks us to think how this man would perceive the earth and the universe. He goes on to explain that, by looking at the clouds, the flora, the fauna, mountains, rivers, wind, the sun, the moon and the stars and the amazing events taking place all around him, he has to come to the conclusion that there is a

117. Hume and Smith, *Dialogues Concerning Natural Religion*.

118. See Aristotle et al., *The Metaphysics*, xiii.

marvelous, intelligent, eternal, all-good being behind all these phenomena. Aristotle calls this being "God."

Later, in the thirteenth century, Aquinas devised the Five Ways to prove the existence of God. The Fifth Way, drawn from the governance of the world, was clearly what we now call the design argument. Aquinas argued that things such as natural bodies lack knowledge but almost always act for an end, in order to obtain the best result. Just as an arrow is pointed by an archer, these mindless bodies are controlled by an intelligent agent, which is called God.

Paley Versus Hume

William Paley (1743–1805), with his watchmaker analogy, produced the plainest formulation of the teleological argument. In his *Natural Theology*,[119] Paley takes his reader for an imaginary walk on a heath. The walker, when he stumbles on a stone, probably does not pay much attention to it. However, if he finds a watch he cannot help thinking that it is designed for a purpose by a designer. None of the watch's components, such as springs, cogs, arrows or screws, has a mind. Yet, when they come together they serve a very specific purpose. Since there is no way specifically designed and built parts can intelligently come together by themselves, there has to be an intelligent external agent, who, according to Paley, is God himself.[120]

Today, some philosophers and scientists present another version of the design argument, which is called the "Fine Tuning of the Universe." With the advance of physics, astronomy, and mathematics, two elements of fine-tuning became more apparent. These are [1] the constants of nature, and [2] arbitrary quantity in the universe. Some philosophers argue that both these concepts strongly indicate that there has to be an intelligent agent making life, Earth and the rest of the universe possible. Craig, for instance, emphasizes the fact that life on earth requires this fine-tuning. In his lengthy January 2011 lecture on the subject, he presented some scientific data to back up the fine-tuning argument.[121]

Hume, surprisingly, had given an answer to the design argument even before Paley formulated it. Hume's objection came in his *Dialogues*

119. See Paley, *Natural Theology, or, Evidences of the Existence and Attributes of the Deity Collected from the Appearances of Nature*. 99–104

120. See the extract of Paley's *Natural Theology* in Hick, *The Existence of God*, 99–104.

121. Craig, *Teleological argument for the existence of God*, podcast, 03/01/2011, www.reasonablefaith.org

Concerning Natural Religion,[122] posthumously published in 1779. Cleanthes asserts the design argument to Philo thus:

> Look round the world. . . . You will find it to be nothing but one great machine. . . . The curious adapting of means to end, throughout all nature, resembles exactly, though it much exceeds, the production of human contrivance; of human design, thought, wisdom, and intelligence. Since therefore effects resemble each other, we are led to infer, by all the rules of analogy, that the causes also resemble each other; and the Author of nature is somewhat similar to the mind of man though possessed of much larger faculties, proportional to the grandeur of the work, which he has executed. By this argument a posteriori and by this argument alone, we do prove at once the existence of a Deity, and his similarity to human mind and intelligence.[123]

Philo raises five objections to Cleanthes, which are also the basis of modern-day arguments for the non-existence of God. These are:

1. The analogy between natural order and artifacts is not really close enough to make theism a good explanation of natural order.
2. The alternative hypotheses of order in nature, such as generation and vegetation, eventually weaken the design argument.
3. Even if the argument proves the intelligent designer, the intelligent designer himself needs explanation.
4. The moral components, such as the existence of evil alongside the good, weaken this argument.
5. And finally, the design argument is useless for explaining life after death, and punishment and reward.

The Problem of Evil

The problem of evil and suffering in the world, which is closely associated with Epicurus, Hume and Mill, is probably the most common question put to theists. As in all theistic beliefs, God is always described as omnipotent, omniscient, benevolent, etc. The theist assumes that the attributes of God are the necessary condition for his existence. In other words, if the atheist

122. See Hume and Smith, *Dialogues Concerning Natural Religion*.

123. For this extract from Hume's *Dialogues*, see Mackie, *The Miracle of Theism: Arguments for and against the Existence of God*, 134.

can prove that God is not omnipotent, they automatically prove that He does not exist. This issue is also known as the Epicurean problem since it was first formulated by Epicurus.[124] Epicurus (341–270 BC), the Greek philosopher whose ideas concerning the ethics of reciprocity influenced the French Revolution, and whose idea of egalitarianism influenced the American Independence Movement, was the earliest atheist in the history of philosophy. The Epicurean argument is as follows:

> Is God willing to prevent evil, but not able to?
> Then, he is not omnipotent.
> Is he able but not willing?
> Then he is malevolent.
> Is he both able and willing?
> Then whence cometh evil?
> Is he neither able nor willing?
> Then why do we call him God? [125]

This is the master-weapon in the atheists' arsenal. Hume, in his fourth objection to the design argument, has similar arguments, which were mentioned above.

John Stuart Mill (1806–73) challenged the theists, especially Christians, head-on in his 1874 work *The Nature and Utility of Religion*.[126] He starts with the evil in human behavior such as killing and torture, and moves on to list all the sufferings caused by nature. He talks about earthquakes, hurricanes, floods, and many other natural disasters in great detail. He quotes from the Pope and the Bible to show the contradiction between what theists claim and what really happens in nature. Mill then asks the question:

> . . . a Creator assumed to be omnipotent who, if he bends to a supposed necessity, himself makes the necessity which he bends to. If the maker of the world can all that he wills, he wills misery, and there is no escape from the conclusion.[127]

The theist camp was left with the need to come up with some logical and convincing answers regarding the problem of evil and suffering.

124. See Konstan, '*Epicurus*,' *The Stanford Encyclopaedia of Philosophy*, http://plato.stanford.edu/archives/spr2009/entries/epicurus.

125. See Epicurus et al., "Principal Doctrines," (2001) 19.9

126. See Mill, *Nature, the Utility of Religion, and Theism.*

127. Hick, *The Existence of God*, 119.

The Poor Design Argument

The poor design argument is completely based on recent scientific findings of anomalies and non-optimal features in organisms. Darwin's *Origin of Species*, in which Darwin implies that it is evolution rather than an intelligent design that is the cause of nature,[128] has inspired many more scientists and philosophers to refute creationists like Paley. The argument is associated with the German biologist and philosopher Haeckel, who was the main promoter of Darwin's ideas in Germany.[129] Later, Wise, who introduced the term "incompetent design," worked systematically to reveal poor design in the natural world.

The gist of the poor design argument is thus:

1. If God, who is omnipotent, omniscient, and benevolent, created living things (organisms), they have to be at optimum efficiency.
2. Some organisms have characters, which is less than optimal.
3. Therefore, either God is not omnipotent, omniscient, and benevolent, or God did not create organisms.

Apologists for the poor design argument put forward two categories of inefficiency in nature. The first concerns male and female reproductive systems. Here, in accordance with recent medical findings, they argue that female pregnancy is problematic, especially the labor and the birth part of it. For example, a baby's skull can easily be damaged during birth since the birth canal is seriously obstructed by the pelvic bone. Also, the male reproductive system is likely to cause medical conditions such as gangrene or prostate cancer.

The second group of examples is from nature in general. There are signs of poor design in certain animals like giraffes and pandas, which cause inherent problems. Also, these apologists list other, extremely technical and complex biological conditions to back up their theory.

Dawkins, along with most of the modern-day atheists, articulates these points in most of his works.[130] However, their level of soundness remains questionable.

128. See Gale, *Evolution without Evidence.*

129. For the ideas of Haeckel, see Haeckel, *The Evolution of Man.*

130. For example see Dawkins, *The Selfish Gene.*

The Argument from Morality and Consciousness

The forth most popular argument for the existence of God is the moral argument. It is considered to be "small but powerful." The argument takes its premises from the universally accepted fact of the existence of moral values and duties, which is not rejected even by atheists. The argument asserts that moral values and duties require a supreme "reference" who gives these codes.

Kant And Rashdall

Immanuel Kant, previously rejecting all three of the above arguments on the grounds that pure theoretical reason cannot establish the reality of transcendent entities, contends that God exists as a postulate of practical reason.[131] Kant is considered to be the philosopher who established the moral argument in philosophy. Having a clear disagreement with Christianity and the Bible, Kant tried to establish his argument outside the sphere of religious belief. The highlight of Kant's argument is this:

> . . . *summum bonum* (the highest good) is possible in the world only on the supposition of a Supreme Being having a causality corresponding to moral character. Now, a being that is capable of acting on the conception of laws is an *intelligence*, and the causality of such a being according to this conception of laws is his *will*; therefore, the supreme cause of nature, which must be presupposed as a condition of the *summum bonum*, is a being which is the cause of nature by *intelligence* and *will*, consequently its author, that is God. . . . It is morally necessary to assume the existence of God.[132]

Following Kant's establishment of the moral argument in modern times, Hastings Rashdall (1858–1924) formulated it in a form which is still used by many others today. The simple formulation of the moral argument is as follows:

Premise 1: If God does not exist, objective moral values do not exist.
Premise 2: Objective moral values and duties do exist.
Premise 3: Therefore, God exists.

131. Coincidentally, Kant's work on morality has the same title in Kant, *Critique of Practical Reason*, Book II, Chapter II, Section V, translated by Abbott.

132. See Immanuel Kant, "God as a postulate of practical reason" in Hick, *The Existence of God*, 137–43.

The argument clearly appeals to common belief and common reasoning. It is surprising to observe that famous atheists like Dawkins and Hitchens seem to agree with the existence of moral values and duties. However, like all atheists, they claim that moral values do not necessarily require a rule-maker, namely God. They suggest that people would have established these definite codes anyway.[133]

The Problem of Hell and Free Will

The problem of Hell has a premise very similar to that of the problem of evil, which was discussed above. Skeptics argue that there is a conflict between the concept of an all-loving, all-caring, all-good God and the existence of Hell. How can an omnipotent god send his creation into a place for eternal punishment? Jonathan Kvanvig[134] and Joel Buenting[135] have dedicated a whole book to this popular issue in philosophy. There are different types of answers to this question. Since the question clearly targets monotheistic faiths, Christian, Muslim, and Jewish theologians have come up with specific answers. From a general philosophical point of view, this argument seems to be self-destroying when one considers that God is also all-just. If God is just, He clearly has to provide justice, which either happens here in this world or elsewhere. This makes the existence of Hell necessary.

Among many answers, arguably the most reasonable one is the *Free Will* defense. Apologists such as Kvanvig and Hunt suggest that human beings possess the right to choose, including the right to choose to act in an evil way, and consequently, free will makes the existence of Hell necessary in order to punish them.

Moral Nihilism

The term "nihilism" is derived from the Latin word "*nihil*," which means nothingness. Nihilism is essentially the complete rejection of all values, and exposes the meaninglessness of life. The classical view of the creationists puts God at the very center of morality and the meaning of life. God is the essential element of all moral values. As Dostoyevsky's character Ivan

133. In *God is Not Great*, Hitchens goes one step further and argues that religion is the source of all evil, not the source of goodness. See Hitchens, *God Is Not Great*, 13.

134. See Kvanvig, *The Problem of Hell.*

135. See Buenting, *The Problem of Hell.*

Fyodorovich summed it up, "If there is no God, everything is permitted."[136] Nihilists, on the other hand, believe that nothingness prevails and that the world is meaningless.[137]

The term "nihilism" was used for the first time by Ivan Turgenev in his 1862 book *Fathers and Sons*,[138] but as a philosophical theory it is strongly associated with Nietzsche. Nietzsche shows his complete rejection of the teleological argument by asserting that there is no objective order or structure in the world except for what we give it.[139]

The positions of atheists and nihilists differ regarding morality. Atheists believe that there is no good evidence for believing in a deity. Hence objective values are not derived from God; they simply exist objectively. They claim that their values are generated from feelings and from relationships with other people. This—in contrast to what atheists claim—makes them subjective (i.e., it is changeable from person to person). Yet the atheist point of view is not a denial of the existence of moral values and morality, but only of the divinity of their source. To put it in context, some atheists say that torturing a small child is wrong not because a deity imposes it on us as wrong but because it is objectively wrong to do so.

Nihilists, on the other hand, argue that morality does not exist as something inherent in objective morality. If it exists it is an artificial construction; therefore, no one action is necessarily preferable to another. For example, killing, for any reason, is not inherently right or wrong.

Arguments from Miracles and Religious Experience

Both miracles and the religious experience of individuals are used as evidence for the existence of God by theologians such as A. E. Taylor and many ordinary believers alike. The main standpoint of the argument from miracles is that the known laws of nature are broken by extraordinary incidents. Since the laws of nature are implemented by the creator and the controller of the universe, i.e., God, these incidents or miracles could only be achieved with His permission. Since the miracles exist, God must exist.

Hume sets out two conditions that must be fulfilled for an incident to be counted as a miracle. First, it has to transgress the laws of nature, and, secondly, this act of transgression must have been produced by an act and

136. See Dostoyevsky and Garnett, *The Brothers Karamazov*, 134–35.

137. See Thielicke, *Nihilism; Its Origin and Nature, with a Christian Answer.*

138. See Turgenev and Garnett, *Fathers and Sons.*

139. See Nietzsche, Kaufmann, and Hollingdale, *The Will to Power.*

will of God.[140] Swinburne, however, argues that extraordinary events do not necessarily count as miracles, unless they show religious significance.[141] For instance, water running uphill defying gravity in certain parts of the world is not necessarily a miracle, but Moses' parting of the sea is certainly a miracle, because it has a religious significance. Miracles and personal experience are not accepted by skeptics as sound proofs for the existence of God. Skeptics argue that there are always more comprehensible scientific explanations for what is perceived as a miracle. They see incidents which science cannot explain as unexplained phenomena rather than as miracles.

Conclusion

This chapter has outlined the most common arguments for the existence of God and the counter-arguments to refute them. The first argument, i.e., the ontological argument, is arguably the least convincing and the most criticized of all. Skeptic philosophers develop reverse arguments; using the same method as the advocates of the ontological argument such as St Anselm's to demonstrate the weakness of this argument. If Anselm and Descartes could claim the existence of God through a definition of God, so the skeptics could claim the existence of a "perfect island" or a "shunicorn."

The cosmological arguments, on the other hand, pose more serious challenges to the mind. There are three distinctive versions of cosmological argument. The *kalām* version focuses on the principle of determination for a creator in time; the Thomist version argues from causality; and the Leibnizian version is based on sufficient reason. Theists, who argue from cosmology, claim that since infinite regress is not possible, the universe has to have a beginning, an uncaused cause or sufficient cause to have brought the universe into existence. There seems to be no dispute between theists and atheists as to how the universe came into existence. The Big Bang theory is currently the most popular explanation. However, a dispute has emerged about who caused the Big Bang. Theists argue that the necessarily existent God created the contingent universe out of nothing. Atheists such as Stephen Hawking, on the other hand, claim that there is no need for a god to explain the Big Bang and the universe coming into existence. How it happened can be explained within the laws of quantum physics. However, *why* the universe came into existence at all is yet to be explained

140. Hume, *Enquiries Concerning Human Understanding, and Concerning the Principles of Morals*, 115

141. Swinburne, *Miracles*, 6.

The teleological argument, which is possibly the most popular defense of theism, suggests that the apparent design and purposefulness of the universe require a designer. Proponents of the teleological argument also claim that the orderliness and regularities in the universe, and the existence of life permitting fundamental physical forces, are the work of a cosmic intelligence. This intelligent designer, according to theists, is God. Atheists, on the other hand, argue that non-theistic theories, including Darwin's theory of evolution, are more realistic. The design argument pulls into the debate more people from the scientific domain than from the philosophical domain. Theists claim that naturalistic explanations for order and design in the universe are mathematically highly improbable. However, atheists argue that it is still more reasonable to believe in their version rather than in the theists' version, which is unverifiable, untestable and un-provable.

The moral arguments assert that the existence of objective moral values and duties within the human mind and conscience is an indication of the existence of God. They argue that moral codes are given by a supreme moral giver; that is God. Atheists reject the idea that a god is necessary for people to be good and righteous. They argue that human intelligence is well enough equipped to distinguish between right and wrong. Good is inherently good and evil is inherently bad. Therefore, for atheists, reason alone is enough to establish correct moral codes and morality does not require God.

Miracles and religious experience are the last two tools used by the apologetic of theism. Although most philosophers consider them two separate arguments, they are closely connected in the case of prophets and revelations. Followers of the Abrahamic religions present the miracles of their prophets and the scriptures given to them as solid evidence for the existence of God. There is more history and psychology involved in these arguments than pure philosophy. Critics of theism argue that the evidence presented for the authenticity of the scriptures is not reliable. All known scriptures, they claim, are the work of their bearers, not of a divine entity. Prophets may well have existed as influential historical figures, but atheists reject the idea that the existence of prophets is a sound proof of the existence of God.

2

A Brief Biography of Saïd Nursi

Introduction

Bediüzzaman Saïd Nursi[1] (1877–1960) is probably one of the most influential intellectuals that Turkey produced in the twentieth century. This chapter examines his life via discussion of the historic and political perspectives that shaped his discourse. It presents an analysis of Nursi's intellectual shift from sociological concerns into philosophical challenges of materialism and atheism, rather than a chronological account of his life. This chapter also gives the analysis of certain terminology such as self (*anā*), self-referential meaning, other indicative meaning, book of universe etc. used by Nursi. The aim of this chapter, therefore, is not to give the reader a chronological life story of Nursi but to recreate the scene in which Nursi developed and introduced his ideas to make the reader understand better how and why Nursi took this certain discourse.

Nursi was born in eastern Anatolia[2] in 1877.[3] At the time, the region where he was born was called Kurdistan and was within the borders of the Ottoman Empire. Nursi's life spread over two completely different regimes: first, the Ottoman Empire, which was a theocratic monarchy with a parliament, and then the Turkish Republic, a secular democracy built on the ashes of the Ottoman Empire in 1923. As the child of Kurdish parents, Nursi

1. The conventional English version, "Said Nursi," is commonly used instead of Saïd Nursi.

2. In order to avoid confusion between the geographic east of the Ottoman Empire and the Republic of Turkey, I use the geographical name of Anatolia.

3. There is a disagreement about Nursi's exact date of birth, owing to Hijri–Gregorian calendar conversion and lack of precise records. Vahide accepts 1877 as more accurate than others. See Vahide and Abu-Rabi, *Islam in Modern Turkey: An Intellectual Biography of Bediuzzaman Said Nursi*, 3.

spoke the local Kurdish language, Ottoman Turkish which was the language of the court and the government,[4] as well as Arabic, the language of science, knowledge and religion. This rather small detail on Nursi's ethnicity and cultural background is to for the foundation of his solutions to the problem of intolerance in the wider world and the problem of Ottoman Education system in particular.

In accordance with these factors, Nursi's life is conventionally divided into three periods. The first is from his birth in 1877 to 1920. Nursi himself calls this thirty-seven-year part of his life the Old Said era. The second period is from 1920 to 1950, when Nursi produced his *magnum opus*, The *Risale-i Nur* (The Epistles of Light). Nursi called this part of his life the New Said era. The last ten years of his life, from 1950 to 1960, are known as the Third Said period.

The Old Said Period (1877–1920)

Nursi spent the first thirty years of his life in eastern Anatolia studying various disciplines in different *madrasas* (religious schools). As a gifted student, Nursi needed only a short time to complete all the courses he attended. Hence, he managed to study almost all the taught-sciences fairly quickly. He read and memorized most of the texts, including those that were not even part of the *madrasa's* curriculum. He was an outstandingly brilliant student. As a result, the nickname *Bediüzzaman* (Wonder of the Age) was given to him by one of his early teachers in Siirt, Mullah Fethullah.[5]

The end of the nineteenth century and the beginning of the twentieth century represented a challenging period for the six hundred-year-old Ottoman Empire. It was fighting wars on different fronts, and facing economic hardship, rising nationalism and many other political problems.

Nursi quickly awakened to the facts that the Empire was in decline and that there were a great many problems to solve. He identified what the main flaws in the education system were and formulated his own solution. At the time, the education system had two tiers. One was strictly religious education and the other was modern sciences (i.e., medicine, engineering, etc.). This caused a chasm between religious scholars who possessed little or no

4. The Rise of the Turks and the Ottoman Empire, [Excerpted from *Turkey: A Country Study.* Paul M. Pitman III, ed. Washington, DC: Federal Research Division of the Library of Congress, 1987] available at http://www.shsu.edu/~his_ncp/Turkey2.html, last accessed on 23 October 2013

5. Vahide and Abu-Rabi, *Islam in Modern Turkey: An Intellectual Biography of Bediuzzaman Said Nursi*, 13.

knowledge of modern science and scientists who had little or no religious knowledge.

Nursi came up with a project for a university called "*Madrasat uz-Zahrā*" which would bring these two tiers, that is, traditional religious teaching and modern science, together. He suggested that his university should have its central campus in Bitlis, one campus in Van and another campus in Diyarbakır. All the Arabic, Turkish and Kurdish languages would be used simultaneously. In *Munāẓarāt,* he writes:

> . . . in this university the language of Arabic is obligatory, the language of Kurdish is acceptable and the language of Turkish is necessary . . .[6]

This idea would arguably have been the solution to the Kurdish Problem that remains to this day. In order to realize his ambitious project,[7] Nursi went to Istanbul, the capital city of the Empire, in 1907. He met Sultan Abdulhamid II and presented his proposal[8] to him. This was a very turbulent time in Ottoman history since the Second Constitution was about to be proclaimed. After submitting his proposal, Nursi did not receive a welcoming treatment. In fact, he was arrested and briefly detained in prison on the grounds of being mentally unfit.[9]

In 1908, the Constitutional Revolution took place, led by the Young Turks. The fruit of the revolution was the reinstatement of Parliament, which had been suspended by Sultan Abdulhamid II in 1878. The revolution saw the union of all the opposition parties against the Sultan. All nationalists, secularists, reform-minded persons and pluralists joined forces. It seemed to be a positive step towards democracy, but it led to the events that eventually completely destroyed the Ottoman Empire. Nursi, like many

6. Nursi, *Münazarāt*, 28.

7. On Nursi's education reform project, Şükran Vahide writes, "It might be noted here that his ideas about educational reform were far-reaching and radical. Besides the joint teaching of the religious education and modern physical sciences, already mentioned, Nursi proposed reconciling and bringing together in the *Madrasat uz-Zahrā*,' the three main educational traditions of the time, the *medreses* or 'religious schools,' the *mektebs* or 'modern secular schools' and the Sufi *tekkes*, and the disciplines they represent. It would thus heal the rifts between them and the resultant division of society . . . he was also a strong advocate of students specializing in subjects for which they had an aptitude, a radical departure from established practice."

8. In his proposal, Nursi writes: "The religious sciences are the light of the conscience, and the modern sciences are the light of the reason. The truth becomes manifest through the combining of the two. The students' endeavor will take flight on these two wings. When they are separated it gives rise to bigotry in the one, and wiles and skepticism in the other."

9. Şahiner, *Bilinmeyen Taraflariyla Bediüzzaman Said Nursi: Kronolojik Hayati*, 93.

other Islamists, supported constitutionalism. Only through freedom and constitutional government could the empire be saved, progress achieved and Islamic civilization established, he believed.[10]

Nursi became a well-known public figure. He gave open public speeches, and wrote articles in support of constitutionalism. He became a founder member of *Ittihad-i Muhammedi Cemiyeti* (Muḥammadan Union for Muslim Unity). After the Thirty-First of March Incident[11] in 1909, he was arrested, court martialed, and acquitted after having served twenty-four days in prison. In 1910, Nursi published his first book, *Nutuk* (Speech), which was a collection of his articles and speeches.[12] In 1911, he published the defense he had presented to the Court Martial under the same title, *Divān-ı Harb-i Örfî*. It was reprinted the following year.[13]

Nursi left Istanbul and headed to the east of Anatolia to live among Kurdish tribes again. He defended democracy and constitutionalism as a way forward. His ideas and exchanges were later published in two books. *Muḥākamāt* (Reasoning) addressed the ʿulamā (scholars), and *Munāẓarāt* (Debates) addressed the general public. These two works were published in 1911 and 1913 respectively. Nursi impressed both scholars and the public with his diagnosis of the three diseases and three cures of the East. The three diseases, he said, were "ignorance, poverty and internal conflict," and they had to be fought with the three cures of "education, industry and unity."

He then travelled to Damascus[14] in Syria, where he gave his notable Damascus Sermon in the Umayyad Mosque to an audience of some ten thousand people, including one hundred and fifty scholars.[15] In his sermon in Arabic, Nursi identified six illnesses and offered remedies from "the pharmacy of the Qur'an." He said:

> In the conditions of the present time in these lands, I have learnt a lesson in the school of mankind's social life and I have realized that (at the origin of) what has allowed foreigners, Europeans,

10. Mürsel, *Bediüzzaman Said Nursi Ve Devlet Felsefesi*, 223–35.

11. The Thirty-first of March Incident was a revolt against *İttihad ve Terakki* (The Young Turks) who took charge of government after the Second Constitutional Revolution. It occurred on 31 March 1325 on the Rumi calendar (13 April 1909), hence called The Thirty-first of March Incident.

12. Vahide and Abu-Rabi, *Islam in Modern Turkey: An Intellectual Biography of Bediuzzaman Said Nursi*, 59.

13. Abu-Rabi, *Islam at the Crossroads*, xviii.

14. Syria was part of the Ottoman Empire in 1911. Following World War I Syria separated and went under the French Mandate as the Ottoman Empire lost the War.

15. Nursi himself reports this event in *The Rays* and gives these figures. See Nursi, *The Rays*, 1148.

> to fly towards the future (with the wings of) progress while it arrested us and kept us, in respect of material development, in the Middle Ages, are six dire sicknesses. The sicknesses are these:
>
> Firstly: the rise to life of despair and hopelessness in social life.
>
> Secondly: the death of truthfulness in social and political life.
>
> Thirdly: the love of enmity.
>
> Fourthly: not knowing the luminous bonds that bind the believers to one another.
>
> Fifthly: despotism, which creeps, becoming widespread as though it was various contagious diseases.
>
> Sixthly: restricting endeavor to what is personally beneficial.
>
> I shall explain, by means of six words, the lesson I have learnt from the pharmacy of the Qur'an, which is like a faculty of medicine. This lesson constitutes the medicine to cure our social life of those six dire sicknesses.[16]

At his stage, Nursi still mainly concentrated on the social problems of the Empire. He wanted to elucidate the ills and cures of the times' social problems. His famous Damascus Sermon was printed twice in Arabic and later reprinted in Turkish as well. Nursi left Damascus and went back to Istanbul to join the new Sultan, Mehmed Rashad, on his Balkan Journey. The mission was to gain the support of Balkan nations still living under the Ottoman flag. Although the trip was successful in the sense that it refreshed the old bonds, the upcoming events of the World War I led eventually to the separation of the Balkans from the rest of the Empire. By Nursi's own account, this Balkan trip helped him to secure the funding for *Madrasat uz-Zahrā* (the Islamic Modern University in the East), the foundations of which were eventually laid in Van in 1913. The project was abruptly halted when World War I broke out in 1914. Nursi had to join the militia to defend the Eastern provinces with his students. Now, his *madrasa* was both a school and a military base. Accounts by visitors to his *madrasa* describe how books and rifles were hanging on the walls side by side.[17]

Just before the turn of the twentieth century, the British Secretary for the Colonies, Gladstone, openly declared war on the Qur'an, which, he said, was the main obstacle to British imperialist ambitions.[18] Despite all

16. See *Hutbe-i* Şāmiye (Damascus Sermon) in Nursi, *Hutbe-i Şamiye*, 1961–62.

17. Şahiner, *Bilinmeyen Taraflariyla Bediüzzaman Said Nursi: Kronolojik Hayati*, 165

18. The British Secretary for the Colonies, Gladstone, said: So long as the Muslims have the Qur'an, we shall be unable to dominate them. We must either take it from them, or make them lose their love of it. See Vahide, *Biography of Bediuzzaman Said Nursi*, 47.

the political and social turbulence, Nursi had always wanted to refresh the truths of Islam and the Qur'an, to dispel the doubts spread by the enemies of religion, and to repulse the underground fears exploited by externalists and extremists.[19] He explained his life mission in *The Words*:

> One time I had a dream: I was at the foot of Mount Ararat. The mountain suddenly exploded, scattering rocks the size of mountains all over the world, shaking it.
>
> Then a man appeared at my side. He told me: "Expound the aspects of the Qur'an's miraculousness you know, concisely and succinctly!"
>
> I thought of the dream's meaning while still dreaming, telling myself: the explosion here symbolizes a revolution in mankind.
>
> As a result of it the guidance of the Criterion of Truth and Falsehood will be exalted everywhere, and will rule. And the time will come to expound its miraculousness![20]

According to Nursi, Qur'anic exegesis (*tafsīr*) should consist of three main parts: (1) the Element of Reality (*haqīqah*), (2) the Element of Rhetoric (*balāghah*), and (3) the Element of Doctrine (ʿaqāid).

The early writings of Nursi, such as *Munāẓarāt* and *Muḥākamāt,* place great emphasis on the element of reality in Islam. Nursi was well aware of the fact that Islam had been polluted by *Isra'illiyāt* (Judaic or Judea-Christian legends in the early Islamic literature) and ancient Greek philosophy. This caused confusion to externalists. He tried to explain that modern sciences and the Qur'an do not conflict at all.[21] Some of the expressions in the Qur'an are representational, not factual.

Nursi started working on *al-ʿIshārāt al-I'jāz*, which is dedicated to demonstrating the Qur'an's miraculous eloquence, in 1913. This work was never completed as he intended, owing to his capture by the Russian army in 1916. In the two hundred or so pages that Nursi managed to write, he commented on the first verses of the Qur'an with a great knowledge of the art of the Arabic language. Vahide relates contemporary scholars' admiration for Nursi's subtlety in expounding the Qur'an's word-order (*naẓm*),

19. See Vahide, in Abu-Rabi, *Islam at the Crossroads*, 8.

20. Nursi, *The Words*, 336.

21. See Said Nursi, *Muhakemat* (Reasoning). Nursi dedicated almost this entire book for the reality of Islam. For example, he explained verses like Qur'an 18:86: "Until when he reached the place where the sun set, he found it going down into a black sea, and found by it a people. We said: O Zulqarnain! either give them a chastisement or do them a benefit." and Qur'an 51:48: "And the earth, we have made it a wide extent; how well have we then spread (it) out."

subtlety which in places surpasses that of the great masters of the past such as Jurjani and Zamakshari.[22] After having spent around two years in Kostroma on the River Volga as a prisoner of war, Nursi escaped from Russia to Istanbul via Warsaw and Austria.[23] Since Germany was the ally of the Ottoman Empire in the war, Nursi received some help from the Germans and made his way back to Istanbul. During the last few years of the Old Said period, Nursi produced several small books: *Sunūḥāt*, *Lemaāt*, *ʿIshārāt* and *Hutuvat-i Sitte*. He was also involved in the creation of the Madrasa Teachers' Association (1919), whose aim was to maintain and raise educational standards in the *madrasas*. To fight the spread of alcoholism, Nursi took part in the foundation of the Green Crescent Society (1920). When World War I ended in 1918, the Ottoman Empire had lost the war and was invaded by foreign troops. Nursi worked for the removal of the invaders and for independence. He eventually went back to Anatolia and withdrew into solitude. This was effectively the end of the Old Said era and the beginning of the New Said.

The New Said Period (1920–50)

During his solitude, Nursi decided to take the Qur'an as his only guide and free himself from the negative influence of philosophy. He began writing his *al-Mathnawī al-ʿArabī al-Nūriyah*, which was translated into Turkish later. This book was the first of the New Said's lifetime struggle to fight atheist and materialist philosophy championed by Nietzsche, Darwin, Comte, Büchner, etc. Out of the six thousand pages of Nursi's work, the *Risale-i Nur* Collection, [24] the main body was written after 1920. *The Words*, *The Letters*, *The Flashes*, *The Rays*, as well as *al-Mathnawī al-ʿArabī al-Nūriyah*, are the fruits of the New Said era. Describing Said Nursi's *magnum opus*, the *Risale-i Nur*, Vahide writes:

> . . . *Risale-i Nur* is Qur'anic interpretation . . . expounding the teachings of Qur'an on the truth of belief that incorporates the traditional Islamic sciences and modern scientific knowledge, and while instilling those truths, effectively refutes the basis of

22. See Şükran Vahide, *Towards the Intellectual Biography of Said Nursi*, in Abu-Rabi, *Islam at the Crossroads*, 9.

23. See Vahide, *Bediüzzaman Said Nursi: The Author of the Risale-i Nur*, 129.

24. See Appendix 1: Chronology and the Diagram of Said Nursi's *Risale-i Nur* Collection.

> materialist philosophy . . . [in a] unique way in the Islamic world for the renewal of belief.[25]

In other words, the *Risale-i Nur* is a Qur'anic exegesis (*tafsīr*), or a topical commentary on the Qur'an, with a unique, characteristic approach. It is evident from the textual analysis that Nursi dedicated the main body of the *Risale-i Nur* to proving the four main aims of the Qur'an: (1) the existence of the Single Maker, i.e., God, (2) prophethood, (3) the resurrection of the dead, and (4) justice.

It is clear from a historical perspective why Nursi shifted his attention from social issues to philosophy, and more specifically to the refutation of materialist philosophy. With the proclamation of the Republic of Turkey in 1923 by Mustafa Kemal Atatürk, a new secular country was born out of a theocratic empire.[26] This new regime took the Kemalist ideology as its official state philosophy. This ideology was characterized by six principles: republicanism, populism, nationalism, revolutionism, secularism, and statism.[27] The progress of the new nation state, according to Atatürk, had to be guided by education and science-based progress on the principles of positivism, rationalism and enlightenment. The new regime abolished the office of Caliphate in 1924 and introduced the Latin alphabet to replace the Arabic alphabet, which had been in use for several centuries. This had a devastating effect on the public at large. The positivist ideas of Auguste Comte and the materialism of Ludwig Büchner and others, which had initially become popular among secular schools in the early 1900, was now the official ideology of the new republic. [28] Islam was quickly removed from public life with the banning of the Arabic call to prayer and the ban on the dervish lodges (*tekkes).* Materialist philosophy entered schoolbooks together with evolutionary theories, while religion was labeled as backwardness. There was a common unpleasant reaction against these extreme actions of the new regime. After the Sheikh Said[29] revolt of 1925, Nursi was arrested and

25. Vahide, *Towards the Intellectual Biography of Said Nursi* in Abu-Rabi, *Islam at the Crossroads*, 1.

26. It is arguable that The Ottoman Empire had better liberal and democratic characters than many so-called democratic countries. However, it has been considered as theocratic in the sense that Sharia laws based on the Qur'an were in force in running the empire.

27. Webster, *The Turkey of Ataturk: Social Process in the Turkish Reformation*, 245.

28. Hanioglu, *Bir Siyasi Dusunur Olarak Dr Abdullah Cevded Ve Donemi*, 370–72.

29. Said Nursi and Sheikh Said were both popular Kurdish personalities, but they should not be confused. Sheik Said led a revolt against the newly formed Turkish Republic in order to gain Kurdish independence. The Kurdish rebels of some fifteen thousand strong were crushed by some fifty thousand Turkish troops. Sheikh Said was

sent into exile at Burdur, even though he opposed the rebellion.[30] There he started writing short treaties to answer local people's questions on religion. During the first three years of his exile in Barla, he completed *The Words.* In the following years, his individual treaties were brought together to form two more books, *The Letters* and *The Flashes.* Since the main aim of these books was to revitalize for people the Islamic faith, Nursi quickly became the enemy of the regime. The state's decision to contain him in a remote village of Barla[31] did not apparently work, since he managed to gather a large audience and spread his treaties, thanks to followers copying them by hand. Nursi once again was summoned and relocated to another exile in Isparta in 1934. Although his teachings were not political, they displeased the Kemalist regime intensely because of their religious contents. The unity of the Maker (God), prophethood, resurrection, and the miraculousness of the Qur'an—these were subjects the Kemalist regime did not like at all. The Kemalist regime was to eradicate Islam and its values from public life and promote a new Western, secular and materialist lifestyle in Turkey. In 1935, Nursi and one hundred and twenty of his students were arrested and charged with "opposing the reforms and belonging to a secret political organization . . . exploiting religion for political ends, forming an organization that constituted a possible threat to public order and giving instruction in Sufism".[32] The court acquitted ninety-seven of his students but sentenced Nursi to eleven months in prison on the grounds of opposition to dress code.[33] Nursi was to be exiled in Kastamonu after having served his sentence in Eskişehir. During the Kastamonu exile, he wrote *The Supreme Sign* and some parts of *The Rays.* He was once again arrested along with one hundred and twenty-six of his students and sent to Denizli. Charges similar to those used in the Eskişehir trial were brought against him, but this time Nursi and

captured and executed.

30. Badıllı writes about Nursi's response to Shaikh Said thus, 'The struggle you are embarking on will cause brother to kill brother and will be fruitless. For the Kurds and Turks are brothers. The Turkish nation has acted as the standard-bearer of Islam for centuries. It has produced millions of saints and given millions of martyrs. The sword may not be drawn against the sons of Islam's heroic defenders, and I shall not draw mine!

See Badıllı, *Bediüzzaman Said-I Nursi, Mufassal Tarihçe-I Hayatı*, 660. Quoted from Selahaddin Çelebi's biographical notes (1946).

31. Barla, at the time, was a very small isolated village on the other side of the lake Eğirdir. In his *Tarihçe-i Hayatı* (Nursi's Biography), Nursi reports how a little boat transferred him to Barla across the lake, as there was no road access.

32. See Vahide, A Chronology of Said Nursi's Life, in Abu-Rabi, *Islam at the Crossroads*, xxi.

33. Atatürk introduced the new dress code in 1925, which made the use of the hat obligatory. Anyone refusing to put a hat on was punished severely.

his students were all acquitted and the *Risale-i Nur* was cleared. However, during the trial, which lasted some nine months, they were kept in harsh conditions in Denizli Prison. *The Fruits of Belief* was written in the prison during this difficult time. Nursi was forced to stay in Emirdağ where, by 1947, the *Risale-i Nur* was completed. Nursi was detained once again and sent to Afyon Prison where he served another twenty months, on the same charges he had previously faced. Although he and the *Risale-i Nur* were cleared once again, the process was deliberately slow in order to keep him in prison as long as possible. Now, Nursi was over seventy years of age, and owing to his periods of exile and stays in prison his health was very poor. According to the accounts of his students, the regime was deliberately trying to kill him, by means of poisoning and by exposing him to extreme cold in his prison cell.[34] The new state was run by Mustafa Kemal Atatürk and his Republican People's Party (RPP)[35] up until 1950. This twenty-seven-year period in the history of modern Turkey, known as the single-party period, is still very controversial. For some, it was a brutal dictatorship, for others, it was a necessary step towards establishing a new state. It was a period when philosophy-based ideologies were becoming increasingly influential in political systems and when Islamic societies underwent the most radical changes in the whole history of Islamic civilization.[36]

Owing to his enforced exile, Nursi rarely made contact with people outside his close circle of students. His main means of communication was through his letters and treaties. During the second period of his life (the New Said period) he hardly made any public speeches other than his court defenses. Hence, his only option was to promote the *Risale-i Nur* rather than his own leadership and charisma. On many occasions, he called himself "a student of the *Risale-i Nur*" rather than the author of it. From 1926 on, Nursi started building up a large number of followers of his *Risale-i Nur*, corporately called the *Risale-i Nur Movement*, or *Nurcus*. Although the new regime abolished the use of the Arabic alphabet in favor of the Latin, Nursi wrote his treaties and letters using the Ottoman alphabet (Arabic), which made them readily understandable by the public at large. Here, it is important to note that the *Risale-i Nur* was printed in the modern Latin alphabet only in 1956, after all charges against it by the Afyon Court were dropped.

34. See Şahiner, *Bilinmeyen Taraflariyla Bediüzzaman Said Nursi: Kronolojik Hayati.*

35. The Republican People's Party was established by Atatürk on 9 September 1923. It was the only party without opposition until the General Election of 1950. The ideology of the party is Kemalism and Social Democracy.

36. See Ahmet Davutoglu, *Bediuzzaman and the Politics of the 20th Century* at http://www.nur.org/en/nurcenter/nurlibrary/Bediuzzaman_and_the_Politics_of_the_20th_Century_198 last accessed on 25 October 2014

Especially after the ban on Sufi lodges (*tekkes)* and religious schools (*madrasas)*, the public experienced a vacuum and a lack of guidance. The *Risale-i Nur* filled this gap and it was widely accepted and its text reproduced by people in and around Isparta.

The *Risale-i Nur* and Nursi's Terminology

According to Nursi, the *Risale-i Nur* inspired directly by the Qur'an,[37] is a genuine spiritual commentary on the Qur'an's meanings (*manevi Tafsīr*).[38] In *al-*ʿIshārāt *al-I'jāz*, Nursi highlights four main purposes (*maqāṣid-i 'arba'*) that the Qur'an expounds. These are: the oneness or unity of God (*tawḥīd*), the nature of and the necessity for prophethood (*nubuwwah*), the resurrection of the dead (*ḥashr*), and justice and worship (*'adalah and* ʿibādah).[39] In order to clarify the Qur'an's exposition of these four elements, Nursi explains certain themes in his writings. Turner and Horkuç argue that six of these distinct themes appear in Nursi's writings.[40]

The Book of Universe (*Kitāb-i Kāināt*) and the Beautiful Names of God (*Al-Asmā Al-Husnā*)

Throughout the *Risale-i Nur*, Nursi meticulously comments on the universe being a book written by God. He explains that, just like a mirror, the universe reflects all the different beautiful names and attributes[41] of its Creator. To Nursi, all beings have been created for a purpose and are the signs (*āyāt*) of their Creator.[42] Therefore, the purpose of man's creation is to attain belief in God, which may be achieved by the correct interpretation of the cosmic narrative.

The very first verses of the Qur'an in *Surat al 'Alaq* revealed to Prophet Muḥammad ordered him to read in the name of his Lord. At first the verse might look to the ordinary reader that he or she needs to learn to read, i.e., become literate. However, based on Nursi's way of thinking one might easily reinterpret this very first Qur'anic verse rather differently. The verse might

37. Nursi, *The Letters*, 527.

38. Nursi, *Tarihçe-i Hayatı*, 2225.

39. Nursi, *Isharat-ul I'caz*, 1167.

40. Turner and Horkuc, *Said Nursi*, 53.

41. Nursi mentions more than the classical ninety-nine beautiful names of God listed in the *hadīth*.

42. This particular theme is also Nursi's first way of arguing for the existence of God, i.e., the teleological (design) argument, which is the focal topic of Chapter 3.

actually mean to read the cosmic book or what Nursi calls *kitāb-ı kāināt* with its true meaning which, according to Nursi, is *ma'nā-i ḥarfī*. This particular interpretation of the Qur'an also set the foundations of Nursi's philosophy. He makes his position very clear in several pieces in his *Risale-i Nur*, such as the Twelfth Word and the Thirtieth Word. Nursi elucidates that there are only two ways of reading the cosmic narrative, one is the way of materialist philosophy which only reads the universe with its self-referential meaning and the other one is the Qur'anic and Prophetic reading which reads it with its other indicative meaning, i.e., witnessing God's names and attributes in every event and in every being.

The Self, or the Human "I" (*Anā*)

According to Nursi, *anā* is the trust given to man by his Creator. The first function of *anā* is to understand the beautiful names of God. Secondly, *anā* is a key given to man wherewith to unlock the secret of creation. *Anā,* the human "I," is a comparison tool given to man so he can see where God stands in contrast to where he stands. In *Anā Risalesi,* The Thirtieth Word, Nursi writes:

> The All-Wise Maker gave to man as a Trust an "I" which comprises indications and samples that show and cause to recognize the truths of the attributes and functions of his dominicality, so that the "I" might be a unit of measurement and the attributes of dominicality and functions of Divinity might be known. However, it is not necessary for a unit of measurement to have actual existence; like hypothetical lines in geometry, a unit of measurement may be formed by hypothesis and supposition. It is not necessary for its actual existence to be established by concrete knowledge and proofs.[43]

Nursi's interpretation of self seems to very different from almost everyone else in non-Islamic tradition. Materialist philosophy locates self at the center of the universe, while Nursi locates God at the center of the universe. Again the Twelfth Word and the Thirtieth Word give strong clues on Nursi's understanding of the purpose of men's existence. Self in Nursian thinking is an essential tool to understand not only the existence of God but is greatness in his attributes. One can start off with faculties and capacities in himself or herself, then realizes he or she is not fully capable. He or she then concludes, or at least this is what Nursi expects, that there has

43. Nursi, *The Words*, 241.

to be a higher more capable being, that is God. Unlike what the materials philosophy suggests the true purpose of self (*anā*), according to Nursi, is to understand the nature of God.

The "Self-Referential" and the "Other-Indicative" (*Ma'nà-i Ismī*, and *Ma'nā-i Ḥarfī*)

To aid understanding of the meaning of life and the nature of the universe, Nursi introduced the concepts of *m'anā-i ismī* (the significative or self-referential meaning of things), and *m'anā-i ḥarfī* (other-indicative meaning). He explains that cosmos and life can be understood correctly only through the window of *m'anā-i ḥarfī*[44] (the meaning that signifies something other than itself). In *The Words*, he explains that the Qur'an mentions beings "not for themselves, but for another." That is, it speaks of the universe as evidence for Almighty God's existence, unity and sublimity.[45] It is apparent from the Tenth Word on Resurrection that Nursi bases his arguments mainly on facts such as order in the universe, purpose in all creatures, and the absence of waste in the cosmos. These are two well-known theistic arguments in the philosophy of religion, the cosmological argument and the teleological argument, also known as the argument from design, which will be examined in the following chapters.

In line with the previous concepts, it can be argued that Nursi systematically tries to teach his readers how to use faculties given to them in order to read the universe correctly to attain the knowledge of God. Nursi seems to create a mind set in his readers mind that continuous creation happening

44. Nursi writes in the *Addendum of the 26th Word*: "According to the apparent meaning of things (*m'anā-i ismī*), which looks to each thing itself, everything is transitory, lacking, accidental, non-existent. But according to the meaning that signifies something other than itself (*m'anā-i ḥarfī*) and in respect of each thing being a mirror to the All-Glorious Maker's Names and charged with various duties, each is a witness, it is witnessed, and it is existent. The purification and cleansing of a person at this stage is as follows:

In his existence he is non-existent, and in his non-existence he has existence. That is to say, if he values himself and attributes existence to himself, he is in a darkness of non-existence as great as the universe. That is, if he relies on his individual existence and is unmindful of the True Giver of Existence, he has an individual light of existence like that of a fire-fly and is submerged in an endless darkness of non-existence and separation. But if he gives up egotism and sees that he is a mirror of the manifestations of the True Giver of Existence, he gains all beings and an infinite existence. For he who finds the Necessary Existent One, the manifestation of Whose Names all beings manifest, finds everything."

See ibid., 211.

45. Ibid., 282.

in the universe and by using the tools of intellect one can constantly observe the evidences of God's existence and him being in charge at all times.

Causality

Nursi tries vigorously to convince his readers that there is no necessary connection between cause and effect independent of God. Scientific materialism, which Nursi considers the greatest threat to humankind, claims that the effective cause of what is actually happening now is the combined result of the previous causes. For example, when a burning match touches dry paper, the paper burns as a result of fire caused by the match. Nursi seems to be maintaining *Ash'ari's* approach to causality, which was also endorsed by Al-Ghazzālī. The *Ash'ari*–Al-Ghazzālī line of thought dictates that the actual cause for the piece of paper burning is not the match but God's creating a new set of conditions to realize the new effect. God is the creator of all causes (*musabbib al-asbāb*).[46]

Nursi explains that people misread nature and natural events in terms of causality. He explains that God is the absolute and continuous creator. According to Nursi, there are two types of creation. These are *ibdā* (creation out of nothing) and *inshā* (gradual building from existing material). In *The Flashes*, Nursi writes:

> Beings are created in two ways: one is creation from nothing called origination and invention; and the other is the giving of existence through bringing together existent elements and things, called composition and assembling. When in accordance with the manifestation of divine singleness and mystery of divine oneness, this occurs with an infinite ease, indeed, such ease as to be necessary. If not ascribed to divine singleness, it would be infinitely difficult and irrational, difficult to the degree of impossibility. However, the fact that beings in the universe come into existence with infinite ease and facility and no difficulty at all, and in perfect form, self-evidently shows the manifestation of divine singleness and proves that everything is directly the art of the Single One of Glory.[47]

46. Nursi expounds on this issue in his Thirty-Second Word while explaining the Qur'an 21:22: "Had there been within the heavens and earth gods besides Allāh, they both would have been ruined. So exalted is Allāh, Lord of the Throne, above what they describe." See ibid., 268–73.

47. Nursi, *The Flashes*, 808.

For Nursi, in order to maintain the element of test (*sırr-ı teklif*), God uses causes to veil his actual power and majesty, yet He expects people to understand that He is the absolute creator and controller of the events that scientific materialism explains otherwise.[48]

One can argue that Nursi was trying to establish a new vision or new way of thinking against the materialist approach to the natural events. Though he is not the first Islamic scholar to expound on the idea of *ibdā* and *inshā*, he is surely the one reintroducing into the twentieth century people whose minds had been polluted by the scientific materialism.

Belief and Submission (Īmān–Islam)

According to Nursi, the true salvation of humanity can only be achieved through a perfect balance between belief and submission. Thus, man is required to attain true belief through investigation and research. Throughout the *Risale-i Nur*, Nursi tries to make his readers move from *taklidi īmān* (belief through emulation) to *tahkiki īmān* (belief through investigation, true belief).[49] Aware of the threat of scientific materialism, Nursi develops a reverse theme of science and nature being the evidence of their Creator. This aspect of Nursi's writing is highly visible in pieces such as *The Treatise on Nature (Tabiat Risalesi)*[50] and The Supreme Sign (*Ayāt al-Kübra).*[51]

It seems that Nursi is not content with people having only *taklidi īmān* or being in the religion of Islam without having any genuine faith, i.e., *tahkiki īmān*. It can be argued that one of the main motives of the *Risale-i Nur* is teaching people how to attain true faith (*tahkiki īmān).*

Closed Doors of Creation

The last theme that Nursi elaborates on is the "closed doors of creation," which is closely connected to the second theme of *anā* (the human "I"). In *The Words*, Nursi explains:

> The key to the world is in the hand of man and is attached to his self. For while being apparently open, the doors of the universe

48. In *The Words*, Nursi writes: Yes, dignity and grandeur demand that causes are a veil to the hand of power in the view of the mind, while Divine unity and glory demand that causes withdraw their hands and have no true effect. See Nursi, *The Words*, 122.

49. See *Emirdağ Lahikası* in Nursi, *Risale-i Nur Külliyati* 2, 1681.

50. See Nursi, Nursi, *The Flashes*, 677–86.

51. See Nursi, Nursi, *The Rays*, 895–931.

> are in fact closed. God Almighty has given to man by way of a Trust, such a key, called the "I," that it opens all the doors of the world; He has given him an enigmatic "I" with which he may discover the hidden treasures of the Creator of the universe. But the "I" is also an extremely complicated riddle and an enigma that is difficult to solve. When its true nature and the purpose of its creation are known, as it is itself solved, so will be the universe.[52]

The Nursian view is that the purpose of human existence is to investigate and explore life and the universe so as to try to unlock the doors of creation in order to attain true belief (*tahkiki īmān).*[53] That is to say one needs to investigate the nature and the universe to attain the knowledge of God, and with the help of the Prophets and the Revelations understand the true meaning of the creation.

Attaining the Knowledge of God

The Third Sign in *the Thirty-second Word* reveals Nursi's difference from *kalām* philosophers. He explains that attaining the full knowledge of God has eight steps. The first step is simply by observing the universe. One sees artefacts and works (*āsār*) which is certainly the result of an action (*fi'il*) as every effect must have a cause. Intelligence asserts that action necessitates the existence of a doer (*fāil*). The doer must certainly have personal names and titles (*ism*) as well as traits and attributes (*siffah*). There is clearly perfection in the universe which self-evidently points to the perfection of the doer's functioning essence (*shu'ūn*), because it is from the functioning essence that the attributes proceed. Finally, the perfection of essential functions point at the degree of "knowledge of certainty" to the perfection of the functioning essence. They point to perfection so worthy that although the light of the perfection passes through the veils of functions, attributes, names, actions, and works of art, it still demonstrates the goodness, beauty, and perfection to be seen to this great extent in the universe.[54]

In other words, there is a continuous relation between *āsār*, *fi'il*, *fail*, *ism*, *siffah* and *shu'ūn*. Nursi's philosophy seems to be aimed at attaining the full understanding of the true nature of God (*Dhāt*) whereas mainstream

52. See Nursi, Nursi, *The Words*, 241.

53. Turner and Horkuc discuss these themes in greater detail. See Turner and Horkuc, *Said Nursi*, 53–84.

54. Nursi, *The Words*, 283.

kalām philosophers especially in their kalām cosmological arguments attain the knowledge that a doer is necessary in explaining the universe.

In pursuance of attaining the full knowledge of God, Nursi employs four arguments. The table below illustrates the chronological development of Nursi's arguments.

Table 1: Nursi's arguments for the existence of God in chronological order

Book	Al-Mathnawī al-'Arabī al-Nūrī		The Words
Date	(circa 1918)	(circa 1919)	(circa 1928)
Period	The Old Said		The New Said
Piece	Reshalar	Nokta	19th Word
1	*Kitāb-ı kabīr-i kāināt*	*Nubuwwah*	*Kitāb-ı kabīr-i kāināt*
2	*Nubuwwah*	*Kitāb-ı kabīr-i kāināt*	*Nubuwwah*
3	*Qur'an*	*Qur'an*	*Qur'an*
4		*Wijdān*	

It is evident in the above table that Nursi developed two different sets of arguments. In his New Said period, he seems to stick to his very first version which appears in *Reshalar* in *Al-Mathnaāwi al-Nūrī*. Nursi somehow changed the order of his arguments in *Nokta* putting prophethood as the first argument and adding conscience as a new addition to the list. Later he dropped the fourth argument which is built around conscience and put the book of universe argument as his first. This might be due to the fast changing political atmosphere of Anatolia which was now governed by secular republic. One can argue that since the Kemalist regime based its doctrine on the teachings of Büchner's materialism and Comte's positivism, Nursi felt obliged to develop parallel counter arguments based on reason and intellect.

Nursi's Style and Method

It is evident to any reader that Nursi wrote the treaties in *The Words* in very simple language compared to his other writings. He uses allegories to make the context clear to readers who were not highly educated. Then, he reveals the truth via the allegory. By way of proof of the Maker, Nursi tells the story of two men travelling through a land. One man is empty-headed and represents the atheist philosophy, and the other is wise and represents the theist philosophy. To the empty-headed man rejecting the Deity, the wise man replies:

> Every village must have its headman; every needle must have its manufacturer and craftsman. And, as you know, every letter must be written by someone. How, then, can it be that so extremely well-ordered a kingdom should have no ruler? And how can so much wealth have no owner, when every hour a train arrives filled with precious and artful gifts, as if coming from the realm of the unseen? And all the announcements and proclamations, all the seals and stamps, found on all those goods, all the coins and the flags waving in every corner of the kingdom — can they be without an owner? It seems you have studied foreign languages a little, and are unable to read this Islamic script. In addition, you refuse to ask those who are able to read it. Come now; let me read to you the king's supreme decree.[55]

While the first pieces were written in a fashion which is suitable for an entry-level reader, Nursi seems to have increased the level gradually. This becomes evident when treaties in the first ten *Words* and the treaties in *The Letters* and *The Flashes* are compared.

In terms of methodology, Nursi's style resembles that of Plato. In the *Laws*, Plato uses two imaginary characters, Cleinias and the Athenian Stranger, to represent opposing ideas. Similarly, Hume, in his *Dialogues Concerning Natural Religion*, speaks from the mouths of Demea, Cleanthes, and Philo to represent the cosmological theist, the experimental theist and the skeptic.

Nursi uses the word philosophy (*falsafa*) in a deprecatory sense, meaning negative philosophy (i.e., materialist, naturalist, and atheist). In order to denigrate this philosophy, he makes the Qur'an speak. He never uses the expressions "atheist philosophy" or "theist philosophy." He often presents a clash between *falsafa* (philosophy) and the Qur'an.[56]

It is clear in Nursi's writings that he adopts a Qur'anic method to convey his messages. For instance, the Qur'an tells in various verses that God gives examples so that people can understand better. Throughout the *Risale-i Nur*, it is evident that Nursi bases his arguments on three pillars. He speaks to the intelligence of his readers, urges them to judge his argument objectively. Once he establishes the logic of his argument he invokes the help of the Qur'an and the *hadith*. It can be argued that Nursi almost always

55. Ibid., 20.

56. For example, see The Twelfth Word in ibid., 49–52. And The Thirtieth Word in ibid., 241–46.

tries to synchronize heart and mind of his readers, in a way this is combining mysticism and philosophy.

In fact, he gives the clues of his method in his early writings such as *Muḥakamāt* where he elaborates on three essential elements of an effective expression. It seems that he puts the theoretical knowledge he wrote in his *Muḥakamāt* into practice in his later writings.

The Third Said Period (1950–60)

Perhaps one of the most important events in the history of modern Turkey was its first democratic, multi-party elections in 1950, after twenty-seven years of single-party rule by the Republican People's Party (RPP). Now, the opposition Democratic Party (DP) was allowed to challenge the RPP and it won the elections with a landslide.[57] One of the first actions of the DP was to lift the ban on the Arabic call to prayer. This was clearly a massive positive step forward in terms of ending anti-religious oppression. Although the DP seriously improved democracy in Turkey, public prosecutors, brandishing the old Article 163 of the Penal Code,[58] were still free to press charges against Nursi. Indeed, the charges against the *Risale-i Nur* and the *Nurcus* kept coming until the removal of Article 163 from the Penal Code in 1991. The shift towards democracy and the rise of communist Russia after World War II gave Nursi the opportunity to promote the *Risale-i Nur* so as to fight the imminent threat of communism. Nursi saw atheism as the common enemy of the all monotheistic religions. In 1953, he met the Greek Orthodox Patriarch and offered his views on uniting forces against aggressive atheism.[59]

Another important turning point in Nursi's life was the 1956 court acquittal of the *Risale-i Nur*, which was consequently printed and duplicated *en masse* in the Latin alphabet in both Ankara and Istanbul. Nursi called this "The *Risale-i Nur* Festival."[60] He said: "From now on, there is no need for me to work in the service of the *Risale-i Nur*. That is to say, the *Risale-i Nur* and its students will perform my duties."[61]

57. The results of the 1950 elections were: Democrat Party: 52.68 percent (415 seats), Republican People's Party: 39.45 percent (69 seats).

58. Article 163 of the old Turkish Penal Code, which was removed in 1991, outlawed politically motivated religious activities and prohibited the establishment of religious organizations and political parties aimed at creating an Islamic republic.

59. On the issue of Nursi's Muslim–Christian dialogue, see Saritoprak, "Said Nursi on Muslim-Christian Relations Leading to World Peace."

60. Şükran Vahide, *A Chronology of Said Nursi's Life* in Abu-Rabi, *Islam at the Crossroads*, xxiii

61. Nursi, *The Rays*, 1094.

In the last few years of his life, Nursi was a free man; his ideas and books were freely available to everyone, and he had followers in thousands. He travelled through the places that had marked his life with important memories. In 1960, he arrived in Urfa in eastern Turkey where, at the age of eighty-three, he died peacefully of old age in his hotel room.

Conclusion

This chapter has looked at the life and discourse of Saïd Nursi in order to put his philosophy into a historical perspective and clarify some terminology he developed. Nursi lived through three distinctive periods of Turkish history, which affected his philosophy of life. During the last few decades of the Ottoman Empire, he was mainly concerned with saving the falling Empire. Nicknamed the "sick man," the Ottoman Empire had been the target of other imperialist states, which saw it as a major threat to their expansion in many parts of the world. This was mainly due to the fact that the Ottoman Sultan also held the post of Caliph, the official head of the Muslims. Gladstone openly declared war on the Qur'an as the main obstacle to British imperialist ambitions. Nursi's thoughts took a first turn here. He committed himself to acquiring all the knowledge available to understand the Qur'an and prove its truth. The Old Said period, which coincides with the last years of the Ottoman Empire, is Nursi's most politically active period. He was advocating a reform of the education system that would help stop the collapse of the Empire and in addition solve other social issues.

With the collapse of the Empire, Nursi turned to fight the materialist philosophy that became the official ideology of the new Turkish Republic. It is clear in the *Risale-i Nur* that there is a great shift towards a *kalām*-style refutation of atheism in works like *The Word*, *The Letters* and *The Flashes*, which were all written during the first years of Kemalist Turkey. Nursi did not object to secularism, since he considered it to be a guarantor of freedom of faith; however, he was seriously concerned with materialism and its negative effects on a mainly Muslim public. He developed a unique way of *kalām*, where he merged modern science and the traditional Islamic knowledge of the *madrasa* to address the question of doubts surrounding the Qur'an. Unlike works such as *Muḥākamāt*, and *al-*ʿIshārāt *al-I'jāz*, which were addressed to scholars, Nursi's writings in the New Said period were mainly aimed at the ordinary public. Nursi explained that every reader could benefit from the *Risale-i Nur* according to his or her abilities. Although he did not make any systematic reference to the materialist philosophers by name, a large proportion of his work was dedicated to refuting their philosophy.

In general, he condemned philosophy on the basis that it did not submit to revelation. He also criticized famous Muslim philosophers such as Ibn-i Sinā and al-Fārābi regarding their judgments. Nursi's position may be seen as more in line with the thought of Al-Ghazzālī, who was given the honorary title of *al ḥujjat-ul Islam*, which literally means "the proof of Islam."

Al-Ghazzālī's criticisms of Ibn-i Sinā and al-Fārābi, and Ibn-i Rushd's criticism of Al-Ghazzālī, and Nursi's praise of Al-Ghazzālī give us a clue of certain allegiance among these scholars.

Having laid out the foundations of theistic and atheistic arguments, and locating Nursi among other thinkers, the study shall now focus on the Nursian arguments and attempt to extract novel ideas developed in his writings.

3

The Teleological Argument

Introduction

Perhaps one of the clearest arguments that appear in Nursi's writings in defense of theism is the argument from design and order in the universe. The design argument is also known as the teleological argument. The term "teleological" derives from the Greek word *telos*, which means "goal" or "purpose," implying that there is an end-purpose in everything in the universe. This argument was originally considered a part of the cosmological argument in general, since they both try to prove the existence of a Deity from evidence found in the cosmos. However, there is a distinction between the cosmological argument and the teleological argument, in the sense that the former starts off from the bare fact that there are contingently existent beings in the universe who require a maker with power to justify their existence, whereas the latter focuses on the properties of the end-product and tries to justify the existence of an intelligent mind behind the apparent design.[1]

The emergence of the teleological argument in ancient Greek philosophy started with Socrates. Socrates argued that forethought in the design of living creatures undoubtedly implies that they are the work of choice or design.[2] Plato, although he rejected the idea of creation out of nothing (*ex-nihilo*), defended the existence of a demiurge who designs the universe and gives order to the chaos in it. For Plato, the universe has always existed;

1. See Ratzsch, "Teleological Arguments for God's Existence."
2. See Xenophon et al., *The Memorable Thoughts of Socrates.*

gods, who act as artificers, only put it in order.[3] This idea was embraced by many subsequent thinkers.[4]

There are clear similarities between Cicero's, Aquinas's and Paley's formulations of the design argument, even though they lived centuries apart. In *De Natura Deorum,* Cicero writes:

> When you see a sundial or a water clock, you see that it tells the time by design and not by chance. How then can you imagine that the universe as a whole is devoid of purpose and intelligence, when it embraces everything, including these artefacts themselves and their artificers?[5]

Aquinas's fifth way, which is the proof from the governance of the universe, is very similar to Cicero's argument. In *Summa Theologiae*, St Thomas tells us:

> We see that things, which lack knowledge, such as natural bodies, act for an end, and this is evident from their acting always, or nearly always, in the same way, so as to obtain the best result. Hence it is plain that they achieve their end, not fortuitously, but designedly. Now whatever lacks knowledge cannot move towards an end, unless it be directed by some being endowed with knowledge and intelligence; as the arrow is directed by the archer. Therefore, some intelligent being exists by whom all natural things are directed to their end; and this being we call God.[6]

The difference between Cicero and Aquinas is that, like most ancient Greek philosophers Cicero believes there is intelligence behind the apparently purposeful design of the universe and its content, but this intelligence is not necessarily the God of Paley or Aquinas. As Ashqar points out, the concepts of God in ancient Greece and in monotheistic religions are completely different.[7]

3. See T. Brickhouse and N. D. Smith, "Plato" (April 21, 2005) *Internet Encyclopaedia of Philosophy.* Retrieved 11.22.2011.

4. For instance, Hume argues that the artificers work on pre-existing materials. For example, the carpenter shapes the pre-existing wood, the watchmaker shapes the pre-existing piece of metal and so on. Therefore, the teleological argument actually fails to prove the existence of a Deity who creates out of nothing. See Hume et al., *Hume's Dialogues Concerning Natural Religion..*

5. See Cicero and Cicero, *The Nature of the Gods; and, on Divination*, Book II, XXIV.

6. See Aquinas, *Summa Theologiae.* Also online text at http://www.ccel.org/ccel/aquinas/summa.FP_Q2_A3.html

7. See Ashqar and Khattab, *Belief in Allah*, 431.

The philosophical dispute between theists and atheists also emerges here. The theist position is such that the intelligence and the power behind the apparent design is the God of monotheistic religions. However, atheists claim, without rejecting *a priori* that there might be design involved, that it is not God but other elements such as natural selection, evolution, or bare chance that lie behind the apparent design of things.

In modern philosophy, William Paley is associated with the teleological argument, which was described as "the oldest, clearest and the most accordant with the common reason of mankind" by Kant in *The Critique of Pure Reason*.[8] Paley's "watch and the watchmaker" analogy puts Cicero's and Aquinas's perspectives into context. In *Natural Theology*, Paley writes:

> Suppose I found a watch upon the ground, and it should be inquired how the watch happened to be in that place, I should hardly think . . . that, for anything I knew, the watch might have always been there. Yet why should not this answer serve for the watch as well as for a stone that happened to be lying on the ground? For this reason, and for no other; namely, that, if the different parts had been differently shaped from what they are, if a different size from what they are, or placed after any other manner, or in any order than that in which they are placed, either no motion at all would have been carried on in the machine, or none which would have answered the use that is now served by it.[9]

Hume presents some imaginary characters in his *Dialogues Concerning Natural Religion*, and Nursi uses a similar method in most of his work. He speaks through the mouths of two friends, two brothers or two soldiers such as he portrays especially in *The Words*.[10] Unlike Hume, Nursi's characters do not have any names. The first usually represents the agnostic or skeptic point of view, as Hume's Philo does, and the other is usually, like Hume's Cleanthes, the virtuous creationist, who represents Nursi's own point of view.

Nursi, like many other scholars, uses metaphor in his writings. For instance, in *The Eight Word*[11] he tells the story of a man who became scared of a lion and fell into a well while running away from it. He then interprets

8. Kant et al., *The Critique of Pure Reason ; the Critique of Practical Reason, and Other Ethical Treatises ; the Critique of Judgement*, 520.

9. See Paley, *Natural Theology; Selections*. Also online text at http://mind.ucsd.edu/syllabi/02-03/01w/readings/paley.html

10. See Nursi, *The Words*, 3–52.

11. Ibid., 12–15.

what every object and event symbolizes. We find the same story in Tolstoy's *Confessions.*[12]

This particular technique of Nursi's reveals what kind of audience he wanted to address. He first sets the scene to make the text accessible even to readers with only a basic capacity for understanding, and then moves to the real philosophical meaning represented in the story. He seems to have been relatively successful in doing this judging by the popularity of his writings. One of the most noticeable examples of metaphor appears in The Tenth Word,[13] which concerns the subject of resurrection and the Hereafter. It is also a simple, straightforward version of Nursi's argument from design and order.

Nursi starts off by telling the story of two men, who reach a village during their travels. They realize that the doors of the properties are not locked and that valuables are left all over the place. The first man starts to help himself to everything freely available, denying the existence of an owner. The second man argues that the two have to show respect to the properties, as there must be an owner somewhere. The first man insists that there is no owner because he cannot see him. The second, the wise man, replies:

> Every village must have its headman; every needle must have its manufacturer and craftsman. And, as you know, every letter must be written by someone. How, then, can it be that so extremely well-ordered a kingdom should have no ruler? And how can so much wealth have no owner, when every hour a train arrives filled with precious and artful gifts, as if coming from the realm of the unseen? And all the announcements and proclamations, all the seals and stamps, found on all those goods, all the coins and the flags waving in every corner of the kingdom — can they be without an owner?[14]

Nursi tries to prove not only the existence of God, but also that He possesses names and attributes such as a*l-Wāhid* (The One), *al-'Alīm* (The Knower of All), *al-Ghafur* (The Forgiver), *al-Ghani* (The Rich One), *al-Fard* (The One), *al-Samed* (The Eternal), *al-Haiy* (The Ever Living), etc.[15] It is clear in his writings that he rarely refers to God with his most common name *Allāh*. He rather uses His particular attribute relating to the context.

12. See Tolstoy and Kentish, *A Confession and Other Religious Writings.* or Tolstoy, *Itirafları*, 28.

13. Nursi, *The Words*, 19–42.

14. Ibid., 20.

15. See Appendix 2: Names and Attributes of God in Islam.

Nursi argues that it could only be God—All-Knowing, All-Powerful—who makes different products from the same ingredients. In nature, there are one hundred and fourteen basic elements, but there are thousands of different plants and organisms which are made up of these basic elements. For example, Nursi tells us that soil, with the help of air and light, makes plants grow, i.e., through the process of photosynthesis. The basic composition of plant seeds is almost always the same, that is, the embryo, nutrients and the coat. However, when two similar-looking plant seeds are planted in the soil, they might grow into completely different plants. Botanists explain that the genetic codes in the embryo tell the seeds what kind of plant they should grow into. How, Nursi asks, is it possible to create so many different plants out of the same soil and the same chemical composition? He concludes that there has to be an intelligent mind behind all these biological events. Since the seeds and the soil are unintelligent entities, it could only be God who creates endless variety of plants out of these basic elements.[16]

Hume came up with a set of objections to the design argument many years prior to Paley and Nursi, who both argue that an artifact requires an artificer. In *The Dialogues Concerning Natural Religion*, Cleanthes tells Philo:

> . . . Since therefore the effects resemble each other, we are led to infer, by all the rules of analogy, that the causes also resemble; and that the Author of Nature is somewhat similar to the mind of man; though possessed of much larger faculties, proportioned to the grandeur of the work which he has executed. By this argument *a posteriori,* and by this argument alone, do we prove at once the existence of a Deity, and his similarity to human mind and intelligence.[17]

Hume's first criticism is that this analogy is very poor. He observes that the universe is not like a man-made artifact. It is not like a machine, but more like a living organism. Secondly, if an analogy is made between man and God, this makes it impossible to justify the omnipotence and omniscience of God because the problem of evil immediately emerges. However, these two criticisms, according to Ratzch, are not regarded as being fatal to the teleological argument.[18] Nursi himself sees "the problem of evil and the existence of pain, suffering, and calamities" as supporting the existence of God. According to Nursi, God's different attributes require a certain physical situation where the function of the particular attribute is fulfilled. In *The Flashes*, Nursi writes:

16. Nursi, *Al-Mathnawi Al-Nuri*, 1356.
17. Hume and Smith, *Dialogues Concerning Natural Religion*, 47–48.
18. See Ratzsch, "Teleological Arguments for God's Existence."

> God Most High has made the garment of the body with which He has clothed man a manifestation of His art. He has made man to be a model on which He cuts, trims, alters and changes the garment of the body, thus displaying the manifestation of various of His Names. Just as the Name of Healer makes it necessary that illness should exist, so too the Name of Provider requires that hunger should exist. And so on . . .[19]

Hume's third criticism, however, sounds fairly challenging to the theists. Hume argues that if we assume an artificer who designs the universe must exist, why should he be one god, why not many gods? For example, Nursi tells us that a needle requires a needle-maker, and a village requires a village head.[20] Hume, on the other hand, might accept the idea of a needle-maker for the sake of argument, but not necessarily a unique needle-maker; instead of one ruler, why not a committee of village rulers? The Humean position could be put in context as follows. Suppose that you see a recently built house. Would you assume that it has been built by a single person, or would you rather assume that it has been built by a team of people? The answer is more likely to be "by a team of people." Nursi and Hume seem to be in complete conflict here. Nursi defends the idea that the maker or the ruler has to be one person; otherwise, multiple makers or rulers would fall into conflict and spoil the work completely. In *The Words*, in supporting his argument with the Qur'an 67:3, Nursi explains:

> Who other than One possessing boundless power, all-encompassing knowledge, and infinite wisdom could interfere in this administration, which is wondrous to the utmost degree. For if one who cannot administer and raise all together these species and nations, which are one within the other, interferes with one of them, he will throw the lot into disorder. Whereas according to the meaning of Qur'an 67:3, "So turn your vision again, do you see any flaw?" there is no sign of confusion. That means not so much as a finger can interfere.[21]

In contrast to the Nursian view, Hume suggests that it is perfectly feasible to assume that the roofer works on the roof, while the plumber fits the bathroom and the gardener does the landscape in the garden. Similarly, several gods could work in harmony to design the universe.[22]

19. Nursi, *The Flashes*, 581.

20. Nursi, Nursi, *The Words*, 20.

21. Ibid., 300.

22. See Hume and Smith, *Dialogues Concerning Natural Religion*, Part II-VIII and Part XII.

Hume's third argument is much in line with that of the ancient Greeks. Most atheists, like most of the polytheistic ancient Greeks, acknowledge the fact that there is apparent design in the universe. They, unlike theists, argue that it is not necessarily the God of Judaism, Christianity, or Islam who is behind the universe. Atheists attribute some *seeming* intelligence to nature in the guise of natural selection and evolution.[23] Natural selection and evolution could explain order and apparent design. The ancient Greeks explain them by the existence of many gods in charge of certain aspects of the universe, such as Aether, the god of air and atmosphere, Thalassa, god of seas, etc.

Hume's other criticism of the theists is that the god of Christianity must be very amateurish, since there are design deficiencies in the universe.[24] This idea was later developed by other scientists and embraced by atheists to defend their point of view.[25]

Nursi, however, claims that materialist philosophy fails to understand the meaning of life and the universe, since it only sees them through their apparent meaning. Here, we find two original terms introduced by Nursi into philosophical thinking about the universe. The first is *mʿanā-i ismī,* which is the apparent or direct meaning of things, or the nominal meaning, and the second is *mʿanà-i ḥarfī*, which is the signifying or indirect meaning of things, or the other-indicative meaning. For example, when someone looks at a flower he can see its beauty. If he says "This is a beautiful flower," he is seeing the apparent beauty through the nominal meaning (i.e., *mʿanā-i ismī*), whereas if he says "This flower has been made beautifully," thus acknowledging the work of the Artificer, he is seeing it through its significative meaning (i.e., *mʿanā-i ḥarfī*). Nursi criticizes mainstream philosophy as examining nature and the universe through the glasses of *mʿanā-i ismī.*[26] That is to say, *falsafa* (philosophy) sees everything in its literal meaning only, whereas Nursi sees the universe through the glass of *mʿanā-i ḥarfī* (i.e., in the sense that it is the reflection of the Maker's art).[27] These two different viewpoints, according to Nursi, constitute the main difference between the teaching of *falsafa* (philosophy) and the Qur'an.

23. See Ashqar and Khattab, *Belief in Allah*, 130.

24. See Hume and Smith, *Dialogues Concerning Natural Religion*, Part II-VIII.

25. For instance, Dawkins argues that the poor designs in mammals such as the retina in the eye which faces backward, and the long route of the tube from testes to penis, are strong evidence of evolution and the absence of an intelligent designer. See Dawkins' Interview at http://www.youtube.com/watch?v=aUFOlyt7ErE at 19:00.

26. Nursi compares the wisdom of the Qur'an with the wisdom of philosophy and science in The Twelfth Word. For the full argument, see Nursi, *The Words*, 49–52.

27. Nursi, *Al-Mathnawi Al-Nuri*, 1364.

Nursi's View of the Teleological Argument and His Challenge to Atheism

Leaving the scientific details to the scientists, Nursi points out the apparent order and harmony in the universe to the ordinary reader.[28] Rather than making a direct attempt to prove the existence of a Maker, Nursi takes the indirect route, which is refutation of the opposite claims. He targets, without naming them, materialist philosophers such as Epicurus, Democritus, Marx, and Darwin, and naturalists such as Bacon and Voltaire.

In his landmark work *The Twenty-Third Flash—On Nature*, Nursi first identifies what he believes are three false claims by the above-mentioned non-creationists. He writes:

> You should be aware that there are certain phrases, which are commonly used and imply unbelief. The believers also use them, but without realizing their implications. We shall explain three of the most important of them.
>
> The First: "Causes create this."
>
> The Second: "It forms itself; it comes into existence and later ceases to exist."
>
> The Third: "It is natural; nature necessitates and creates it."[29]

As the fourth possibility, Nursi tells us that the universe is created through the power of One All-Powerful and All-Glorious God. Since the refutation of the first three postulations implies the truth of the fourth one, Nursi proceeds to produce three arguments for each of these three postulations in order to invalidate them.

The First Postulate: Causes Create This Thing (*A'wjadathu Al-Asbāb*)

The first postulation to explain creation is that of "*causes being the creator*." In other words, things come into existence as a result of the collaboration between certain causes. For example, the existence of a flower, according to this view, is the result of teamwork between sufficient light, warmth and water. The atomists, such as Leucippus and his pupil Democritus, defended the

28. Unlike modern scientist-philosophers such as Dembski, Behe, or Dawkins, Nursi does not go into the scientific details of the universe and its content. He simply tries to explain what might be the cause behind the visible universe.

29. Nursi, *The Flashes*, 677.

notion that there is always a scientific or mechanical explanation for every event in the universe, as opposed to cosmologists like Plato and Aristotle who sought explanation through a Prime Mover, First Cause or Purpose.[30] Democritus rejects the role of a demiurge and insists that nature is a result of pure chance.[31] Nursi argues that this theory is flawed, and in three steps attempts to explain why.

The First Impossibility

Nursi tells his readers that it is mathematically fallacious to accept that the excellent order and design in nature occurs as the result of some unintelligent chance. Following the classical design argument method, he asks the reader if he would accept that the medicines in a pharmacy came into existence by pure chance. Although the common-sense answer to this assumption is always "no," since all the medicines are the products of physical and chemical combinations of certain substances in certain proportions, the atheist philosophy maintains the possibility of creation as the result of pure chance. Atheists claim that there might have been billions of unsuccessful events until one in a billion happened and gave us the current result. They do not deny that it is extremely difficult to bring all the necessary conditions and elements together to create a certain product by chance, yet they argue that it is still possible and that is how life on earth came into existence. Dawkins, for instance, admits that it would have been very hard for the initial conditions to come into existence. However, once life has started, evolution through natural selection takes charge and makes life on earth evolve into life as we know it now.[32]

As a counter-argument, the contemporary *Risale-i Nur* authority Abdullah Aymaz points out that chemical reactions require not only the random mix of substances but also require certain conditions such as temperature and pressure, which doubles or trebles the impossibility of existence by chance.[33] Nursi summarizes his argument as follows:

> The vital substances in this vast pharmacy of the universe, which are measured on the scales of Divine Determining and Decree of the All-Wise and Pre-Eternal One, can only come into existence

30. For a detailed study of ancient Greek atomism, see Leucippus, Democritus, and Taylor, *The Atomists, Leucippus and Democritus: Fragments: A Text and Translation with a Commentary.*

31. For the detailed views of Democritus, see Cartledge, *Democritus*, 9–20.

32. Dawkins, *The God Delusion*, 113–19.

33. Abdullah Aymaz, Interview, 11 January 2011, Frankfurt.

> through boundless wisdom, infinite knowledge and all-encompassing will. The unfortunate person who declares that they are the work of blind, deaf and innumerable elements and causes and natures, which stream like floods; and the foolish, delirious person who claims that that wondrous remedy poured itself out when the phials were knocked over and formed itself, are certainly unreasonable and nonsensical. Indeed, such denial and unbelief is a senseless absurdity.[34]

Nursi clearly tries to expose how irrational to accept a theory whereby all wondrous creations come into existence by blind chance.

The Second Impossibility

Nursi turns our attention to minute organisms such as a mosquito fly. It is utterly false, he claims, to assume that nature and most of its elements and causes, which are naturally hostile to each other, come together intentionally and intelligently to make this fly. For example, the organisms consist of elements such as magnesium, iron, oxygen and hydrogen,[35] some of which are reactive with each other. Technically speaking, bringing these elements together normally results in a violent chemical reactions such as burning or explosion. Yet, they exist in organisms side by side without any trouble. One of the best examples of this is the chemical formation of water. Water molecules consist of Hydrogen and Oxygen, which occur in nature in the gaseous state. Hydrogen is a highly flammable gas which is used as fuel, and Oxygen is the essential gas for burning—NASA uses liquid Hydrogen and liquid Oxygen to create a combustion reaction to launch rockets into space—but in the formation of water molecules these two reactive substances can stay together to form a new substance, which demonstrates a complete set of different properties. Nursi suggests that an intelligent creator interferes and overruns certain properties of basic elements in order to create a new substance. Furthermore, continuous design patterns on artifacts, according to Nursi, imply the possible source of them. For example, when we see the same branded watches, we assume that they were all made in the same factory. Otherwise, we should accept the suggestion that each watch was made in a different factory, which requires the existence of as many factories as watches. In the former assumption, the existence of a single watch-factory reasonably explains how all these watches came into existence. In the latter case, since it is impossible that there should be as many watch-factories

34. Nursi, *The Flashes*, 678.

35. See Appendix 3: Elements in the Human Body.

as there are watches to be made, we have to accept the theory that each and every watch is the product of a single watch-factory. Similarly, in the observable universe, we see things coming into existence such as the growth of a plant or the birth of a baby. There is a chain of scientific explanations for how events lead to each other. The Nursian viewpoint is that all these products came out of the hands of the same producer: God.[36] The opposing view (i.e., that of naturalist philosophy) claims that the collaboration of sufficient causes as a result of chance is the reason behind the existence of beings in the universe. In other words, naturalists assume that nature and its constituents are within every organism (i.e., each and every organism is the maker or creator of itself). This is an idea which, Nursi claims, is utterly absurd. Hence, Nursi concludes, "Everything has to be attributed to the All-Powerful and All-Glorious One, Who is the Single One of Unity".[37]

The Third Impossibility

Nursi's third argument comes in two parts. The first part is the argument of *unity and continuity* in organisms. If random reasons in nature created the organisms, they would come in various shapes with completely different properties. However, we observe consistency in organisms. For example, every species in nature always has the same biochemical and physical characteristics. The example of a painter is a very good analogy with which to explain this argument. Imagine different artists are asked to paint the same object. On the basis of their ability, expertise and artistic sense, they would paint differently. Likewise, if we see very similar paintings, we conclude that they have all been painted by the same artist. Nursi then suggests that without an Intelligent Artist, the universe would have to be completely messy and chaotic, the completely opposite of how it is now. This, for Nursi, is an indication of the same Intelligent Maker, not the product of random causes of nature. Nursi sums up his argument in his supplication to God in *The Rays* thus:

> . . . I have understood that just as the heavens, atmosphere, earth, seas and mountains, together with their creatures and all they contain, recognize You and make You known; so too do all the trees and plants, together with all their leaves and flowers and fruits. All their leaves, with their ecstatic movements and recitations; all their flowers, which describe through their decoration the Names of their Maker; and all their fruits, which

36. See the Thirtieth Word in Nursi, *The Words*, 299–316.

37. Ibid.

> smile with their agreeableness and the manifestation of Your compassion, testify—through the order within their wondrous art, which is utterly impossible to ascribe to chance, and the balance within the order, and the adornment within the balance, and the embroideries within the adornment, and the fine and various scents within the embroideries, and the varying tastes of the fruits within the scents—so clearly as to be self-evident to the necessary existence of an infinitely Compassionate and Munificent Maker. At the same time, their similarity and mutual resemblance throughout the earth, and their bearing the same stamps on their creation, and their being related in their administration and organization, and the coincidence of the creative acts and dominical Names connected with them, and the innumerable members of their one hundred thousand species being raised one within the other without confusion, form a testimony through them as a whole to the unity and oneness of their Necessarily Existent Maker."[38]

The second part of the third argument is the *argument of the internal complexity* of organisms. Here, Nursi explains that the random causes of nature ought to affect the exterior of organisms through direct contact or touch. However, there is more technical complexity inside the organisms where the material causes of nature cannot reach.[39] Evolutionary biologists object to this on the grounds that nature can manipulate the exterior of organisms as well as the interior. Nursi might have meant that the molecular structures, or the genetic DNA structures, could not successfully be mutated from the outside by nature.

Nursi's internal complexity argument was corroborated by some biochemists a few decades after he put it forward through what is often referred to as the "Irreducible Complexity Argument" and the "Fine Tuning Argument." In his 1996 book, "*Darwin's Black Box*," Michael Behe defines his term "irreducible complexity" as follows:

> A single system which is composed of several interacting parts that contribute to the basic function, and where the removal of any one of the parts causes the system to effectively cease functioning.[40]

Behe maintains Nursi's position that, should the most basic component of an organism change, the whole system would cease to function. There is no

38. Nursi, *The Rays*, 869.
39. Nursi, *The Flashes*, 678.
40. Behe, *Darwin's Black Box: The Biochemical Challenge to Evolution*, 39.

dispute about the fact that physical and chemical causes affect and change the character of organisms. Both Nursi and Behe argue that, should this happen, it would most probably cause disease or death rather than more complicated and successful forms of life. In the mousetrap analogy, Behe explains that if one of the five basic components of a mousetrap—spring, base, bar, catch, or hammer—were removed, this would only cause the device to malfunction or to cease functioning completely; it would certainly not improve it. The mousetrap analogy was quickly criticized by Miller. In his book *Only a Theory*, Miller argues, against Behe's theory that a broken mousetrap could actually function as something completely different. For example, its spring fixed on a baseboard could make a very good catapult.[41]

Here, Behe presents the modern-day teleological argument in the form of Intelligent Design (ID)[42] and argues that everything is designed by an Intelligent Designer in such a way that the removal of even the most minute component would cause a catastrophe, as in the mousetrap analogy. Intelligent Design apologists support their theory with further examples, such as the eye, the immune system, and bacterial flagella. Indeed, to this day, scientists have yet to come up with any satisfactory alternatives to ID's claims. Dawkins thinks science must keep working towards explanations. Ignorance, according to Dawkins, cannot be the answer. He accuses creationists of taking a short cut. In *The God Delusion*, Dawkins writes:

> . . . If you [the theists] don't understand how something works, never mind: just give up and say God did it.[43]

The apparent weakness of Nursi's argument is that he only seems to consider the external factors as "manipulants." In *The Flashes*, Nursi writes:

> If we leave this impossibility aside and assume that material causes have effects, these effects can only occur through direct contact and touch. However, the contact of natural causes is with the exteriors of living beings. And yet we see that the interiors of such beings, where the hands of material causes can neither reach nor touch, are ten times more delicate, well-ordered and perfect as regards art than their exteriors. Therefore, although tiny animate creatures, on which the hands and organs of material causes can in no way be situated, indeed they cannot touch

41. For the evolutionist objection to the Intelligent Design, and Irreducible Complexity Arguments, See Miller, *Only a Theory*.

42. Behe's *Darwin's Black Box* has the subheading of *Biochemical Challenge to Evolution* where he argues how evolution cannot be the cause of extremely complex biochemical molecules. See, ibid.

43. Dawkins, *The God Delusion*, 132.

> the creatures' exteriors all at once even, are more strange and wonderful as regards their art and creation than the largest creatures, to attribute them to those lifeless, unknowing, crude, distant, vast, conflicting, deaf and blind causes can result only from a deafness and blindness compounded to the number of animate beings.[44]

The evolutionists could give an unforgiving reception to Nursi's argument, since it is scientifically accepted that natural conditions such as temperature, pressure, moisture, etc., cannot only affect the physical exterior, but also affect the chemical, biological, or genetic interior of organisms.

The Second Postulate: Things Create Themselves (*Tashakkala Bi Nafsihi*)

The second postulation proposes *the self-creation of things*. In other words, the second postulation suggests that the minute elements of an organism take decisions independently and intelligently to produce a successful result. The idea might have developed from the observation of cell division. Scientists have successfully explained that there are two types of cell division common to most organisms. If we focus on fertilization, birth, and the growth of mammals, two crucial cell cycles become apparent. The parents' bodies produce gametes, that is, sex cells (sperm and egg), as a result of meiosis cell division, which produces four cells with half the chromosomes of the parents' cells. The opposite sex cells fuse as a result of fertilization, which takes twenty-three chromosomes from each of the parents; therefore the offspring display similar yet not identical characters to the parents. The growth of the newly fertilized body is the result of another type of cell division, called mitosis. In mitosis, each cell divides into two identical cells which function exactly as the parent cell. Although this explanation is highly accurate in terms of biochemical events taking place within the cell, Nursi would no doubt argue that it does not tell us anything about the decision-making process. It is hardly logical to suggest that the organs of a cell, i.e., nucleus, membrane, chromatin, etc., have their own mind with which they decide how to function and to start the cell-division process. Biologists are widely agreed that these organs are pre-programmed and act on this program. Yet, Nursi would have argued that science is unable to explain where the programs come from and who installed them there. Now, the scientific issue turns into a philosophical question. What, or who,

44. Nursi, *The Flashes*, 678.

is responsible for this entire, highly complex biochemical event? Is it the organism, or is it God?

Nursi's strategy here is very clear. He objects to Darwin and Wallace's idea of evolution through natural selection in his three-step argument in order to strengthen his theistic position.

The First Impossibility

The first fallacy that Nursi detects in the postulate "things create themselves" is brought into light by use of *logic*. If one does not accept the authority of the Program Maker, i.e., God, one has to accept the logically unsound assumption that each and every part of an organism has all the knowledge necessary to act intelligently in order to operate the amazing body machine. Nursi asserts that:

> You would have to ascribe to each particle an intelligence equivalent to that of a hundred geniuses, sufficient to know and recognize all your past and your future, and your forbears and descendants, the origins of all the elements of your being, and the sources of all your sustenance. To attribute the knowledge and consciousness of a thousand Plato's to a single particle of one such as you who does not possess even a particle's worth of intelligence in matters of this kind is a crazy superstition a thousand times over![45]

Here, Nursi clearly attempts to ridicule the suggestion that the constituent particles of a matter have got intelligence to take their own decision.

The Second Impossibility

What Nursi also defends is essentially the *argument from lack of conflict* within organisms. In this argument, Nursi refers to the competitive nature of living things. For example, two identical trees planted in a limited space with limited sunlight tend to run against each other to make the most of the available resources. It is also valid in the animal kingdom. Two sibling cubs from the same pack fight each other to get the largest share of the kill. This could be taken as a general rule of nature. Nursi then shifts our attention to the human body, which he describes as a "thousand-domed wondrous palace in which the stones stand together in suspension and without support".[46]

45. Ibid., 679.

46. Ibid.

In this analogy, the stones represent the building blocks of the body (i.e., the cells). Because of the theory of competition,[47] these cells are supposed to struggle with each other. The cells forming the feet should fight the cells forming the head since it is much harder to be the feet than the head. Similarly, the tissues of muscles, which are part of some unpleasant organs, should fight to get a better location, as the theory requires. However, unlike what is the common occurrence in nature, this struggle does not happen in the body. Every cell and tissue seems to have been subdued into staying where it had been appointed to work. This only means, according to Nursi, that they are ordered by a "Necessarily Existent Controller."[48]

The Third Impossibility

Nursi's third argument against the naturalist atheism is the *argument from ease* in the nature. Here, Nursi contends that if a letter is written by a pen whose holder has got power and intelligence, it is very easy to produce this perfect letter. However, if we do not accept this first proposition, and claim that it is writing itself or that nature is writing the letter, then the writing process for this letter will be extremely difficult. The second proposition requires an incredible amount of knowledge and hardware. For every character in the letter, there has to be one iron letter as in the old-fashioned printing machines, and for every word there has to be a printing-block consisting of several iron letters. These conditions are impossibly difficult to put together, as opposed to one Intelligent Hand with a pen writing a letter effortlessly.[49]

47. The term "survival of the fittest," i.e., competition-based life, was introduced by Herbert Spencer in 1864, and was used by Charles Darwin later to describe natural selection. For Darwin's use of the term, see Darwin, *On the Origin of Species by Means of Natural Selection ; or, the Preservation of Favoured Races in the Struggle for Life.*

Kropotkin, though being an atheist, objected to the theory of competition. He argues extensively for the cooperation in nature rather than competition in his book *Mutual Aid: A Factor of Evolution*. See Kropotkin, *Mutual Aid: A Factor of Evolution.*

48. Capitalized descriptive nouns are Nursi's trademark preference to refer to God. There are countless examples of these names throughout Nursi's writings.

49. Nursi, *The Flashes*, 679.

The Third Postulate: Nature Creates Things (*Iqtaẓathu Al-Ṭabīʿah*)

The third postulate considers *nature as a creator.* Thales was the first scientist-philosopher of ancient Greece who tried to explain nature and natural events without referring to mythology,[50] thus introducing the idea of naturalism. According to naturalist philosophy, everything arises from natural properties and causes, and supernatural or spiritual explanations are excluded or discounted.[51] During the Enlightenment, naturalist philosophical viewpoints became popular among the secular scientists of Europe. Laplace, for instance, insisted that there is no room for the supernatural when explaining celestial mechanics.[52] Later, in the twentieth century, naturalist philosophers such as Kurtz argued that, rather than a supernatural being; it was nature and its laws that were the causes in the universe.[53] Nursi takes the idea of naturalism and tries to falsify it in three steps by demonstrating three impossibilities in their postulates.

The First Impossibility

Nursi attempts to refute the idea that nature is self-intelligent. Imagine, he asks, hundreds of droplets of water and pieces of glass scattered on the ground. You see that the light is being reflected on them. Would you say:

> i. It is one light source, i.e., the sun, whose light is being reflected on these shiny objects or,

50. For the origin of naturalism, see O'Grady, *Thales of Miletus.*

51. Simpson, Weiner, *The Oxford English Dictionary.*

52. Rouse Ball writes Laplace-Napoléon dialog as follows: Laplace went to Napoleon to present a copy of his work, and the following account of the interview is well authenticated, and so characteristic of all the parties concerned that I quote it in full. Someone had told Napoleon that the book contained no mention of the name of God; Napoleon, who was fond of putting embarrassing questions, received it with the remark, "M. Laplace, they tell me you have written this large book on the system of the universe, and have never even mentioned its Creator." Laplace, who, though the most supple of politicians, was as stiff as a martyr on every point of his philosophy, drew himself up and answered bluntly, *Je n'avais pas besoin de cette hypothèse-là.* ("I had no need of that hypothesis.") Napoleon, greatly amused, told this reply to Lagrange, who exclaimed, *Ah! c›est une belle hypothèse; ça explique beaucoup de choses.* ("Ah, it is a fine hypothesis; it explains many things.") See Ball, *A Short Account of the History of Mathematics.*

53. Kurtz, "Darwin Re-Crucified: Why Are So Many Afraid of Naturalism?" 17.

ii. Each of these mindless, soulless, dead objects has got extremely complicated mechanical systems inside and they generate light, or

iii. There are as many light sources up in the sky as the number of reflections on the ground?[54]

To Nursi, the obvious answer is the first one. Consequently, ascribing all power and will to nature is irrational as this would imply that every particle, atom, cell, and/or organism, let alone non-living beings such as stars, planets and rocks, ought to have their own mind, will and power in order to act for an end-purpose. Therefore, according to Nursi, logic tells us that there has to be an Intelligent Creator of nature and the universe.

The Second Impossibility

Nursi again attacks what he believes is the absurdity of the naturalist idea of creation. He starts out with the basic constituents of all plant seeds. All seeds consist of an orderless, formless, paste-like mixture of oxygen, hydrogen, carbon and nitrogen. We plant different seeds in the same flowerpot, which holds a small amount of soil. After providing some essential conditions (i.e., light, warmth, and moisture), we observe that all these different seeds germinate into certain plants. How do we rationally explain this? Is it that this small amount of soil has got the intelligence of a thousand biologists, chemists and botanists with the incredible high-tech machinery of a sophisticated factory? Or is it that an Intelligent Creator programs the seeds and instructs the soil, air, water and light to work as they are ordered? Here, Nursi says, any reasonable mind would reject the first proposition, as it would be clearly illogical to accept it.[55] In conclusion, Nursi writes: "To attribute all beings to the Necessarily Existent One is so easy as to be necessary. While to attribute their creation to Nature is so difficult as to be impossible and outside the realm of reason."[56]

The Third Impossibility

In the third impossibility, Nursi tackles the naturalist idea of nature as creator with two examples. The first example is the metaphor of an ignorant,

54. Nursi, *The Flashes*, 680.
55. Ibid., 681.
56. Ibid.

savage caveman. This man comes across a palace in the middle of a desert. He walks into it and, to his fascination, he witnesses some fantastic piece of architecture, the perfect design and functionality of the palace. He starts looking round in search of the builder. Yet to his disappointment, he cannot find any intelligent builder. He turns his attention to the inside of the palace and looks for a possible maker. Then, he finds a book where the statistics, plans and rules of the palace are written. He concludes that the book seems to be the most intelligent thing there; therefore, it has to be the designer, maker, and maintainer of this palace. Nursi then dismisses the naturalist idea. Naturalists claim that the most seemingly intelligent thing within the universe is nature. Since they do not accept the possibility of a Deity as creator, they conclude, like the caveman in the palace, that nature has to be the cause of everything. Nursi then directly addresses naturalists by pretending to speak to one of them:

> O you mistaken unfortunate! Your foolishness exceeds anything imaginable! Lift your head out of the swamp of Nature and look beyond yourself! See an All-Glorious Maker to Whom all beings from particles to planets testify with their different tongues and Whom they indicate with their fingers! Behold the manifestation of the Pre-Eternal Inscriber, Who fashions the palace and Who writes its program in the notebook.[57]

The second example tackles the ideas of nature being the order-giver where, again, Nursi tells the story of the same ignorant man who goes into an army training ground. He observes that a certain number of soldiers come together to form certain units (i.e., platoons, battalions, regiments). They are moving in perfect harmony, firing exactly simultaneously as a single body at the command, etc. This ignorant man thinks that all these soldiers are tied up to each other with a thread; as a result, they do the same thing at the same time. What actually happens is that there is a commander who forms the small units of the army, gives them commands and controls them. Nursi explains that, contrary to what atheists believe as a result of the misguidance of materialism and naturalism, nature is like a giant army, which is controlled by a Commander. Nature, Nursi exclaims, can at the very most be a work of art; it cannot be the Artist! It is embroidery and cannot be the Embroiderer. It is a set of decrees; it cannot be the Issuer of the decrees. It is a body of the laws of creation and cannot be the Lawgiver. It is but a created screen to the dignity of God and cannot be the Creator. It is passive and created, Nursi continues, and cannot be a

57. Ibid.

Creative Maker. It is a law, not a power, and cannot possess power. It is the recipient and cannot be the source.[58]

The refutation of these three assumptions, therefore, leaves one final possibility, which is not only the existence but also the eternal presence and eternal activity of a Creator.

Although Nursi considered that naturalist philosophy was defeated by his *Treatise on Nature*,[59] naturalist philosophers hold the opposite view.

In Defense of Naturalism

Ever since the introduction of Thales' idea of naturalism, philosophers at both ends of the scale have always focused on nature and science to justify the existence or non-existence of a Deity. The theists, especially from the Christian tradition, see nature as the secondary cause. In other words, God is always the first cause, using nature as the secondary cause.[60] One of the most remarkable Christian scientists, Galileo, who is considered to be the father of observatory astronomy,[61] explains that the universe never violates the orders given to her by God,[62] the complete opposite of Laplace's idea.

Francis Bacon was one of the leading figures of enlightenment naturalism. He objected to the teleological arguments on the grounds that they are inductive arguments made by simple enumeration and likely to lead to the wrong conclusion. In his parable, he tells the story of a census officer who was to record all the inhabitants of a Welsh village. He records the inhabitant of the first house as William Williams. The inhabitant of the second house is also called William Williams and so are those in the third, the fourth and the next houses. Soon, he concludes that all inhabitants are called William Williams and he gives up his quest and simply records all inhabitants as William Williams. But in fact, one of the inhabitants was actually called John Jones.[63] The census officer had drawn the wrong conclusion. Bacon despised syllogism; he called it "blind rule".[64] Therefore he was hostile to Aristotle, but thought very highly of Democritus. To him, everything ought

58. Ibid., 682.

59. The Twenty-third flash in *The Flashes* is also called "*Treatise on Nature*." See ibid., 677–86.

60. See McGrath, *Christian Theology: An Introduction*.

61. Singer, *A Short History of Science to the Nineteenth Century*, 217.

62. Lindberg and Numbers, *When Science & Christianity Meet*, 267.

63. Russell, *A History of Western Philosophy*, 499.

64. Klein, *A History of Scientific Psychology; Its Origins and Philosophical Backgrounds*, 36.

to be explained necessarily from efficient cause. In the investigation of a phenomenon, writes Bacon, we should neither be like a spider which spins things out of its own bowels, nor like an ant which simply collects. We should be like a bee, which collects and arranges. In order to avoid a quarrel with the authorities, Bacon never openly rejected God, but insisted that scientific enquiry and revelation have to go hand in hand; revelation alone is not sufficient to reach a solid conclusion.

Voltaire, on the other hand, maintained a more hardline opposition to religion. Rather than making a philosophical point, he openly criticized the church because of its poor treatment of people. He had equally hostile views regarding all religions. Despite his hostility to religions, he seemed to have a fair belief in the existence of a deity. To Voltaire, Newtonian mechanics was of great importance when it came to explaining and understanding the universe. For Voltaire, the universe is governed through the universal laws of physics. As a deist, he defended the *clockwork universe theory*, which states that God created the universe and stepped aside, but set it like a clock so that it runs itself automatically.[65]

Kurtz argues that there is no purpose in the universe. He rejects the supernatural. To him, nature and natural phenomena are best explained by reference to material principles (i.e., mass, energy, and other scientifically accepted physical and chemical properties). In his article "Why are we afraid of naturalism?" Kurtz writes: "To introduce a supernatural or transcendental cause within science is to depart from naturalistic explanations. On this ground, to invoke an intelligent designer or creator is inadmissible."[66]

Kurtz ideas on naturalism are also worth considering. Kurtz explains that every theory has to be examined and scrutinized through scientific inquiry. He objects the idea of scientific explanation involving the supernatural. Kurtz maintains a position where he defends scientific endeavors excluding God, rather than making a case against the existence of God. He writes:

> To introduce a supernatural or transcendental cause within science is to depart from naturalistic explanations. On this ground, to invoke an intelligent designer or creator is inadmissible.[67]

According to Kurtz and other naturalists, everything has to be explained within the boundaries of the known natural sciences. Quinn argues

65. See Fellows, *From Voltaire to La Nouvelle Critique: Problems and Personalities*, 64, or Quine, *Ontological Relativity, and Other Essays.*

66. Kurtz, "Darwin Re-crucified," 17.

67. Kurtz, "Darwin Re-crucified," 17.

that science is the highest tribunal. There is absolutely nothing higher than science with which to judge or to reach the absolute truth.[68]

Plantinga, however, objects to the methodology of the naturalists. The weakness of naturalist philosophy, according to Plantinga, is that it limits itself to empirical involvement. In *Science and Technology News*, he explains:

> If you exclude the supernatural from science, then if the world or some phenomena within it are supernaturally caused—as most of the world's people believe—you won't be able to reach that truth scientifically.[69]

Plantinga and Nursi hold parallel thoughts as regards to involving the supernatural alongside the natural in order to reach the truth. They argue that every available tool has to be used in order to reach the truth. Indeed, having two torches rather than one makes more sense while searching for an item in the dark.[70]

Nursi's point of view on nature as a secondary cause is clearly seen in *The Rays*, where he writes:

> Yes, dignity and grandeur demand that in the view of the mind causes are veils to the hand of power. While unity and oneness demand that causes abstain from having any real effect.[71]

In other words, Nursi acknowledges the fact that causes are everywhere in nature, and an ordinary observer could mistake them for primary causes. However, to Nursi, they are in reality just the veils hiding the real Actor, that is, God.

Analysis of Nursi's Substantiations for Defending Theism

There are two independent, conspicuous pieces of writing by Nursi in which teleology is the focal subject. In *The Flashes*, Nursi mainly tries to rebut the atheist argument by attacking materialist and naturalist philosophy, as was discussed above. In *The Words*, he systematically formulates his teleological argument, to which we now turn.

The Twenty-Second Word in *The Words* in the *Risale-i Nur* is completely dedicated to demonstrating the existence of God from order and

68. Quine, *Theories and Things*, 72.
69. Plantinga and Sennett, *The Analytic Theist: An Alvin Plantinga Reader*, 300–305.
70. http://www.discovery.org/a/3331
71. Nursi, *The Rays*, 980.

design (i.e., the teleological argument). At the beginning of this treatise, Nursi sets out two common views of nature and the universe in philosophy. The first is the theist or creationist point of view. The second is the point of view of the atheists. The second viewpoint equally represents the materialist, naturalist, and agnostic position. Here, Nursi sets the scene with the metaphor of two friends who find themselves in a strange town in the middle of nowhere. They look around and observe an extremely orderly settlement. They see strange creatures carrying out intelligent tasks and communicating in a language that they cannot understand. The first friend is an intelligent man and represents the theistic view, which is also Nursi's own understanding of the universe. The second friend is a foolish man and represents the atheist view.

The first, intelligent man, being fascinated by the design and order of the town and its contents, interprets it as follows:

> This strange world must have someone to regulate it, and this orderly country must have a lord, and this fine town, an owner, and this finely made palace, a master builder. We must try to know him, for it is understood that the one who brought us here was he. If we do not recognize him, who will help us? What can we await from these impotent creatures whose language we do not know and who do not heed us? Moreover, surely one who makes a vast world in the form of a country, town, and palace, and fills it from top to bottom with wonderful things, and embellishes it with every sort of adornment, and decks it out with instructive miracles wants something from us and from those that come here. We must get to know him and find out what he wants.[72]

What the intelligent man suggests obviously requires the fulfillment of duties and responsibilities. Finding out the ruler of the land means accepting his authority and abiding by his rules. However, denying the existence of the ruler and his authority means not obeying his rules. This second position, i.e., not obeying the rules, looks fairly easy and reasonable. We shall be analyzing it in greater detail in Chapter 6, which focuses on morality and consciousness. To return to Nursi's story, the intelligent man declares that denying a ruler is irrational and dangerous as it might put the friends in a very unpleasant situation with the law enforcement authorities of the land. The foolish man says: "Either prove to me decisively that this large country has a single lord and a single maker, or leave me alone."[73] Nursi, through the

72. Nursi, Nursi, *The Words*, 115.

73. Ibid.

mouth of the intelligent man, determines the following arguments to argue for the existence of God. He calls each of his arguments "the proof."

The First Proof

This is based on basic *observation of plants* in nature. For example, a tiny seed grows into a massive pear tree, which yields fruit a thousand times heavier than the original seed. Also, vine trees climb onto other stronger trees, since they cannot support their own body weight. All these and many other examples in nature, according to Nursi, are clear evidence of a Hidden Hand of God. Otherwise, Nursi suggests, we have to believe that it is a miracle of nature, which is just groundless superstition.[74]

The Second Proof

Here, Nursi points out the fact that *The Maker has got his signs* on everything in nature. For instance, a tiny seed grows into a fantastic work of art, as shown in the shape, pattern and color in its leaves and flowers. It produces a taste sweeter than any man-made sweet, and tastier than any man-made food.[75]

The Third Proof

This is the extreme *similarity between the universe and humans and animals.* Every human or animal body is a miniature universe. It contains all the elements of the universe. Therefore, Nursi contends, the Maker of the whole universe and the Maker of every creature has to be the same person.[76]

The Fourth Proof

The fourth proof is the *communication and cooperation* between plants and animals. Nursi tries to demonstrate this by describing the cooperation between an egg-laying fly and a tree. When the fly lays eggs on the leaf of a tree, the tree gives food and protection to the eggs in order to facilitate their hatching into baby flies. There are two possible explanations

74. Ibid.
75. Ibid.
76. Ibid., 116.

for this biological event. It is either the fly and the tree communicating and agreeing on cooperation, or the Hidden Ruler ordering the tree to look after the fly's egg. Assume, Nursi says, that the first proposition is correct. Although it might work on one single occasion, there would be complete overall chaos in nature in the wider perspective if vegetables and animals had to take the initiative to cooperate. If there were no unity in command, every organism would act randomly, causing a complete mess. As Nursi explained earlier, harmony requires unity in command. Because of the present harmonious appearance of nature, he says, we can only conclude that there is only one Commander.[77]

The Fifth Proof

Here, Nursi attracts our attention to the *art and design in nature*, which, he notes, exceeds all artificial art and design. The best painting of a dexterous painter can never match the beauty of the real object. In order to explain the existence of better artwork in nature, atheists have to resort to the nonsensical idea that unconscious causes, blind coincidence and deaf nature have got more intelligence and talent than a painter. Every piece of artificial art refers to its artist. Hence, Nursi asserts, all the art in nature refers to its Artist.[78]

The Sixth Proof

The sixth proof is the proof from *orderliness in nature*. Although there is continuous change in nature, there is never any mistake in the order of events. For example, similar types of plants follow the exact same routine every spring. That is to say, they first grow green leaves, then flowers and fruit. There is never any maverick tree that decides to skip one of the stages and do things its own way. According to the naturalists, however, nature has its own mind.[79] If we put ten people in one room, they would move around according to their own will; they would never follow the same pattern of action unless they worked towards it intelligently. How then, Nursi asks, do billions of individual plants and animals follow the same pattern every spring?[80]

77. Ibid.

78. Ibid., 117.

79. Hall, *The Ingenious Mind of Nature: Deciphering the Patterns of Man, Society, and the Universe*, 4.

80. Nursi, *The Words*, 117.

The Seventh Proof

Here, Nursi shows us the *cooperation and interconnectedness* in nature. For example, plants produce more lush leaves and fruit than they themselves need; the surplus is not for their own benefit but for the animals that feed off them. Animals help out their offspring and the other animals in terms of the food chain, and the sun provides all living things with light and warmth. All these different elements are cooperative, and they are all interconnected. Therefore, since they cannot decide by themselves, Nursi claims that there has to be an Unseen hand setting up this brilliant cooperation between these different elements.[81]

The Eight Proof

In this proof, Nursi explains the Oneness of the Maker. If we see some identical products with the same label, he says, we understand that they are produced in the same factory by the same machine. Similarly, in nature, all the art of beings indicates the Oneness of their Creator. In order to dress up a soldier, a clothing factory needs to be set up to manufacture soldier's clothes. If there is one factory and a million soldiers, it is not hard to fabricate a million clothes. If there is no oneness, there needs to be a million different factories to manufacture each piece of clothing. If the unbeliever does not accept the Oneness of the Maker, he needs to defend the idea of billions of complicated factories and machineries creating each and every thing in nature. This claim, he asserts, is obviously illogical, and insupportable.[82]

The Ninth Proof

This is essentially the continuation of the previous proof. Nursi argues that it is easier to recognize the existence of one Maker than to refuse his existence. Imagine, he says, an apple tree with a thousand fruits on it. If we recognize that all the fruits are connected to one tree trunk, it is easy and coherent to understand that they all come from the same origin. Otherwise, we have to defend the opposite idea, which is the existence of a thousand trunks, each of them supporting one fruit.[83] Nursi's eighth and ninth proofs are in line with the Ockham's Razor principle, which asserts that, in explaining a thing,

81. Ibid., 118.
82. Ibid.
83. Ibid.

no more assumptions should be made than are necessary.[84] Swinburne also argues in line with Nursi. He writes:

> . . . the simplest hypothesis proposed as an explanation of phenomena is more likely to be the true one than is any other available hypothesis, that its predictions are more likely to be true than those of any other available hypothesis, and that it is an ultimate a priori epistemic principle that simplicity is evidence for truth.[85]

The Tenth Proof

The tenth proof is perhaps the most striking argument among the twelve. Nursi's argument is this:

> For the causes of things disappear along with them. Whereas, the things which we attribute to them, which follow on after them, are repeated. That means those works are not theirs, but the works of one who does not perish. Just as it is understood from the bubbles on the surface of a river disappearing and the bubbles which follow on after them sparkling in the same way that what makes them sparkle is a constant and elevated possessor of light, in the same way, the speedy changing of things and the things that follow on after them assuming the same colors shows that they are the manifestations, inscriptions, mirrors, and works of art of one who is perpetual, undying, and single.[86]

In other words, when a set of causes, which the atheists claim to be the creator, dies, a new set of causes comes along. The result of this new set of causes ought to be totally different from the result of the previous set. However, there is a continuity in species over millions of years. This argument gives a stronger hand to the theists.

84. Encyclopaedia Britannica's definition: Ockham's razor, also spelled Occam's razor, also called law of economy or law of parsimony, principle stated by William of Ockham (1285–1347/49), a Scholastic, that *Pluralitas non est ponenda sine necessitate*, "Plurality should not be posited without necessity." The principle gives precedence to simplicity; of two competing theories, the simpler explanation of an entity is to be preferred. The principle is also expressed as "Entities are not to be multiplied beyond necessity."

85. Swinburne, *Simplicity as Evidence of Truth.*

86. Nursi, *The Words*, 119.

Although there is no evidence that they directed their criticisms at Nursi, it is clear that Flew, Mackie and Everitt follow the Humean tradition of objecting to the Nursian proofs.

Design Versus Evolution

For centuries, creationists have been defending the position of what the Holy Books, i.e., the Torah, the Gospels, and the Qur'an, claimed, that is, creation out of nothing, *creatio ex nihilo*. The creation theory states that God created every species independently out of nothing. Christian creationists, especially, take Genesis, that describes the creation of the first man and woman as well as of all plants and animals in the Garden of Eden, literally.[87] The common ground of all monotheistic religions is the belief that no species has developed from any other.[88] As a theist, Nursi also believes that it is God who created the universe and everything in it. However, he does not agree with the concept of creation from absolute nothingness. He suggests that absolute nothingness contradicts the attributes of God. The creation of things, according to Nursi, is effectively a transfer from the universe of relative absence into the universe of visible bodies. In other words, things have always existed in another universe, of God; they are simply given physical and visible bodies and transferred into this universe.[89]

The Aristotle-Aquinas-Paley line of thought (i.e., the teleological argument) had been the dominant explanation for the existence of the universe until the nineteenth century, when Darwin and Wallace came up with an alternative theory, which is the *theory of evolution* through *natural selection*. Many philosophers and scientists believe that the mark of design, the detailed structure of plants and animal bodies and their adaptation to the conditions they live in, can be better explained by the Darwinian theory of evolution through natural selection.[90] Shortly after Paley's *watch and watchmaker* analogy, Darwin's voyages to the Galapagos Islands prompted him

87. Genesis, Chapter 1, verses 24–25 reads: And God said, "Let the land produce living creatures according to their kinds: the livestock, the creatures that move along the ground, and the wild animals, each according to its kind. And it was so. God made the wild animals according to their kinds, the livestock according to their kinds, and all the creatures that move along the ground according to their kinds. And God saw that it was good."

88. Everitt, *The Non-Existence of God*, 101.

89. For the detail of Nursi's argument of creation from relative nothingness, see Nursi, *The Rays*, 857.

90. Mackie, *The Miracle of Theism: Arguments for and against the Existence of God*, 135.

to produce a countering theory, in which he tries to explain where different species might have come from. In *The Origin of Species*, Darwin linked most animals to each other to explain the parallels between them. He defended the idea that they might have had the same root in history (i.e., species might have developed from one another).[91]

In his 1887 book *The Descent of Man*, Darwin took one step further in his theory of evolution and suggested that "humans and other currently existing species such as chimpanzees both developed from a single earlier species of primates." In the concluding chapters, he writes:

> . . . I believe that animals have descended from at most only four or five progenitors, and plants from an equal or lesser number.[92]

Darwin's theory of evolution suddenly became the most powerful tool for the atheists. Dawkins believes that it is a fatal blow to the design argument.[93] Although it was initially meant to be a piece of research in biology and botany, it suddenly fell into the field of philosophy, and more precisely into the field of theology. It has been argued for and against by thousands of thinkers to date. Darwin's core idea is the rejection of creationism and the existence of a Maker. Darwin's ideas about evolution can be simplified in the following three ways.

Assume we are trying to justify the origins of the long necks of giraffes. One possible explanation could be that God intervened in each succeeding generation of short-necked herbivores, making the neck of the following generation slightly longer until the full giraffe form was reached.

The second explanation is what Lamarck calls "the theory of acquired characteristics,"[94] which is this: each generation of originally short-necked herbivores kept stretching their necks to suit the purpose. Then, these acquired characteristics passed on to the next generation, which repeats the same process until they achieve the desired length.

The third possible explanation is Darwin's choice of preference. It is probably the best-known theory: the theory of *natural selection*. This is the key element of the Darwinian theory of evolution. The gist of the theory of natural selection is this: Imagine that an animal produces two offspring. At birth, they are equal. But in time, one of them gets stronger, hence more competitive in hunting, running away from danger, food-finding and,

91. Ibid.

92. See Darwin, *On the Origin of Species: A Facsimile of the First Edition*, 483.

93. Dawkins, *The Blind Watchmaker*, 1–18.

94. Packard, *Lamarck, the Founder of Evolution*, 431. For his life and thoughts, see Lamarck, *Zoological Philosophy: An Exposition with Regard to the Natural History of Animals*, 113.

inevitably, in mating. Since the offspring with stronger characteristics keeps mating, he can pass his good-quality characteristics to the next generation, eliminating the weak offspring. Therefore, only the strongest survives.[95]

Almost all well-known modern atheist thinkers, such as Mackie,[96] Flew[97] and Everitt,[98] endorse Darwin's theory. They regard the modern theory of evolution as a more plausible theory than that of the theists.

There are three main criticisms that may be made against Darwin. The first is that evolution through natural selection makes seeming design a matter of "blind chance." In defense of the "blind chance" criticism, Everitt claims that the term "blind" is a hostile expression and systematically used by theists in order to imply absurdity to the Darwinian theory. Everitt defends Darwin, arguing that the apparent design in the universe is a product of "chance" in the sense that it was not pre-planned. For instance, two people go to a meeting independently from each other. Their meeting at the venue can be considered a chance one since it was not pre-planned. Everitt concludes that:

> that is true in one sense of "chance," just as most things that happen are a matter of chance. But it is false in the other sense of "chance," since natural selection says that there is a perfectly good explanation of how and why the seeming design in nature appears and is maintained.[99]

The second criticism of Darwin is that the theory of evolution does not disprove the existence of God. Darwin would arguably have been surprised to find out how many people genuinely took his theory as a fact, although it is only a theory. A theory, by definition, is "a *supposition* or a system of ideas intended to explain something, especially one based on general principles independent of the thing to be explained."[100] There have been many attempts of debunking Darwin's theory of evolution on scientific grounds,[101] some of them are considered to be quite successful and convincing.

95. Everitt, *The Non-Existence of God*, 102.

96. Mackie, *The Miracle of Theism: Arguments for and against the Existence of God*, 133, 38, 40, 41, 45, 46, 96.

97. Flew, *God & Philosophy*, 60, 61, 62, 73.

98. Everitt, *The Non-Existence of God*, 104–5.

99. Ibid., 105.

100. See Simpson, Weiner, *The Oxford English Dictionary*.

101. See Yahya, *Atlas of Creation*. Fossils have discredited evolution. See Simmons, *What Darwin Didn't Know*. See Spetner, *Not by Chance! Shattering the Modern Theory of Evolution*.

Now, let us turn our attention back to Nursi and find out what his thinking is regarding the theory of evolution and natural selection.

There is no mention of Darwin or his theory of evolution in the *Risale-i Nur*, although Nursi tackles the issue indirectly in various treatises. One of the first negations of Darwin's theory comes as the "*power–hardship relationship*" in nature. Nursi talks about extremely able animals, like lions, cheetahs, sharks, and eagles, very clever animals, like foxes, ravens, and rats, and very weak animals, like fruit worms. Here, he argues that the Maker designed nature and the animals in such a way that every animal has to work, in order to get fed, in proportion with its capacity. For example, the success ratio of big cats in hunting is roughly four out of ten. This means that they have to work really hard to hunt prey in order to survive. In complete contrast, extremely weak animals like apple worms have to make very little effort to reach their food. The Creator put them right at the center of their food. Clever animals, like foxes, need to work much harder for their survival. Nursi tells us that abundance of food and the ability to obtain it are inversely proportional. The stronger the animal, the harder it is for it to get food. The weaker the animal, the easier it is for it to get food.

Throughout the *Risale-i Nur*, we see that Nursi's obvious vantage point on nature is through *mʿanā-i ḥarfī*. In every being in nature, he sees the signs of what he calls *the Magnificent, All-Powerful Creator*.

There are some inconsistencies in Everitt's argument from scale,[102] which is meant to refute theism. What it actually does is to falsify the atheist position, as it appears in Dawkins' *Climbing Mount Improbable*.[103] The gist of Dawkins' argument is that the universe is so old that the current changes in organisms might have had a very, very long time to evolve through time. In other words, rather than jumping upward to the sheer top of the cliff, evolution climbs up the steady slope of the hill on the other side of the mountain.[104] What Everitt defends as being the possible scientific life of mankind (which is about one hundred thousand years, as opposed to some sixteen billion years of the Earth) automatically refutes Dawkins' argument. In other words, although the earth has existed for billions of years, mankind only walked the earth some one hundred thousand years ago, which is a fairly short time for a complex organism such as man to evolve to his current form.

102. See Everitt, *The Non-Existence of God*, 213–25.

103. See Dawkins, *Climbing Mount Improbable*.

104. In an interview at the Edinburgh International Book Festival on Monday 11 August 2008 conducted by Paula Kirby, Dawkins used the analogy of an escalator to explain how organic life has evolved over billions of years, as opposed to the invisible, unexplainable hand of God, as in the representation of a skyhook.

One of the most conspicuous arguments in Nursi's writings is the mathematical impossibility of existence by chance, which is surprisingly in line with the argument of an atheist philosopher. Hoyle's Fallacy argues the impossibility of a hurricane's creating a Boeing 747 by sweeping across a scrapyard.[105] Developing Hume's "Who created the creator?" thesis, Dawkins proposes his "Ultimate Boeing 747 Gambit," which claims that designing a super-complex designer requires even more complex intelligence. Therefore, according to Dawkins, evolution through natural selection is more feasible than positing an ultra-complex designer.[106] The Ockham's Razor principle is used by both parties, each claiming that their way of explanation is simpler, hence more plausible.

Recent, more scientific explanations of the existence of God look more appealing to scientifically oriented minds. Equally, Dennett's "skyhook and cranes" analogy, which is used by Dawkins, appeals to the same audience as well.

Nursi acknowledges the apparent fact that the causes seem to be the reason behind the wonders in the universe. However, he maintains the position that natural and materialist causes cannot intelligently act for a purpose. To him, they could only be the executive officers of the Ruler of the land.

Although, given the current evidence, the atheist position seems to be less plausible than the Nursian view, it is still premature to draw conclusions such as "Evolution is a blow to God,"[107] or "this (meaning the *Risale-i Nur*) breaks the backbone of disbelief."[108]

Conclusion

This chapter has extended the arguments introduced in Chapter 1 and gone into the analysis of Nursi's teleological argument. Like most theologians, Nursi takes his stand on the apparent design and purpose in the universe in order to demonstrate the existence of God. The teleological argument is the first of four arguments he puts forward. Owing to the ever-changing landscape of the late nineteenth and early twentieth centuries, materialist and naturalist philosophy and the advance of Darwinism, Nursi appears to ascribe great importance to the design argument in his works. He briefly

105. See Dawe, *The God Franchise: A Theory of Everything*, 299.

106. See Dawkins, *The God Delusion*, 113.

107. http://online.wsj.com/news/articles/ Dawkins, *The Blind Watchmaker*.

108. It has been reported that Nursi used this phrase upon the completion of The Tenth Word on Resurrection in Barla in the late 1926.

touches on the argument in his very early work *Al-Mathnawī al-Nūriyah* and gradually developed the argument from there on. For example, he clearly sets out his teleological proof in *The Words*, and he carefully handles objections to it in *The Flashes* and later in *The Rays*. In this regard, he seems to be elaborating around "Why it is God" theme in his early writings and "Why it is not others" theme in his later writing. This particular method of making a case first and tackling the challenges later, one could argue, is evident throughout the *Risale-i Nur*. It is also quite airtight in terms of holding a philosophical stand.

The teleological argument seems throughout time to have been of interest not only to philosophers and theologians, but also to scientists. All parties have equally been involved in the defense or rebuttal of this argument. Recently, both the critics and the defenders of the argument have mainly been scientists, like Dawkins and Behe.

In the historical perspective, the teleological argument seems to have enjoyed a long-lasting monopoly without any major criticism until Hume's *Dialogues Concerning Natural Religion* of 1779. Hume's approach is apparently a philosophical one. However, Darwin came up with a greater challenge to the theists with his 1859 work *On the Origin of Species*, where his alternative argument against the traditional idea of creation is purely a scientific one. Hence, creation versus evolution through natural selection is still a fresh battleground for theists and atheists today.

Although embraced by most atheists as their main defense, the first plausible alternative to creation, i.e., evolution through natural selection, has its own weaknesses. As the fiercest of defenders of evolution through natural selection, Dawkins admits that the theory needs a starting point, i.e., a water-borne microorganism which has to come into existence by chance in order to progress gradually. Plantinga argues that the theory of natural selection does not necessarily refute the existence of God. He defends that God might well have chosen natural selection as a biological process.

Nursi, like many other Islamic scholars such as Al-Ghazzālī and Ibn-i Rushd, suggests that the species were created in their current shape and form. He and they acutely reject the theory of evolution from the outset. Here, Nursi is in conflict with another theologian, Plantinga, who believes that the Darwinian explanation might be partly true.

Two strands of Nursian way of arguing in favor of the teleological argument have been analyzed. The first one is essentially an attempt to refute three materialist postulates namely; causes being the creator, self-creation and the nature being the creator. The second strand is to argue for the validity of the teleological arguments from bottom to top.

The chapter concludes that Nursi's most frequently used arguments to demonstrate the existence of God in his works is the teleological argument. Nursi simply resonates and elaborates on what has already been out there. Most of his arguments have roots in ancient and modern philosophy. What Nursi does is simply to make the existing arguments accessible to ordinary public to strengthen their faith.

4

Prophethood

(*Nubuwwah*)

Introduction

Historically speaking, there have been people who have claimed to be the messengers of God, and whose job it is to guide people according to God's orders given to them via revelations from God himself. These people (i.e., the prophets) argued for the existence and the oneness of God. Therefore, the argument for the existence of God always goes hand in hand with the argument from Revelation (*waḥy*) and the argument from prophethood (*nubuwwah*). There is hardly any theist who stands for the existence of God yet rejects the Divine Revelations or the prophets.[1] The Nursian proof of the existence of Divine Revelations; i.e., the Holy Books such as the Torah, the Gospels and the Qur'an, is the subject of Chapter 5 of this book, where the matter is discussed at length.

This chapter, however, focuses on the Nursian interpretation of prophethood and discusses the philosophical and social issues surrounding it. Issues such as "Do people need prophets?" and "Is it provable whether the prophets are genuine messengers of God?" are explored from a Nursian perspective.

The chapter begins with an assessment of the Argument from Religious Experience, and of how it has been developed as a tool to argue for the existence of God. The second section focuses on the characteristics of

1. Although there are disagreements among the monotheistic religions about the prophets, there is almost total recognition of each other's prophets. For example, despite the historical rejection of the Islamic Prophet, Christians generally recognize the prophethood of Muḥammad.

prophets in general, and the Prophet Muḥammad[2] in particular. It examines his life before and during his prophethood, his personal qualities, his teachings, and the serious social transformation he brought to nomadic Arab tribes.

Then, Nursi's argument for the Prophet Muḥammad's prophethood is analyzed. Nursi argues that the apparent design in the universe requires a Designer,[3] who then requires prophets in order to communicate with his creations. For Nursi, therefore, the existence of God necessitates the existence of prophets, which reciprocally prove each other.

Nursi develops his thesis of Muḥammad being a genuine prophet around four themes. The first theme is that the religious experience of Muḥammad is veridical since Muḥammad's personal characteristics before and after his claim of prophethood match those described by philosophers and scholars. Nursi's second theme is that miracles support his prophethood. The third theme concerns Nursi's own interpretations of some verses of the Bible and Torah which, for Nursi, indicate Muḥammad's arrival and his being the last prophet. The fourth theme Nursi employs is that the social transformation that Muḥammad brought about within twenty years could only strengthen further his claim to be a genuine prophet of God.

Next, philosophical criticisms to the Argument from Religious Experience in general are discussed. After that the focus moves to the criticisms of the Prophet Muḥammad made by people such as Gautier de Compiegne, Ramón Marti, Andrea Biglia, Theodore Bibliander, and Humphrey Prideaux. The Nursian stance on popular issues such as the Prophet's marriages, his battles, and his miracles, such as the Splitting of the Moon and the Night Journey (*Isrā wa al-Mi'rāj*), are considered.

Outline of the Argument from Religious Experience

One of the most frequent arguments for the existence of God from the theistic point of view is the Argument from Religious Experience, or the ARE. Although, strictly speaking, it is not a theistic proof *per se*,[4] or a piece of reasoning for the existence of God, the ARE always appears as a supporting pil-

2. It is a compulsory practice in Islamic culture to say "Peace be upon him" when the Prophet Muḥammad's name is mentioned. However, I shall not indicate "p.b.u.h." each time mention the prophet's name is mentioned, leaving it to the reader to acknowledge it.

3. See Chapter 3: Nursi on the Design Argument.

4. In Davis, *God, Reason and Theistic Proofs*, 121. Davis explains that in order for an argument to be considered a philosophically accepted theistic proof, its conclusion must be "God exists."

lar to the other more philosophical arguments, such as the teleological and moral arguments. Everitt explains that for an atheist or agnostic to convert to theism on the basis of religious experience is hardly common. However, he goes on, the argument does offer additional confirmatory evidence to those who already accept the existence of God.[5]

The main tenet of the ARE is the God-signaling interpretation of certain events and occurrences by religious or religiously inclined individuals. The doctrine of all monotheistic religions is based on their prophets' religious experiences, that is, their speaking to God, or experiencing his presence or the presence of other certain spirits such as angels, and thus receiving messages and revelations from God. For instance, the Bible narrates Moses' encounter with God as follows:

> Now Moses was tending the flock of Jethro his father-in-law, the priest of Midian, and he led the flock to the far side of the wilderness and came to Horeb, the mountain of God. There the angel of the Lord appeared to him in flames of fire from within a bush. Moses saw that though the bush was on fire it did not burn up. So Moses thought, "I will go over and see this strange sight—why the bush does not burn up."
>
> When the Lord saw that he had gone over to look, God called to him from within the bush, "Moses! Moses!"
>
> And Moses said, "Here I am."
>
> "Do not come any closer," God said. "Take off your sandals, for the place where you are standing is holy ground." Then he said, "I am the God of your father, the God of Abraham, the God of Isaac and the God of Jacob." At this, Moses hid his face, because he was afraid to look at God.
>
> The Lord said, "I have indeed seen the misery of my people in Egypt. I have heard them crying out because of their slave drivers, and I am concerned about their suffering. So I have come down to rescue them from the hand of the Egyptians and to bring them up out of that land into a good and spacious land, a land flowing with milk and honey —the home of the Canaanites, Hittites, Amorites, Perizzites, Hivites and Jebusites. And now the cry of the Israelites has reached me, and I have seen the way the Egyptians are oppressing them. So now, go. I am sending you to Pharaoh to bring my people the Israelites out of Egypt."[6]

5. See Everitt, *The Non-Existence of God*, 150.
6. Exod 3: 1–7.

In the Gospels, Isaiah, who is also considered to be one of the prophets of God, describes his encounter with God as follows:

> In the year that King Uzziah died, I saw the LORD, high and exalted, seated on a throne; and the train of his robe filled the temple. Above him were seraphim, each with six wings: With two wings they covered their faces, with two they covered their feet, and with two they were flying. And they were calling to one another: "Holy, holy, holy is the LORD Almighty; the whole earth is full of his glory."
>
> At the sound of their voices the doorposts and thresholds shook and the temple was filled with smoke.
>
> "Woe to me!" I cried. "I am ruined! For I am a man of unclean lips, and I live among a people of unclean lips, and my eyes have seen the King, the LORD Almighty."[7]

The Prophet Muḥammad's religious experience, on the other hand, takes place mainly through the arbitrating Angel Gabriel, except for the final leg of the Night Journey and Descent (*Isrā wa al-Mi'rāj*). The first encounter reportedly occurred in Hira Cave in Mecca, where Muḥammad was secluded for the purposes of self-mediation. One of Muḥammad's wives, Aisha, explains this experience in full detail,[8] relating how Gabriel asked Muḥammad to read, and how Muḥammad replied that he was illiterate, whereupon Gabriel shook him violently and revealed the first three verses of the Qur'an, which are:

> Recite in the name of your Lord (*al-Rabb*) who created man from a clinging substance. Recite, and your Lord is the most Generous.[9]

In the second encounter, the same angel brings to Muḥammad God's message and orders, which read:

> O you who covers himself [with a garment], Arise and warn. And your Lord glorify. And your clothing purify. And uncleanliness avoid.[10]

7. Isa 6: 1–6.
8. See Khan, *Sahih Al-Bukhari*, Vol 1, Book 1:1.
9. Qur'an 96:1–3.
10. Qur'an 74:1–5.

In *The Varieties of Religious Experience*, psychologist and philosopher William James reports similar personal experiences whereby the presence of God or of some exalted spirit is felt by many religious people.[11]

There are two distinctive characteristics of such religious experience which are apparent in almost all such encounters. These are: [1] they are always private (i.e., experienced by only one person, even though other people are present), such as the experience of a seventeen-year-old boy in church[12] reported in James' book, and Isaiah's and Muḥammad's experiences; and [2], there is always a strong sense of God's or the angel's greatness, and of one's own inadequacy or smallness, which is the case in almost every prophetic encounter.

According to the theist philosopher Richard Swinburne, there are several different types of religious experience, which all strengthen the arguments for the existence of God. In the first type, Swinburne explains, the divine reality or the presence of God may be experienced in a normal public setting. For instance, as in Nursi's case, someone might look at the sunset, or a flower, and see it as a powerful revelation of God, or as mediating God's presence.[13]

The second type consists of experiencing the presence of God through unusual (miraculous) events, such as Moses seeing a bush on fire but not consumed, or the ascension of Jesus, or the experience of the Virgin Mary.

In the third type, Swinburne explains, the experience is mediated through a private object such as visions, dreams or voices. The fourth type is personal experience that cannot be described in ordinary sensory language. For instance, someone might feel the presence of God or Jesus near him, but not be able to explain or defend the feeling. The fifth type, according to Swinburne, consists of experiencing God such that the experience does not seem to be mediated by anything sensory at all.[14]

Stephen Davis classifies these religious experiences into two main groups. The first group Davis calls "religious experience," where the strong presence, power and holiness of God is felt through one's ontological

11. James, *The Varieties of Religious Experience: A Study in Human Nature*, Lecture III, Reality of the Unseen. 55–77.

12. In *Varieties of Religious Experience*, 71, William James reports an anonymous seventeen-year-old boy: Sometimes as I go to church, I sit down, join in the service, and before I go out I feel as if God was with me, right side of me, singing and reading the Psalms with me. . . . And then again I feel as if I could sit beside him, and put my arms around him, kiss him, etc. When I am taking Holy Communion at the altar, I try to get with him and generally feel his presence.

13. Swinburne, *The Existence of God*, 250.

14. Ibid., 251.

distinctness from God. The second group, "mystical experience," on the other hand, involves a strong sense of ontological unity with God. This second kind of experience, which is also called monistic (God is the only reality) or unitive mystical experience, includes the disappearance of oneself as a thing distinct from God.[15]

The ARE may be briefly formulated as follows:

Premise 1: Throughout human history, and in very many human societies and cultures, people claim to have experiences of God or some godlike being.

Premise 2: The claim that those experiences are veridical is more probable than the claim that they are delusive.

Premise 3: Therefore, probably, God or some godlike being exists.[16]

Apologists for the ARE stress the fact that the characteristics of the person who experiences the presence of God has the utmost importance. Therefore, these need to be scrutinized closely.

Characteristics of Prophets

The authenticity of the mission of any prophet depends upon his personal characteristics, such as trustworthiness and truthfulness. Skeptics always scrutinize the personal qualities of an individual who claims to be a prophet. Theists claim that prophets are chosen people whose job it is to teach mankind faith, knowledge, morals and laws. Therefore, prophets ought to hold the high ground in terms of having supreme moral qualities.

The Qur'an highlights five essential qualities that all prophets must have. These are as follows:

Truthfulness (*Ṣidq*)

If a person is known to have lied in the past, he cannot be a prophet since he might be accused of lying again. This is also the first test with which to question whether the personal experience of an individual is genuine.

15. Davis, *God, Reason and Theistic Proofs*, 125.

16. Ibid., 128.

Trustworthiness (*Amānah*)

If a person is known to have cheated in the past, he cannot be a prophet. Therefore, this is the second essential test to reveal whether the person is a genuine prophet.

Manifesting Faith (*Tablīgh*)

If a person practices his faith in solitude, he cannot be a prophet. Prophets always call their people openly to God's unity.

High Intelligence (*Faṭānah*)

If a person is weak, uncertain or unintelligent, he cannot be a prophet. Since prophethood requires strong intelligence, people must consider the prophet to be strong and intelligent and look up to him.

Moral Perfection (*'Iṣmah*)

If a person is to known to have committed crime, or to have displayed low moral behavior, he cannot be a prophet. All prophets are pure and innocent.[17]

Since all the prophets were humans, not angels, they have had certain shortcomings in their personal judgments, which were, however, not deliberate acts of evil. For instance, Jonah refused to undertake the task assigned by God for a while and left his tribe, hence his troubles at sea and his return to his tribe.[18] Then there is Moses' fighting and killing the Egyptian,[19] and Adam's eating the forbidden fruit,[20] etc.

The Qur'an tells more about the prophets and their characteristics. The first distinction the Qur'an makes between the prophets is that some of

17. See Appendix 5: The names and the characteristics of the prophets mentioned in the Qur'an.

18. Qur'an, 10:1–109.

19. Qur'an, 28:15: And he entered the city at a time of inattention by its people and found therein two men fighting: one from his faction and one from among his enemy. And the one from his faction called for help to him against the one from his enemy, so Moses struck him and [unintentionally] killed him. [Moses] said, "This is from the work of Satan. Indeed, he is a manifest, misleading enemy."

20. Qur'an, 7:22: So he made them fall, through deception. And when they tasted of the tree, their private parts became apparent to them, and they began to fasten together over themselves from the leaves of Paradise. And their Lord called to them, "Did I not forbid you from that tree and tell you that Satan is to you a clear enemy?"

them are *rasūl* and some of them *nabī*.[21] Those who had a book are called *rasūl*, and those who did not have a book, but carried on the messages of previous prophets, are called *nabī*.

The Qur'an points out that all the prophets had the qualities of sincerity, compassion, honesty, trustworthiness, purity, piety, patience and righteousness. We learn the stories and the qualities of the prophets from the Qur'an and the Prophet Muḥammad's tradition (*ḥadīth*). The Qur'an, for example, tells us about the encounter of the prophet Moses with God on Mount Sinai, and describes Moses' two prophetic quality of penitence and faithfulness, at the end of the verse which reads:

> And when Moses arrived at Our appointed time and his Lord spoke to him, he said, "My Lord, show me [Yourself] that I may look at You." [Allah] said, "You will not see Me, but look at the mountain; if it should remain in place, then you will see Me." But when his Lord appeared to the mountain, He rendered it level, and Moses fell unconscious. And when he awoke, he said, "Exalted are You! I have repented to You, and I am the first of the believers."[22]

Regarding the righteousness of the prophet Abraham, the Qur'an reports:

> And We gave to him [Abraham] Isaac and Jacob and placed in his descendants prophethood and scripture. And We gave him his reward in this world, and indeed, he is in the Hereafter among the righteous.[23]

> In the Qur'an, Jesus is described as a prophet who: is righteous,[24] is held in honor in the world and in the Hereafter,[25] taught the

21. Qur'an, 6:13, 22:75, 29:27, 81:19.

22. Qur'an, 7:143.

23. Qur'an, 29:27.

24. Qur'an, 3:45–46 *Sūrat 'Āli 'Imrān* (Family of Imran): "[And mention] when the angels said, "O Mary, indeed Allāh gives you good tidings of a word from him, whose name will be the Messiah, Jesus, the son of Mary—distinguished in this world and the Hereafter and among those brought near [to Allāh]. He will speak to the people in the cradle and in maturity and will be of the righteous."

25. Ibid.

book and wisdom by God,[26] and is pure,[27] kind[28] and close to God.[29]

There are many accounts of the Prophet Muḥammad's characteristics in the works of Bukhārī, Muslim, Tirmidhī, Abū Dawūd and Qadī Iyāz, and in other Islamic literature. One of the best and the shortest description of his character is contained in the answer his wife Aisha gave when she was asked about the Prophet's character. Aisha replied:

> Don't you read the Qur'an? The character of the Messenger of Allāh was the Qur'an.[30]

The Prophet Muḥammad himself explained that he was the living, practical face of the religion of God (i.e., Islam). He said:

> Allāh has sent me as an apostle so that I may demonstrate perfection of character, refinement of manners and loftiness of deportment.[31]

The Prophet Muḥammad, along with all his predecessors, was reported to be a kind, gentle, softly spoken person. This might be due to the physiological fact that people in general are likely to refuse the message if the messenger is rude or harsh. The Qur'an approves Muḥammad's excellent manners in spreading God's messages. *Sūrat 'Āli `Imrān* (Family of Imran) in the Qur'an reads:

> So by mercy from Allāh, [O Muḥammad], you were lenient with them. And if you had been rude [in speech] and harsh in heart, they would have disbanded from about you. So pardon them and ask forgiveness for them and consult them in the matter. And when you have decided, then rely upon Allāh. Indeed, Allāh loves those who rely upon him.[32]

26. Qur'an, 3:48 *Sūrat 'Āli `Imrān* (Family of Imran): "And he will teach him writing and wisdom and the Torah and the Gospel."

27. Qur'an, 19:19 Sūrat Maryam (Mary): "He said, "I am only the messenger of your Lord to give you [news of] a pure boy."

28. Qur'an, 19:32 Sūrat Maryam (Mary): "And [made me] dutiful to my mother, and he has not made me a wretched tyrant."

29. Qur'an, 3:55 *Sūrat 'Āli `Imrān* (Family of Imran):"[Mention] when Allāh said, "O Jesus, indeed I will take you and raise you to Myself and purify you from those who disbelieve and make those who follow you [in submission to Allāh alone] superior to those who disbelieve until the Day of Resurrection. Then to me is your return, and I will judge between you concerning that in which you used to differ."

30. Muslim, *Al-jami'-uṣ-ṣaḥīḥ*, 1623.

31. Ahmed, *Musnad*, Mishkat.

32. Qur'an, 3:159.

The Prophet Muḥammad is considered to be the perfect man (*insān-i kāmil*), and the perfect servant of God whom every Muslim has to work towards in attaining his qualities. The Qur'an reveals his excellent qualities of being submissive to God,[33] his total devotion,[34] and his fear of God.[35] God puts him in charge of guiding the entire human race rather than his tribe or nation. This is revealed in *Sūrat al-Anbiyā'* (The Prophets) 21:107, where God says: "And We have not sent you, O Muḥammad, except as a mercy to the worlds."[36]

Nursi claims that Muḥammad was the last of prophets appointed by God to guide humanity. He not only relies on Qur'anic evidence, but also builds up his own theory of Muḥammad's prophethood.

Nursi's Arguments for Muḥammad's Prophethood

According to Nursi, the universe has been created by God in an extremely complicated manner.[37] Nursi claims that the purpose of the creation of the universe is that God desired to be known through the eyes and mind of people. He argues that the existence of a powerful and intelligent God naturally requires him to communicate with his subjects (i.e., the human race).[38] This communication, for Nursi, had to be conducted through the most perfect member of humankind (i.e., the Prophet Muḥammad).[39]

33. Qur'an, 3:20: So if they argue with you, say, "I have submitted myself to Allāh in Islam, and so have those who follow me . . . ".

34. Qur'an, 48:29: *Sūrat Al-Fatḥ* (The Victory): Muḥammad is the Messenger of Allāh; and those with him are forceful against the disbelievers, merciful among themselves. You see them bowing and prostrating [in prayer], seeking bounty from Allāh and [his] pleasure. Their mark is on their faces from the trace of prostration. That is their description in the Torah. And their description in the Gospel is as a plant which produces its offshoots and strengthens them so they grow firm and stand upon their stalks, delighting the sowers—so that Allāh may enrage by them the disbelievers. Allāh has promised those who believe and do righteous deeds among them forgiveness and a great reward.

35. Qur'an, 10:15: *Sūrat Yūnus* (Jonah): And when Our verses are recited to them as clear evidences, those who do not expect the meeting with Us say, "Bring us a Qur'an other than this or change it." Say, [O Muḥammad], "It is not for me to change it on my own accord. I only follow what is revealed to me. Indeed I fear, if I should disobey my Lord, the punishment of a tremendous Day."

36. Qur'an, 21:107.

37. See Chapter 3: Nursi on teleological argument for Nursi's arguments for the existence of God from the apparent design in the universe.

38. Nursi, *The Letters*, 387.

39. Ibid.

Nursi claims that the prophethood of Muḥammad could be proved beyond question. Proving Muḥammad's prophethood also spontaneously verifies the authenticity of all the previous prophets, since they are all interconnected and lean against one another.[40] Nursi, then, develops an elaborate web of arguments in order to validate his point.[41]

Muḥammad Reporting the Future (*Ikhbār-i Ghaybī*)

As his first line of defense, Nursi presents some of the Prophet Muḥammad's reports of future events which have been proven historically. For instance, pointing to his grandchild Hasan b. Ali, Muḥammad explained that this little child would settle a great dispute between two Muslim armies.[42] Indeed, history tells us that some forty years later, Hasan b. Ali prevented a war between Muslims by signing a peace treaty with Muawiya b. Abū Sufyan.[43]

On another occasion, the Prophet Muḥammad warned his son-in-law, ʿAli b. Abū Ṭālib, that someone would stain his beard with his blood, implying that he would be murdered.[44] This person, indeed, was ʿAbd al-Raḥmān ibn Muljam the Kharijite. In more general, better-known historical events, the Prophet Muḥammad reported the capture of Cyprus and Constantinople by Muslims, and the fall of the Roman and Persian empires, which all became reality.[45]

Nursi, therefore, claims that the Prophet Muḥammad was an ordinary man, not a soothsayer. However, his prophethood was reinforced by God, who inspired him with some of his eternal knowledge.[46] This, Nursi asserts, is a clear indication that Muḥammad was God's genuine messenger.

Miracles Regarding Food and Water

Among many alleged miracles of the Prophet Muḥammad, Nursi gives a few examples regarding food and water. Nursi reminds the reader that the Arabian Peninsula is naturally very dry and that there is usually a shortage

40. Nursi, *Al-Mathnawi Al-Nuri*, 1224.

41. For the schematic illustration of Nursi's arguments, see Appendix 9.

42. See Bukhari and Khan, *Sahih Al-Bukhari: The Translation of the Meanings of Sahih Al-Bukhari: Arabic-English*, Fitan 20.

43. Nursi, *The Letters*, 392.

44. Wādiʿī, *Rijal Al-Hakim Fi Al-Mustadrak*, 113.

45. For the Prophet Muḥammad's miracles regarding the reporting the future events, see Nursi, *The Letters*, 392.

46. Ibid., 400.

of food and water. Therefore, according to Nursi, the miracles regarding food and water not only provide sustenance to a large number of companions but also strengthen their faith. One of Nursi's examples is the incident reported by Jabir al-Ansari, who reported that during the *Aḥzāb* (confederates) expedition on the celebrated day of *Khandaq* (Battle of Trenches), about a thousand people ate from four handfuls of rye bread and a young cooked goat, yet food was still left over.[47]

Regarding the water miracles, Nursi mentions an incident reported by Abdullah al-Ansari, who said:

> We were one thousand five hundred men on the Hudaybiyyah expedition, and we were thirsty. The Noble Messenger performed the ablutions from a leather water bag called *qirba*, then he dipped his hand into it. I saw that water was flowing from his fingers like a spring. The one thousand five hundred men drank from it and filled their water bags.[48]

Further to these particular miracles, which involved only limited numbers of people, Nursi advances to his next argument, which involves many million people, as well as whole societies and their way of life, in terms of social transformation for the better owing to the Prophet Muḥammad's teachings.

Social Transformation Argument

Arguably, the Prophet Muḥammad's arrival and the introduction by him of Islam has been one of the greatest events in human history in terms of changes and advancements in human civilization. Nursi explains that the pre-Islamic era of ignorance (*jāhiliyyah*) was a time when almost every ill practice of humanity was at its peak. Practices that many civilized individuals despise were considered acceptable. Charging interest on loans (*ribā*), adultery (*zinā*), believing in omens (*tayattur*), astrology (*tanjīm*), seeking blessing from objects (*tabarruk*), and soothsaying (*kahānah*) were some of the customs of *jāhiliyyah*.[49]

In his ambassadorial address, Ja'far Ibn Abū Ṭālib described the lifestyle of pre-Islamic Arabia to the Negus of Abyssinia upon their arrival in

47. Khan, *Sahih Al-Bukhari*, Maghazi 29.

48. Ibid., Menaqib 25.

49. For the general history of pre-Islamic Arabia, see O'Leary, *Arabia before Muhammad*.

For the detailed *Jāhiliyyah* traditions of Arabs, see Haylamaz, *Gönül Tahtımızın Eşsiz Sultanı: Efendimiz (Sas)*, 58–62.

his country in order to seek refuge from the oppression of polytheists of Mecca. He explained: "We were people of *Jāhiliyyah*, worshipping idols, eating the flesh of dead animals,[50] committing abominations, neglecting our relatives, doing evil to our neighbors and the strong among us would oppress the weak . . ."[51]

During *Jāhiliyyah,* some 40 percent of baby girls used to be buried alive, since the common belief was that they bring embarrassment to their fathers. The Qur'an mentions this brutal scene in *Sūrat al-Takwīr* (The Overthrowing), "when the girl [who was] buried alive is asked, for what sin she was killed."[52]

According to Nursi, the transformation of Arab society from the verge of savagery to the high moral ground thanks to the Prophet Muḥammad's teachings could be considered one of his greatest achievements, one owing to the divine origins of his teachings. In *The Letters,* he writes:

> You know that a small habit like cigarette smoking among a small nation can be removed permanently only by a powerful ruler with great effort. But look! This Being (the Prophet Muḥammad) removed numerous ingrained habits from intractable, fanatical large nations with slight outward power and little effort in a short period of time, and in their place he so established exalted qualities that they became as firm as if they had mingled with their very blood. He achieved very many extraordinary feats like this. Thus, we present the Arabian Peninsula as a challenge to those who refuse to see the testimony of the blessed age of the Prophet. Let them each take a hundred philosophers, go there, and strive for a hundred years, I wonder if they would be able to carry out in that time one hundredth of what he achieved in a year?[53]

The philosophical value of Nursi's particular argument here is open to debate. Skeptic philosophers, as well as sociologists, might argue that the transformation of a society does not necessarily entail the conclusion that the forces creating change actually hold right values. For instance, Hitler achieved a certain transformation of German society, and so did Stalin in Soviet Russia. Nursi, however, would have opposed this suggestion, and argued that the social changes occurred in Nazi Germany and Soviet

50. A dead animal here means an animal which died itself some time ago, not one slaughtered to be eaten.

51. Gülen, *Prophet Muhammad: Aspects of His Life,* 1–3.

52. Qur'an, 81: 8–9.

53. Nursi, *The Words,* 93.

Russia were due to the brutal forces of the regimes. By contrast, the Prophet Muḥammad's transformation has been on the basis of voluntary acceptance, at least in most cases.

We now return to particular incidents that occurred during the Prophet Muḥammad's life, the "era of bliss" that Nursi considers as offering miracles and supportive evidence of Muḥammad's prophethood.

Miscellaneous Miracles

In *The Letters*, Nursi details the Prophet Muḥammad's miracles at great length,[54] using well-known miracles in order to support his argument. One of the most popular miracles of prophet Muḥammad was the *moaning of the trunk* incident. This miracle, according to Nursi, became more popular than the miracles concerning food and water since it was witnessed by many people within the mosque of the Prophet in Medina. It was mainly aimed at strengthening the faith of new Muslims. Miracles concerning food and water, by contrast, to Nursi, were more of a matter of survival, and hence became less well known.[55]

The moaning of the trunk incident took place in the Prophet's mosque in Medina. The tree trunk against which the Prophet used to lean to give his sermon became redundant upon the construction of a new pulpit. During a Friday sermon, the congregation in the mosque all witnessed the cry of the trunk owing to the Prophet's not using it any longer.[56]

Nursi exposes further miracles of Muḥammad in *The Letters*. He relates examples of miracles regarding stones talking, trees obeying the Prophet's instructions and moving around, miracles of Muḥammad healing the sick and wounded and miracles of the animals talking to him in order to argue that Muḥammad was a genuine messenger of God.

Nursi on Prophet Muḥammad According to Judaism and Christianity

According to Nursi, Prophet Muḥammad was the last of the chain of prophets (*khatama annabiyyeena*) starting from the first man and the first prophet, Adam. Here, Nursi holds onto a classical theist position, which assumes that

54. See *The nineteenth Letter: The Miracles of Muḥammad* in: Nursi, *The Letters*, 387–451.

55. Ibid., 411.

56. Khan, *Sahih Al-Bukhari*, Menakib 25.

the first man was created by God complete in terms of anatomy and intelligence, as opposed to the atheist, or Darwinian view whereby the human form is alleged to have evolved from a less complicated common ancestor of mammals.[57]

Having acknowledged the truthfulness of all previous scriptures and the prophets, Nursi claims that the prophethood of Muḥammad has been mentioned by the previous Abrahamic religions. For him, this proves the authenticity of the previous Books and the prophets, even though, he claims, their messages have been corrupted. In *The Letters*, Nursi writes:

> Indeed, since those Books (i.e., the Torah, the Bible, the Psalms of David) are revealed scriptures and those who brought them were prophets, it is necessary and certain that they should have mentioned the one who would supersede their religions, change the shape of the universe, and illuminate half the earth with the light he brought. Is it possible that those scriptures, which foretold insignificant events, would not speak of the most important phenomenon of humanity, the prophethood of Muḥammad "peace be upon him"? Yes, since they would certainly speak of it, they would either denounce it as a falsehood and so save their religions from destruction and their books from abrogation, or they would affirm it, and through that man of truth, save their religions from superstition and corruption. Now, both friend and foe agree that there is no sign of any such denouncement in the scriptures, in which case there must be affirmation. And since there is certain affirmation, and since there is a definite reason and fundamental cause for such affirmation, we too shall demonstrate through three categorical proofs the existence of this affirmation.[58]

Nursi presents his case that the Prophet Muḥammad was already affirmed in the Torah, and that the Qur'an clearly challenges the Jews to affirm that Muḥammad is a genuine prophet who was reported in the Torah. Regarding the Jews' rejection of Muḥammad's prophethood, the Qur'an announces, "Say, O Muḥammad, So bring the Torah and recite it, if you should be truthful"[59] and challenges further:

> Then whoever argues with you about it after this knowledge has come to you—say, "Come, let us call our sons and your sons, our

57. In *God Is Not Great*, Hitchens writes "It is because we are evolved from sightless bacteria . . . ." See Hitchens, *God Is Not Great*, 82.

58. Nursi, *The Letters*, 430.

59. Qur'an, 3:93.

> women and your women, ourselves and yourselves, then supplicate earnestly together and invoke the curse of Allāh upon the liars among us.[60]

Nursi maintains that the Prophet Muḥammad and the Qur'an openly challenged the Jews to refute the fact of Muḥammad's prophethood with evidence from their own Holy Book. Since they failed to disprove Muḥammad, they chose the hard way, namely killing or being killed on the battlefield. According to Nursi, the Jews' act of war was actually another evidence of Muḥammad's prophethood being genuine. Otherwise, they would have chosen the easier way, showing evidence from the Torah.

Nursi claims that most Jewish and Christian scholars admitted that their Holy Books mention the upcoming prophets of the Arabs.[61] He narrates an incident before Muḥammad became a prophet in which Monk Bakhira called the uncle of Muḥammad during their journey from Damascus, warned Abū Ṭālib that little Muḥammad was the prophet who was reported in the Torah, and asked him to take extra care in protecting him in case the Jews might want to harm him out of jealousy.[62]

Nursi interprets some verses from the previous scriptures in which, he claims, Prophet Muḥammad's arrival had already been mentioned. In the King James Version of the Gospel of John:

> Took branches of palm trees, and went forth to meet him, and cried, Hosanna: Blessed is the King of Israel that cometh in the name of the Lord[63]

and

> Hereafter I will not talk much with you: for the prince of this world cometh, and hath nothing in me.[64]

and

> Nevertheless I tell you the truth; It is expedient for you that I go away: for if I go not away, the Comforter will not come unto you; but if I depart, I will send him unto you. And when he is come, he will reprove the world of sin, and of righteousness, and of judgment: Of sin, because they believe not on me; Of

60. Qur'an, 3:61.

61. Nursi, *The Letters*, 431.

62. For the details of this incident, see Lings, *Muhammad: His Life Based on the Earliest Sources*, 29–30.

63. John 12:13.

64. John 14:30.

> righteousness, because I go to my Father, and ye see me no more; Of judgment, because the prince of this world is judged.[65]

and

> who also, as Luke says, descended at the day of Pentecost upon the disciples after the Lord's ascension, having power to admit all nations to the entrance of life, and to the opening of the new covenant; from whence also, with one accord in all languages, they uttered praise to God, the Spirit bringing distant tribes to unity, and offering to the Father the first-fruits of all nations. Wherefore also the Lord promised to send the Comforter, they are manifested by the Holy Ghost, who was sent; "that is the Paraclete, of whom the Lord said, "If I go not away, He will not come. And, "If I go not away, that Advocate shall not come to you; but if I go away, I will send him to you."[66]

Nursi argues that terms in the Bible such as *Paraclete* or *Faraqlit* refer to the person who distinguishes truth from falsehood. It is therefore the name of one who in the future will lead people to the truth. This person, Nursi interprets, could only be the Prophet Muḥammad.[67] In Genesis we read:

> Verily God told Abraham that Hagar—the mother of Isma'il—will bear children. There will emerge from her sons one whose hand will be above all, and the hands of all will be opened to him in reverence.[68]

And in Deuteronomy:

> And He said to Moses: "O Moses, verily I shall send them a prophet like you, from the sons of their brothers [the children of Isma'il]; I shall place My word in his mouth, and shall punish whoever does not accept the words of the one who will speak in My name."[69]

And in Isaiah:

> Here is my servant, whom I uphold, my chosen one in whom I delight; I will put my Spirit on him, and he will bring justice to the nations. He will not shout or cry out, or raise his voice in the

65. John 16:7–11.
66. John 16:7.
67. Nursi, *The Letters*, 435.
68 Genesis, Chapter 16.
69 Deut 18:17–19.

> streets. A bruised reed he will not break, and a smoldering wick he will not snuff out. In faithfulness he will bring forth justice; He will not falter or be discouraged till he establishes justice on earth. In his teaching the islands will put their hope.[70]

In short, Nursi asserts that verses like these, and tales from the pre-prophetic era, represent strong evidence that Muḥammad was a genuine messenger of God. This, according to Nursi, also proves that all the previous scriptures and prophets are interrelated and that they are all combined proof of the existence of God, who clearly chose to speak to his subjects.[71]

Although Nursi, along with many Muslim theologians, argues that these verses provide evidence of the Prophet Muḥammad's arrival, outside Muslim circles this claim is uncommon.[72] Furthermore, interpretations of these verses might differ from person to person. Arguably, this could be considered a weakness in Nursi's argument for Muḥammad's prophethood from previous monotheistic scriptures.

Objections to Nursi's Argument from Prophethood

Skeptic philosophers do not accept the theistic argument for the existence of God through prophets. Their objections take two forms. The first is the criticism of the argument from miracles. The second is the criticism of the argument from religious experience. Since the objection to the argument from miracles is dealt with earlier, we will focus in the following section on the argument from religious experience.[73]

Philosophical Objections to the Argument from Religious Experience

Although the argument from religious experience or the ARE became more popular from the twentieth century onwards, it would not be wrong to assume that Nursi's argument from prophethood as being part of the ARE. The ARE usually favors theism, in the sense that the receiving people associate

70 Isa 42:1–4

71. Nursi, *The Letters*, 435.

72. For instance, certain Christian groups, such as Mormons and Jehovah's Witnesses, might consider themselves renewers of God's religion.

73. Arguments for the existence of God through prophethood and through scripture are inseparably connected. Nursi studies these two concepts separately; hence I structure this book following Nursi's methodology. Therefore, I focus on the ARE and the criticisms to ARE in this chapter, and miracles and criticisms of miracles in Chapter 5.

the experience with "the presence of God."[74] Davis rejects this argument outright on the grounds that it contradicts the definition of a theistic proof. For Davis, theistic proof has to be an argument whose conclusion is "God exists."[75] The ARE is held to be an argument for the rationality of theism, not a theistic argument. In *Perceiving God*, Alston makes this point clear.[76] Swinburne, on the other hand, argues that the ARE needs to be considered as a theistic proof, not necessarily on its own but as a complementary part of other theistic arguments.[77]

Davis acknowledges the existence of extraordinary personal experience of hard-to-explain events. However, he disagrees with theists like Nursi that such experience absolutely proves the existence of God. In some cases, people claim to have encountered some god among other gods such as Thor or Zeus, or some impersonal Absolute like Brahman, or the Dharmakaya, or Absolute Emptiness.[78]

Dawkins brings a completely scientific approach to the ARE. He argues that the human brain runs first-class simulation software, which makes people believe in whatever they wish to believe.[79] In this sense, what Nursi claimed to have happened to the Prophet Muḥammad, according to Dawkins, was not necessarily God (through the mouth of Gabriel) speaking to him, but was more likely his brain playing a simulation to him. In other words, Dawkins rejects the validity of the ARE in general and the prophethood in particular.

Freud, sometime before Dawkins, tried to give a psychological explanation of the ARE, in which he claimed that religious experience is the result of psychological need, for example the desire to project a father image onto the universe. Freud went on to explain that, at some stage of life, all children come to recognize that their father, whom they once viewed as infallible and omnipotent, is fallible, human, and finite; but people subconsciously retain the inner need for a father figure who will care for and protect them in this life and the next, and so they project the need onto the universe. Thus they come to believe in an all-powerful and perfectly good God, a cosmic father. To Freud it is a myth: of course no such God exists.[80]

74. Davis, *God, Reason and Theistic Proofs*, 121.

75. Ibid.

76. See Alston, *Perceiving God*, 222, 84.

77. Swinburne, *The Existence of God*, 244–76.

78. Davis, *God, Reason and Theistic Proofs*, 122.

79. Dawkins, *The God Delusion*, 91.

80. Freud, *The Future of an Illusion*.

Here, Freud seems to challenge the Nursian view. Nursi claims that the Prophet Muḥammad was the messenger of God and that his prophethood proves the existence of God. By contrast, Freud implies that the personal experience of the Prophet Muḥammad was the result of his psychological needs resulting from his being an orphan, and did not prove the existence of any gods. Davis, therefore, establishes his first objection to the ARE, and indirectly to the Nursian argument from prophethood: that plausible naturalistic explanations of religious experience, such as those of Freud and Dawkins, are available.

Davis' second objection to the ARE is based on the fact that religious experience is not like ordinary perception. He argues that the perceptions of religious experience yield little information about God. Therefore, no scientific comparison between the descriptions of God through religious experience is possible. The critics of the ARE protest about the lack of descriptive clarity, and explain that nobody wants to say that God is red, or tall, or soft; the idea, rather, is that God has non-sensory properties such as goodness, power and knowledge.[81] Matson adds to this that publicity and corroboration tests are notoriously not met in reports of religious experience. Thus, unless there is an independent reason for us to believe in the existence of God (in which case we might sensibly expect to have experience of God), no report of a religious experience can ever count as a good reason to believe in his existence.[82]

Furthermore, Clark argues that, in cases of religious experience, there is no objectively specifiable set of circumstances such that, should a normal human being find himself in those circumstances, he would have the religious experience in question, were the experience genuine. As a consequence of this, the sort of philosophical treatment that is appropriate for assessing the evidential value of experience, such as seeing colors and feeling pain under normal circumstances, is not appropriate regarding religious experience.[83]

Next, some specific criticisms of Swinburne's position will be examined.

Objections to Swinburne's Principle of Credulity

Swinburne argued that, in the absence of special considerations, if it seems (epistemically) to a subject that X is present, then probably X is

81. Peterson, *Reason and Religious Belief*, 18.

82. Matson, *The Existence of God*, 3–40.

83. Clark, "The Evidential Value of Religious Experiences."

present: what one seems to perceive is probably so.[84] Swinburne further clarifies that the subject has to be a reliable person (i.e., someone who is known for not telling lies in the past, or taking hallucinogenic drugs). This approach to the ARE is parallel to the Nursian way of defending the authenticity of the Prophet Muḥammad's experience. Nursi repeatedly argues that Muḥammad was a very honest and well-trusted man long before his prophethood. Indeed, Muḥammad's nickname was "*al-amīn*" (the trustworthy). Nursi also suggests that Muḥammad never used intoxicating drinks or drugs, and that his mental condition was very healthy. Therefore, with the philosophical support of Swinburne, Nursi believes that Muḥammad's experience was genuine.

One of the critiques of the principle of credulity is that made by Gary Gutting. Gutting explains that religious experiences purportedly of God give *prima facie* evidence of the existence of God, but that further support (rather than merely the absence of reasons to be skeptical) is needed before the *prima facie* evidence can be regarded as convincing evidence.[85]

To discredit the theists' claims, such as that Mother Teresa experienced the presence of Jesus, or that Muḥammad experienced the presence of the Archangel Gabriel, Gutting gives a counter-example. He tells us that he walks into his office and sees his dead aunt. This fulfills all the conditions set by Swinburne (i.e., he has not proved unreliable, he is not under the influence of alcohol or drugs); and the lighting is good. Therefore, he claims that he experiences the existence of his dead aunt. In fact, Gutting says, even though none of the defeating conditions recognized by Swinburne applies, it is obvious that he is not rationally entitled, in the absence of other evidence, to believe that he has seen his aunt.[86]

Although Gutting's arguments seem to weaken the ARE, as Swinburne explained, a healthy conclusion could only be drawn on the basis of cumulative proofs. Swinburne makes it clear that the ARE on its own could not be a sufficient proof, could only be a supporting argument. Similarly, Nursi does not simply construct his argument regarding Muḥammad's prophethood (and hence, indirectly, of the existence of God) on the basis of the ARE. He builds up a web of arguments, only a small part of which is the ARE.

84. Swinburne, *The Existence of God*, 254.

85. Gutting, *Religious Belief and Religious Skepticism*, 147–49.

86. Ibid.

Whose Experience Is Veridical?

One of the problems regarding the ARE is that the followers of certain faiths claim to encounter the certain supreme being of their particular faith. For instance, Catholics tend to experience the Virgin Mary, Vedantic Hindus Brahman. The question is, "What do we do with non-theistic experiences?" or "What do we do with religious experiences which contradict theism?" Gutting tells us that if religious experience is veridical, it can only defeat naturalism, and show that something else besides physical reality exists.[87] Davis, on the other hand, is not as generous to the ARE as Gutting is. He explains that religious experiences are so diverse, with many of them not being theistic at all, that they could not possibly be a proof of theism. He writes:

People who are already theists can certainly use theistic religious experience as a way of corroborating their beliefs; convinced theists as they are, they can simply say that non-theistic religious experience is mistaken, or is an experience of God that is misinterpreted. Or perhaps they can make use of other theistic proofs, or other sorts of arguments from natural theology, to show that Ultimate Reality, or the object of religious experience, is personal rather than impersonal in nature.[88]

In short, skeptic philosophers argue that the faith of an individual directly affects his or her religious experience. Therefore, the ARE is not a satisfactory argument for the existence of God.

Nursi on the Criticisms of Muḥammad

Beyond the philosophical criticisms of the Argument from Religious Experience set out in previous sections, and of the Argument from Miracles set out earlier, Nursi had to tackle specific criticisms pointed at the Prophet Muḥammad. Current critiques of the Prophet Muḥammad can be traced back in history. John Tolan states that almost all of them are sourced from the early writings of hostile historic characters.[89]

The first learned encounter with Islam and the Prophet Muḥammad in the Christian West, Tolan writes, occurred through the *Risālat al-Kindī* (Letter *of al-Kindī*), the writings of an anonymous Iraqi Christian in the twelfth century.[90] In his book, Al-Kindī wrote an imaginary dialogue between a

87. Ibid., 169.

88. Davis, *God, Reason and Theistic Proofs*, 136.

89. See John V. Tolan, '*European Accounts of Muḥammad's Life*' in Brockopp, *The Cambridge Companion to Muhammad*, 232.

90. Ibid.

Muslim and a Christian in which the Muslim tries to convert the Christian to Islam, and a debate develops between them. Although some reliable and more accurate sources were available in the West in the ninth century, such as the work of Theophanes' *Chronographia*,[91] Tolan explains that almost all early knowledge, or rather myths, about Muḥammad was derived from the rather biased *Risālat al-Kindī*.[92] Owing to on-going hostility because of the Crusades, Europeans chose to portray the Prophet Muḥammad as representing an offshoot of Christianity, and as a fake prophet and an imposter.

Armed with knowledge from the aforementioned texts, Gautier de Compiegne wrote his *Otia de Machometi*[93] in 1090. His work consisted of poetry in Latin. Gautier's disparaging work later inspired many more Europeans such as Alexandre du Pont,[94] Adelphus, Embrico of Mainz, and Guibert of Nogent.[95] Other Westerners, such as Ramon Marti, took another route to inform fellow Christians so that they could argue the falsehood of Islam and its prophet. Marti's book *De seta machometi*,[96] written before 1257, examined biblical evidence in order to refute the idea of Muḥammad's prophethood. The hostile tradition of portraying Muḥammad as a fake prophet and an evil man continued into the fifteenth century. Andrea Biglia described Muḥammad as "a horrible beast from Hell," and Favio Bionde depicts Muḥammad as someone who seduced and deceived Arabs with his miracles.[97] The European discourse on Islam was dominated by evil tales from Muḥammad's life well into the eighteenth century. Works such as Dominican Riccoldo da Montecroce's *Contra legem Saracenorum* or Nicholas of Cusa's *Cribratio Alcorani* dominated this era.[98]

In Early Modern Europe, two sets of works became very prominent. First, Theoder Bibliander published a serious of works on Islam and the Prophet Muḥammad in Basel in 1543. These were Robert of Ketton's

91. Theophanes et al., *The Chronicle of Theophanes Confessor: Byzantine and near Eastern History, Ad 284–813*.

92. Brockopp, *The Cambridge Companion to Muhammad*, 232.

93. For the original work of Gautier de Compiègne, see Alexandre du et al., *Le Roman De Mahomet*.

94. Alexandre du Pont translated Gautier's Latin poem into French in 1258. See Alexandre, . . . and Lepage, *Le roman de Mahomet*.

95. See Brockopp, *The Cambridge Companion to Muhammad*, 232.

96. See Hernando, *De Seta Machometi o De origine, progressu et fine Machometi et quadruplici reprobatione prophetiae eius de Ramón Martí*, s.XIII and Tolan, *Saracens*, 236–39.

97. See Tolan, *Saracens*, 173–87.

98. See Riccoldo da Montecroce, *Libellus contra legem Saracenorum*, ed. J. Merigoux, 1–144; see Tolan, *Saracens*, 251–54. Nicholas of Cusa, *De pace fidei and Cribratio Alkorani*, trans. Hopkins.

twelfth-century translation of the Qur'an, the Latin translation of the *Risālat al-Kindī*, and works by Riccoldo da Montecroce, Nicolas of Cusa, and others.[99] The second set was the works of Humphrey Prideaux, an Anglican minister and Oxford-educated doctor of theology. Prideaux published a book called *The True Nature of The Imposture Fully Display'd in the Life of Mahomet* in 1697.[100] Prideaux's book, and the others mentioned above, offered a list of criticisms of Islam, and its Prophet, Muḥammad. In his *Risale-i Nur*, Nursi not only argues for the authenticity of Muḥammad's prophethood, but also tries to fend off the criticisms posed by the skeptics, such as Gautier, Marti, Prideaux, and many others.

Muḥammad's Marriages

Muḥammad's marriages head the list of criticisms directed at him. These criticisms center on numbers, age gaps, and appropriateness. Muḥammad was married for the first time, at the age of twenty-five, to Khadījah, who was forty at the time of marriage in 610 CE.[101] This alleged mismatch, according to Christian polemicists, indicates Muḥammad trying to gain power and influence over Khadījah's tribe, who did not really know the real indication of a prophet.[102] His marriage to Khadījah lasted twenty-five years until her death. Muḥammad was fifty when his first wife died, and he afterwards did not marry for two or three years. He then married Sawdā bint Zam'a, a fifty-three-year-old widow whose husband had died in battle. Sawdā was his only partner for around three years. He then married ʿĀisha bint Abū Bakr, whose age has been, and still is, a great source of debate. Polemicists argue that she was seven at the time of the marriage; other sources suggest she was seventeen.[103] 'Aisha was the youngest of all Muḥammad's wives, and she was the only virgin (i.e., this was her first and only marriage). She reported more than two hundred *ḥadīth* (Prophet's sayings); in this sense, she was the guide and the teacher of Muslim women. All Muḥammad's remaining marriages occurred in the last nine years of his life, after the age of fifty-four. Considering the fact that his generation carried on through his children from his

99. See Theophanes et al., *The Chronicle of Theophanes Confessor*, 464–65.

100. Prideaux, *The True Nature of Imposture Fully Displayed in the Life of Mahomet with a Discourse Annexed for the Vindicating of Christianity from This Charge*.

101. Brockopp, *The Cambridge Companion to Muhammad*, 4.

102. Ibid.

103. Muslim historians such as Martin Lings argue that ʿĀisha's elder sister, Asma, was twenty-seven during the Immigration (*Hijra*). Since Aisha was ten years younger than her sister, she ought to have been seventeen at the time of marriage.

first marriage with Khadījah,[104] one can assume that he had a regular family life with his first wife for twenty-five years from the age of twenty-five till fifty. He had a son, Ibrahim, by Maria al-Qibṭiyya. But Ibrahim died during his infancy. Therefore, according to Nursi, his marriages were not sexually motivated; there were certain reasons behind them. Nursi writes:

> Such vile doubts cannot be harbored against that lofty one! The Messenger (UWBP) was such that from the age of fifteen to forty when the blood is fiery and exuberant and the passions of the soul enflamed, with complete chastity and purity he sufficed and was content with a single older woman, Khadija the Great (May God be pleased with her)—as is agreed by friend and foe alike. His having numerous wives after the age of forty, that is, when bodily heat subsides and the passions are quietened, is decisive, self-evident proof for those who are even a little fair-minded that such marriages were not to satisfy the carnal appetites, but were for other important reasons and instances of wisdom.[105]

For Nursi, then, the reason behind his marriages was the fact that his family life had to be witnessed and reported to Muslim men and women so that they could learn true religion through the example of the Prophet. Nursi also argues that the female-related part of religion constitutes half of the entire religion. In this respect, the Prophet married several women so that they could learn from him and act as teachers of other women.[106]

Unlike many other contemporary Muslim scholars, such as Gülen, Nursi keeps his argument fairly concise. For instance, he does not defend the Prophet's marriages on the grounds of politics. Gülen, on the other hand, argues that politics was one of the factors behind some of the marriages. The Prophet wanted to befriend certain tribes by marrying a woman from them. Another reason, according to Gülen, was to give a social message to the men, to encourage them to marry the widows of martyrs and look after them.[107]

As regards his marriage with Zaynab bint Jaḥsh, who was initially married to the Prophet's adopted son but was later separated, Nursi claims

104. Khadīja gave two sons and four daughters to Muḥammad. The sons Qāsim and Abdullah did not survive. Muḥammad's family tree grew from his daughters Zaynab, Umm Kulthūm, Ruqiyyah and Fāṭima.

105. Nursi, *The Letters*, 357.

106. Ibid.

107. Gülen, *Prophet Muhammad: Aspects of His Life*, 206–7.

that the Prophet entered into it purely on the orders of divine determining.[108] The focal point of Nursi's argument is the Qur'anic verse which reads:

> And [remember, O Muḥammad], when you said to the one on whom Allāh bestowed favor and you bestowed favor, "Keep your wife and fear Allāh," while you concealed within yourself that which Allāh is to disclose. And you feared the people, while Allāh has more right that you fear Him. So when Zayd had no longer any need for her, We married her to you in order that there not be upon the believers any discomfort concerning the wives of their adopted sons when they no longer have need of them. And ever is the command of Allāh accomplished.[109]

Furthermore, Nursi explains that the Prophet was trying to teach Muslims that, contrary to the common view at the time, Islam allows the marriage of an adopted child's ex-spouse. In other words, adopted children do not have all the characteristics of biological children. This justification, however, does not necessarily satisfy critics such as Nasrin, who claims that the Prophet made up these verses for his own advantage.[110]

Alleged Miracles of the Splitting of the Moon

The "Splitting the Moon" miracle of the Prophet was allegedly witnessed and reported by many of his companions, such as ibn 'Abbas, Anas ibn Mālik and Abdullah ibn Mas'ūd. Chapter 54, *Sūrat Al-Qamar* (The Moon), in the Qur'an reports the incident as follows:

> The Hour has come near, and the moon has split [in two]. And if they see a miracle, they turn away and say, "Passing magic."[111]

The most common criticism made for this particular incident is the fact that it has not been reported anywhere else. Nursi argues that the main reason this incident does not appear in any popular history-book is its time, location, and duration. It took place in the middle of the night, in the sparsely populated part of Arabia, for a very brief period of time. Therefore, Nursi explains, the Eastern and Western worlds did not witness the event

108. See Nursi, *Hutbe-i Şamiye*, 357.

109. Qur'an, 33:37.

110. Wagner, *Opening the Qur'an: Introducing Islam's Holy Book*, 233–36. Also see http://taslimanasrin.com/opinion.pdf

111. Qur'an, 54:1–2.

since they were in different time zones (i.e., early morning or early evening), and the sky might have been overcast to stop others seeing it.[112]

Moreover, Nursi clarifies that it was a brief incident, not a lengthy one, so that individuals who witnessed it had to decide about it for themselves. He writes:

> Miracles are for proving claims to prophethood and for convincing those who deny those claims; they are not for compelling people to believe.[113]

Nursi argues that the people who witnessed the event are the only ones whose opinions are to be taken into account. None of them rejected it, but, as Qur'an indicates, some claimed it to be a "passing magic."[114]

Alleged Night Journey and Ascension [*Isrā wa Al-Mi'rāj*]

One of the most controversial claims about the Prophet Muḥammad concerns his night journey from his home in Medina to Jerusalem[115] and his ascent to the Heavens to speak with God. This is a peak example of Muḥammad's religious experience. The incident took place in 621 CE, and was rejected not only by his tribe at the time, but also by critics throughout history. The incident is reported in Chapter 17 of the Qur'an, in *Sūrat Al-'Isrā'* (The Night Journey), as follows:

> Exalted is he who took his servant by night from al-Masjid al-Haram to al-Masjid al-Aqsa, whose surroundings we have blessed, to show him of our signs. Indeed, he is the hearing, the seeing.[116]

Nursi faces a challenge from the skeptics to defend the authenticity of this claim. He admits outright that it is impossible to prove this incident on the grounds of science and reason. He believes that non-believers need to be convinced firstly of the existence and unity of God, and then convinced that Muḥammad was his true messenger.[117] However, he attempts to convince

112. Nursi, *The Words*, 266.

113. Ibid., 267.

114. Qur'an, 54:1–2: The Hour has come near, and the moon has split in two. And if they see a miracle, they turn away and say, "passing magic."

115. The approximate distance as the crow flies in miles from Medina in Saudi Arabia to Jerusalem in Israel is 565 miles or 909 kilometers.

116. Qur'an, 17:1.

117. Nursi, *The Words*, 253.

skeptical believers of the necessity, nature, virtues and benefits of *Isrā wa al-Mi'rāj*.

Nursi expounds that it was necessary for God to lift his messenger to the Heavens so as to communicate with him. In *The Words*, he writes:

> Now we say to the atheist who is in the position of listener: "Since the universe resembles a most orderly country, magnificent city, and adorned palace, it surely must have a ruler, owner, and builder. And since there is such a magnificent, All-Glorious Owner, All-Perfect Ruler, and All-Beauteous Maker; and since there was a human being whose view was universal and who demonstrated a relationship with the entire world, country, city, and palace and was connected to all of them through his senses and faculties of perception; certainly, the Magnificent Maker would have an elevated relationship to the fullest degree with that human being, whose view was universal and consciousness comprehensive, and would favor him with an exalted and sacred address.
>
> Among those who manifested this relationship from the time of Adam (Peace be upon him) up to now, Muhammad the Arabian (Peace and blessings be upon him) demonstrated it at the very fullest degree according to the testimony of his achievements, that is, his having taken half the globe and a fifth of mankind under this direction and control and having transformed and illuminated the spiritual shape of the universe. This being so, the Ascension, which comprised the very fullest degree of that relationship, is most worthy and suitable for him.[118]

Nursi, once again, tries to establish a link between the order and design in the universe and an Orderer and Designer (i.e., God). He explains that God requires someone to convey his messages to humankind; this person (i.e., the prophet) is Muḥammad. Therefore, for Nursi, it is completely feasible that God caused his messenger to ascend to the Heavens so that he could talk to him and show him what most people cannot see but are expected to believe, such as the existence of angels, spirits, Hell, and Paradise.

When faced with the scientific implausibility of such long-distance travel in such a short period of time, Nursi claims that God is so great and so powerful that nothing is beyond his power. Besides, he exclaims, within the limits of science such high-speed travels are possible. He asks:

> According to your science, in its annual rotation a heavy body like the earth cuts a distance of approximately one hundred and

118. Ibid., 255.

> eighty-eight hours in one minute. In one year it covers a distance of approximately twenty-five thousand years. Should an All-Powerful and Glorious One, then, Who causes its regular motion and revolves it like a stone in a sling be unable to convey a human being to his throne? Should a wisdom that causes the body of the earth, which is extremely heavy, to travel around the sun through a dominical law known the sun's gravity like a Mawlawi dervish be unable to raise a human body to the Throne of the All-Merciful One like lightning through the gravity of that All-Merciful One's mercy and the attraction of the Pre-Eternal Sun's love?[119]

As a final line of defense, Nursi cites the *ḥadīth* reported in Sahih al-Bukhāri, in which the Prophet explained how he faced a challenge from his own tribe, who asked him to describe the mosque in Jerusalem where he claimed to have been. The vision of the mosque, the Prophet said, "has been brought in front of my eyes. I looked at it and reported the most minute details of it to my tribe, and those who had seen the mosque confirmed my description of it."[120]

Nursi on Alleged Discrepancies in Ḥadīth

Critics of the Prophet have tried to discredit him by showing some discrepancies in his sayings (*ḥadīth*). They claim that some of his sayings do not make any sense when judged by science and reality. Perhaps the most criticized *ḥadīth* in this respect is that in which the Prophet responded to a question about what the earth rests upon. The Prophet stated that "the earth rests upon a bull and fish."[121] Nursi argues that this *ḥadīth*, and those similar to it, are not necessarily scientifically implausible. One possible reason for this, according to Nursi, is that the Prophet might have used analogies so that ordinary people could understand better.[122] Nursi explains that the bull in this *ḥadīth* might actually mean farming and agriculture, and the fish sea-related activities such as fishing and shipping, since the earth consists of one-third land and two-thirds water.[123]

Nursi further tries to strengthen his position by reference to another incident, in which the Prophet explained, upon hearing a big bang, that it

119. Ibid., 259.
120. Hanbel, *Müsned*, vol. 1, 309.
121. Hâkim, *Müstedrek*, vol. 4, 636.
122. Nursi, *The Flashes*, 629.
123. Ibid., 630.

was the sound of a stone which had been rolling downhill for seventy years and had just hit the bottom of Hell.[124] This explanation at first sounded very unrealistic, until a companion arrived at the scene and reported the death of a seventy-year-old hypocrite (*munāfiq*). In fact, the Prophet portrayed the scene using a metaphor which was not meant to be taken literally. However, some analogies might have changed over time so that they have been taken literally. For instance, the analogy of the earth resting upon a bull and a fish has been understood as a literal explanation. Nursi also indicates that the Prophet once said that the earth rests on a bull and, on another occasion he said that it rests upon a fish, meaning that the Earth is within the constellation of Taurus and Pisces. Nursi, then, writes:

> . . . he (Prophet Muḥammad) indicated a truly profound truth that would be understood only many centuries later, and said in the miraculous prophetic tongue: "On the Bull," because at that time the earth was in the likeness of the constellation Taurus. And on being asked a month later, he replied: "On the Fish," for then the earth was in the shadow of the constellation of Pisces.[125]

In other words, the so-called inconsistencies in the Prophet's sayings, according to Nursi, are due to misinterpretations of metaphors used by the Prophet.

Muḥammad's Defeat in the Battle of Uḥud

Nursi had to defend the Prophet once again when he was questioned as to whether Muḥammad was a genuine messenger of God after his defeats in certain battles. The argument, reformulated as a syllogism, goes like this:

> If Muḥammad had been a genuine prophet, God would have given him miracles.
>
> The miracles ought to have given him power to see the future.
>
> He did not see the upcoming maneuver of the enemy in the Battle of Uhud, and his army was defeated.
>
> Therefore, the authenticity of his prophethood is doubtful.

124. Ibid., 629.
125. Ibid.

> Indeed, it is historically recorded that the Prophet had seen defeats and retreats in certain battles. However, Nursi considers these defeats as natural for a human prophet, rather than as a weakness. If the Prophet had continuously lived his life on the plane of extraordinary miracles, he could not have fulfilled his duty of being "absolute *imām*" and "greatest guide."[126]

The second reason God permitted these defeats, according to Nursi, was to let people choose freely between the way of the Prophet and the way of the Devil. If the Prophet continuously used miraculous powers and defeat the enemy, everyone would be forced into believing his message without using their intelligence. This, to Nursi, is against the nature of religion and free will. In *The Words*, Nursi writes:

> Religion is an examination, a test, which distinguishes elevated spirits from base ones. It therefore speaks of matters that everyone shall see with their eyes in the future in such a way that they remain neither altogether unknown, nor self-evident so that everyone would be compelled to confirm them. They open the door to the reason but do not take the will from the hand.[127]

Famous characters such as Khālid ibn al-Walīd fought in the enemy army, and later converted to Islam. Nursi argues that these conversions were based purely on intelligence and free will. No one could devalue these conversions and argue that these people chose Islam out of fear.[128]

Demanding Privilege to His Family

Critics of the Qur'an and the Prophet Muḥammad contend that there are inconsistencies in verses such as, "Indeed, the most noble of you in the sight of Allāh is the most righteous of you"[129] and "Say, O Muḥammad, 'I do not ask you for this message any payment but only good will through kinship.' And whoever commits a good deed—We will increase for him good therein . . . ."[130]

Although the first verse clearly states that virtue is in righteousness, the second advises believers to show respect for the Prophet's family, implying that there is virtue in doing so. Therefore, it has been argued that the

126. Nursi, *The Words*, 624.
127. Ibid., 147.
128. Nursi, *Hutbe-i Şamiye*, 624.
129. Qur'an, 49:13.
130. Qur'an, 42:23.

Prophet demanded privileges for his family, which is clearly a contradiction of the institution of prophethood.

According to Nursi, this behavior might be justified by two arguments. The first is that the Prophet foresaw that there were going to be great personalities among his descendants who would become light-giving trees in the world of Islam, in terms of providing a true representation of Islam and true guidance to Muslims.[131] Secondly, with his clairvoyance, he foresaw that his family would multiply and reach a great number. Since family kinship requires great partiality, submission and partisanship, the Prophet knew that the members of his family would always embrace Islam and protect it at any cost, even though some of them were less knowledgeable than other Muslims.[132]

Conclusion

This chapter has looked into the argument from religious experience, Prophet Muḥammad in particular. It has outlined the argument from religious experience and counterarguments as to that the ARE is not acceptable as a philosophical argument. It has followed by Nursi's case for Prophet Muḥammad's prophethood mainly based on the reported wonders he displayed as in the existing literature. In the last section, it has analyzed Nursian defense to particular attacks to Prophet Muḥammad.

It is apparent in Nursi's writings that he tries to establish a logical link between order in the universe and an Orderer of the universe, as was discussed in the previous chapter. In this chapter, we have seen how Nursi moves from the existence of God to the necessity of God having prophets. Nursi argues that the existence of prophets, Prophet Muḥammad in particular, is an evidence for the existence of God. He claims that the universe teleologically proves that it has got a Master and a Maker who must communicate with his subjects on Earth. Since communication with a group requires a representative, this person ought to be the most credible, intelligent, consistent and honest among them. Therefore, Nursi asserts, God chooses persons possessing these qualities, i.e., the prophets, in order to talk to them and put them in charge of spreading his message among people.

Like many of his predecessors, Nursi then sets out to argue that the Prophet Muḥammad displays all the necessary characteristics of being a most perfect human, thereby qualifying for prophethood. Starting with Muḥammad's early life, Nursi relates a list of unusual events (*irhāṣāt*), such

131. Nursi, *The Flashes*, 631.

132. Ibid.

as the disappearance of Lake Saveh in Iran, the toppling of the idols in Ka'ba and the dying of the sacred fire of the Zoroastrians (*majūsis*), and claims that Muḥammad's prophethood had already been indicated via these signs. He then moves on to the Prophet Muḥammad's life after his prophethood, and reports some examples of his miracles, his leadership, and his personal life. He then attempts to develop a theme whereby he claims that the Prophet Muḥammad was a man among men, not a supernatural being, in order to set an example to humanity of the way of life prescribed by God in the Qur'an.

Nursi also elaborates on the Prophet Muḥammad's leadership during his short reign in the city-state of Medina. He demonstrates how Muḥammad transformed a fairly uncivilized society into a one which is admired by many. This social transformation is believed by Nursi to be due to the divine source of Muḥammad's teachings

Nursi implies that the personal experience of the Prophet Muḥammad had to be accepted as genuine, since Muḥammad, as an individual, clearly passes the tests set to validate or invalidate one's personal religious experience. Considering Muḥammad's truthfulness, trustworthiness and personal integrity, Nursi believes, there is no room to doubt about his encounters with the angel Gabriel and God.

For Nursi, the combined strength of Muhammad's religious experience and miracles are the evidence of him being an authentic prophet of God which in turn proves the existence of God.

The chapter concludes that a careful analysis of the *Risale-i Nur* reveals that Nursi leans his arguments on the existing literature about the miracles of Prophet Muḥammad which has been the tradition in the Islamic world for centuries. In this respect, it can be argued that there is almost no new material other than Nursi's social transformation argument, against which counterarguments have already been developed.

With regard to defending Prophet Muḥammad against criticisms Nursi invokes the help of the Qur'an as well as simple logic and common sense. Hence, other than making a passionate case for the excellence of Prophet Muḥammad's character and virtues in his actions Nursi does not seem to bring out any new arguments.

5

Revelations

[Waḥy]

Introduction

The third of Said Nursi's four ways of arguing for the existence of God is his argument from scriptures (*kutub*) or revelations *(waḥy)*. Nursi explains how his discourse of life changed upon reading, in 1898, a newspaper article in which the British Secretary for the Colonies Lord Gladstone was reported as saying:

> So long as the Muslims have the Qur'an, we shall be unable to dominate them. We must either take it from them, or make them lose their love of it.[1]

Up until that time, Nursi, who was in his early twenties, was mainly interested in science and other theoretical knowledge taught at *madrasas*, not theology or philosophy. He considered this Western attempt to devalue the Qur'an a greater threat, and declared:

> I shall prove and demonstrate to the world that the Qur'an is an undying, inextinguishable Sun![2]

In other words, Nursi, in turning his attention to theology, set out to argue that the Qur'an is a genuine scripture revealed by God to his final Messenger, Muḥammad.

1. Nursi writes in his biography that he read this newspaper article in Van in 1898, where William Ewart Gladstone, British Secretary for Colonies was reported to say these particular words. See Vahide and Abu-Rabi, *Islam in Modern Turkey*, 30.

2. For Nursi's transformation, see his own narration in Nursi, *Tarihçe-i Hayatı*, 2131

Nursi's intellectual transformation into a scholar of natural theology, especially concerning the origins and the meanings of life and the universe, begins here. He outlines four arguments to prove the existence of God with all his attributes,[3] arguments which, he believes, would help mankind to understand the meaning of the cosmos and human existence. These are: [1] The proof from the universe (*kitāb-ı kabīr-i kāināt*) (i.e., the design argument, which was discussed in Chapter 3); [2] The proof from prophethood (*nubuwwah*), which was discussed in Chapter 4; [4] the proof from the scriptures (*waḥy*), which is the subject of this chapter; and [4] the proof from human conscience (*wijdān*), which will be discussed in Chapter 6.[4]

In the previous chapters, Nursi's arguments from the universe and the prophethood have been discussed. In this chapter, the details of his argument from revelations, and from the Qur'an in particular, will be examined. In philosophy, the argument from miracles deals with the prophethood and the Divine Scriptures together. Therefore, this chapter focuses on the argument from miracles. Also, Nursi contends that the prophets and the scriptures are inseparable. To his mind, the Qur'an and Muḥammad are inextricably interconnected, and they prove the truthfulness each other reciprocally. Since the criticisms of the skeptics are pointed at the prophethood and the scriptures simultaneously, Nursi tries to defend his theistic position and to refute these criticisms. In this respect, Chapters 4 and 5 are closely connected.

The Qur'an as the Genuine Revelation

Abrahamic monotheism accepts three main bodies of texts (*suhuf*) as being revelations from God: the Torah (*at-Tawrāt*), the Gospels (*az-Zabūr* and *al-Injīl*), and the Qur'an, as well as other unknown *suhuf* mentioned in the Qur'an. The Islamic creed commands followers of the Qur'an to believe equally in all the previous revelations and the messengers.[5] If someone de-

3. What makes Nursi distinct from many other *mutakallimūn* such as *Ibn-i Sinā*, and *al-Fārābi* is that Nursi is not only concerned with proving the existence of a Deity, but also interested in his attributes. He believes that philosophy could only achieve proof of the existence of a Supreme Being, whereas his *Risale-i Nur* explains what kind of Supreme Being He is and what he expects from humankind.

4. There are mentions of this set of proofs in several different books of Nursi. For instance; see Nursi, *The Words*, 91. And Nursi, *Al-Mathnawi Al-Nuri*, 1283 and 1368

5. Qur'an, 3:84: Say, "We have believed in Allāh and in what was revealed to us and what was revealed to Abraham, Ishmael, Isaac, Jacob, and the Descendants, and in what was given to Moses and Jesus and to the prophets from their Lord. We make no distinction between any of them, and we are Muslims [submitting] to him."

nies the truthfulness of Jesus or the Bible or any other prophet in this sense, he falls into disbelief (*kufr*).[6] Nursi touches on this matter lightly, since his main concern is the last Prophet and his Book. He bases his argument on the assumption that if the truthfulness of revelation and the prophethood is proven, the content of their message has to be taken as fact. He takes this argument through the root of Islam; therefore, he focuses on the book of Islam (i.e., the Qur'an), and the Prophet of Islam (i.e., Muḥammad). The basis of Nursi's argument is the miraculousness of the Prophet Muḥammad and the Qur'an. In the following, once Nursi's point of view regarding the scripture and the Prophet has been established, the historical and traditional Humean objection, which in recent times has been endorsed by Mackie, Flew, and Everitt, will be examined. Nursi asserts that if one succeeds in convincing the rationalist mind that the Qur'an is a genuine scripture, this automatically entails the existence of God as a genuine fact, not an assumption.

Throughout the *Risale-i Nur*, Nursi systematically refers to the cosmos (*kaināt*), the Prophet, and the Qur'an to present the case for his theism. In *The Words*, The Twenty-fifth Word,[7] which concerns the miraculousness of the Qur'an, is Nursi's focal writing in defense of the Qur'an's divine origins. In this work, Nursi presents his case using a highly systematic structure.[8] It may be said that this treatise on the Qur'an is one of the most elaborate, well-structured and detailed pieces of work Nursi ever produced. One can easily realize upon a close study of the *Risale-i Nur* that Nursi, contrary to many other scholars, presents his expositions in a fairly systematic manners. This is also highly visible in The Nineteenth Letter on the Miracles of Muḥammad.

In order to demonstrate that the Qur'an is not an ordinary book but a Divine Scripture revealed by God to the Prophet Muḥammad, Nursi produces three sets of arguments. In the first set, he explains what he claims are three unique characteristics of the Qur'an: its eloquence (*balāghah*), its comprehensiveness (*jāmi'iyyah*), and its reporting of the unseen (*ikhbār-i ghaybī*). In the second set, he demonstrates the Qur'an's features of fluency or clarity (*fasaha*) and conciseness (ījāz) and finally, in the third set of arguments he argues for the miraculousness (*i'jāz*) of the Qur'an, its superiority over materialistic philosophy, and its superiority over human reason.

6. Qur'an, 4:136: O you who have believed, believe in Allāh and his Messenger and the Book that He sent down upon his Messenger and the Scripture which he sent down before. And whoever disbelieves in Allāh, his angels, his books, his messengers, and the Last Day has certainly gone far astray.

7. See Nursi, *The Words*, 160–204.

8. See Appendix 7: Map of Nursi's Twenty-fifth Word: Miraculousness of the Qur'an.

Nursi's Exposition

One of the most common criticisms of the Qur'an concerns it being allegedly the poetic writings of the Prophet Muḥammad.[9] It is widely argued that the Qur'an is very different from any other book ever written before or after. Clearly, a better appreciation and understanding of the Qur'an's poetic aspect requires some basic knowledge of the Arabic language. Therefore, we shall give meanings and transliterations in order to make the language more understandable to non-Arabic-speaking people.

The Eloquence (*Balāghah*)

The poetic aspect of the Qur'an is probably the most apparent of its characteristics. This is mainly because of the nature of the oral culture of the people of the Arabian Peninsula in the seventh century AD. Poetry was at its peak, and poets were the most respected people in the community. Poetry was so powerful that it could start or end wars between tribes. Nursi reports that, owing to common illiteracy among people, historical events, praising and scorning, as well as moral values, used to be related in the form of poems.[10] This, naturally, makes them easy to memorize and remember. It is also a widespread technique for memorizing important information today. As soon as the Prophet spoke the first five verses of Chapter 96,[11] The Clot (*Sūrat al-'Alaq*),[12] people were astonished by its eloquence. This rhythmical

9. For the arguments for the authenticity, see Bucaille, *The Bible, the Quran and Science*. For the criticism, see Crone and Cook, *Hagarism*.

10. Nursi, *The Words*, 162.

11. The first five verses of the Chapter 96 were the first verses revealed to the Prophet. It is important to note that the chronological revelation order and the text order of the verses in the Qur'an are different.

12. In the first five verses of Chapter 96: The Clot, verses 1 and 2 rhyme; similarly verses 3, 4 and 5 rhyme between themselves.

The Original:

96:1—اقْرَأْ بِاسْمِ رَبِّكَ الَّذِي خَلَقَ—96:1
96:2—خَلَقَ الْإِنسَانَ مِنْ عَلَقٍ—96:2
96:3—اقْرَأْ وَرَبُّكَ الْأَكْرَمُ—96:3
96:4—الَّذِي عَلَّمَ بِالْقَلَمِ—96:4
96:5—عَلَّمَ الْإِنسَانَ مَا لَمْ يَعْلَمْ—96:5

English phonetic readings:

1. Iqra bi-ismi rabbika allathee khalaq
2. Khalaqa al-insana min AAalaq
3. Iqra warabbuka al-akram
4. Allathee AAallama bialqalam

aspect of verses that end with a rhyme is more or less continuous throughout the Qur'an. Although the poetic aspect of the Qur'an is arguably the most visible, Nursi does not elaborate upon this aspect of the Qur'an.

Nursi points out that despite the Qur'an's open challenge in 2:23,[13] no one has ever succeeded in imitating its eloquence.[14] The Signs of Miraculousness (al-ʿIshārāt *al-I'jāz*) is Nursi's first attempt to write a full commentary on the Qur'an. This work had to be left incomplete owing to the outbreak of the First World War and Nursi's exile to Russia as a prisoner of war. However, the existing work examines specific fascinating features of the Qur'an. Although Nursi intended to interpret all the verses of the Qur'an, he only managed to comment on the opening chapter and the first thirty-three verses of the second chapter.[15]

Further to the Qur'an's poetic features, Nursi elaborates on the eloquence of the Qur'an, highlighting some of its apparent aspects. These are: its word-order (*naẓm*), its meaning (*ma'nā*), its literary style (*uslūb*), its use of letters and words (*lafẓ*), and its manner of exposition (*bayān*).

The Qur'an's Word-Order (*Naẓm*)

Regarding the word-order of the Qur'an (*naẓm*), Nursi likens the Qur'an to a clock and explains:

> The way the second, minute, and hour hands of a clock each complete the order of the others, that is the way the entire work explains the order in each sentence and passage of the All-Wise Qur'an, and in each of its words, and in the order in the relationships between the sentences.[16]

---

5. AAallama al-insana ma lam yaAAlam

The Meaning:

1. Proclaim! (or Read!) In the name of thy Lord and Cherisher, Who created
2. Created man, out of a (mere) clot of congealed blood
3. Proclaim! And thy Lord is Most Bountiful
4. He Who taught (The use of) the pen
5. Taught man that which he knew not

13. Qur'an, 2:23: And if you are in doubt about what We have sent down upon Our Servant [Muḥammad], then produce a surah the like thereof and call upon your witnesses other than Allāh, if you should be truthful.

14. Nursi, *Al-Mathnawi Al-Nuri*, 1368.

15. See Nursi's *Signs of Miraculousness* in Nursi, *Risale-i Nur Külliyati* 2, 1155–1274.

16. Nursi, Nursi, *The Words*, 163.

In a fairly complex manner, he breaks down the components of the verses such as "But if a breath of your Sustainer's punishment touches them"[17] and "And spend [in God's way] out of what We have bestowed on them as sustenance."[18] He tries to demonstrate how each letter and word has an extraordinary role in conveying a very efficient message in a very short sentence. Nursi seems to direct his argument to the minds of Arabic grammarians more than to that of an ordinary reader. Nonetheless, the average reader may also appreciate the general line of Nursi's argument.

The Qur'an's Meaning (*Ma'nā*)

As regards the meanings of the Qur'an (*ma'nā*), Nursi explains that verses such as "All that is in the heavens and on the earth extols and glorifies God, for He is the Tremendous, the Wise"[19] give life and consciousness to apparently dead and soulless cosmic objects, and make them extol and glorify God. The Qur'an, in his thinking, transforms the darkness of ignorance into a domain of light. Chaos gives way to order, and futility is replaced by meaningfulness.[20]

The Qur'an's Style (*Uslūb*)

As regards the style of the Qur'an (*uslūb*), Nursi asserts that it is unique and that there has never been anything similar before or after it. One aspect of this uniqueness is the fact that there are opening expressions in some chapters which consist of letters but do not form a meaningful word.[21] Nursi had a great personal interest in the secret meanings of these code letters. In *al-*'Ishārāt *al-I'jāz*, he studies the possible meanings of these unique symbols, and concludes that they cannot be the intellectual product of any human mind.[22] To Nursi, the Qur'an does not imitate anything and nothing could ever imitate it. He believes that the Qur'an's style is strange, original, awe-inspiring, superior, majestic, beautiful, and ever young.[23]

17. Qur'an, 21:46.
18. Qur'an, 2:3.
19. Qur'an, 57:1.
20. Nursi, *The Words*, 165.
21. Some examples are: Qur'an [2:1]: Alif, Lam, Meem. And Qur'an [19:1]: Kaf, Ha, Ya, 'Ayn, Sad.
22. Nursi, *The Words*, 165.
23. Ibid., 168.

To demonstrate the beauty of the Qur'an's style, Nursi gives the example of the verse "Say, 'O Allah, Owner of Sovereignty, You give sovereignty to whom You will and You take sovereignty away from whom You will. You honor whom You will and You humble whom You will. In Your hand is [all] good. Indeed, You are over all things competent.'"[24]

Nursi points out what he calls the majestic style of the Qur'an. For example, Chapter 11 (*Sūrat al-Hūd*) narrates the story of the prophet Noah. The verse, which tells of the end of the storm and the massive flood, goes as follows:

> And it was said, "O earth, swallow your water, and O sky, withhold [your rain]." And the water subsided, and the matter was accomplished, and the ship came to rest on the [mountain of] Judiyy. And it was said, "Away with the wrongdoing people."[25]

This, according to Nursi, is a clear example of a distinctive style of the Qur'an, which not only narrates a past event but also stresses the great control of God over earthly incidents. Similarly, in the opening verses of Chapter 84 (*Sūrat al-'Inshiqāq*),[26] the Qur'an not only reports an event in the future (i.e., the Judgement Day), but also demonstrates God's absolute control over the entire universe.

The Speech of the Qur'an (*Lafẓ*)

Nursi claims that the Qur'an is extraordinarily eloquent in terms of *naẓm*, *ma'nā* and *uslūb* yet outstandingly easy to read, listen to or memorize. This, in his mind, is further clear evidence of the Qur'an's divine origins. He notes that human nature is such that repetition causes boredom after a while. If the same text is read repeatedly, it becomes dull and uninteresting. However, the Qur'an has been read and memorized by millions of people over the

24. It is inevitable that most of Nursi's Qur'anic presentations will be lost in translation. The original verse of Qur'an, 3:26:
قُلِ اللَّهُمَّ مَالِكَ الْمُلْكِ تُؤْتِي الْمُلْكَ مَن تَشَاءُ وَتَنزِعُ الْمُلْكَ مِمَّن تَشَاءُ وَتُعِزُّ مَن تَشَاءُ وَتُذِلُّ مَن تَشَاءُ بِيَدِكَ الْخَيْرُ إِنَّكَ عَلَىٰ كُلِّ شَيْءٍ قَدِيرٌ—3:26
Meaning: Say, "O Allāh, Owner of Sovereignty, You give sovereignty to whom You will and You take sovereignty away from whom You will. You honor whom You will and You humble whom You will. In Your hand is [all] good. Indeed, You are over all things competent."

25. Qur'an, 11:44.

26. Qur'an, 84:1–5: When the sky has split [open]. And has responded to its Lord and was obligated [to do so]. And when the earth has been extended. And has cast out that within it and relinquished [it]. And has responded to its Lord and was obligated [to do so].

years, unlike any man-made texts, but it still feels exciting and fresh. Even very young children can easily memorize it thanks to the wonderful, fluent eloquence of its wording. Nursi exclaims that the Qur'an is the truth and the reality and truthfulness and guidance and wonderfully eloquent; that it does not cause weariness, but preserves its freshness and agreeableness as though preserving a perpetual youth.[27]

To Nursi, then, its freshness, unweariness and perpetual youth is another miraculous aspect of the Qur'an.

Manner of Exposition (*Bayān*)

On the excellence of the Qur'an's manner of exposition (*bayān*), Nursi claims that it has a superiority, conciseness and grandeur that set it over all other discourse.[28] He then goes on to give examples of verses where there are special modes of expositions of praise, deterring, threatening, censure, restraint, proof, and demonstration.[29]

For Nursi, the grandeur and majesty of verses such as "Has there reached you the report of the Overwhelming event?"[30] and "It the earth almost bursts with rage,"[31] and "Qāf. By the honored the Qur'an . . . ,"[32] are a clear indication that the Qur'an is by no means the word of a human being.

The Comprehensiveness (*Jāmi'iyya*)

This aspect of the Qur'an, according to Nursi, is essentially its characteristic of offering distinctive messages to every level of intelligence. Nursi argues that a fairly short verse such as "And the mountains as stakes?"[33] could offer different meanings to different people, such as an ordinary

27. Nursi, *The Words*, 168.

28. Ibid.

29. For threatening, see Qur'an, 88:1: "Has there reached you the report of the Overwhelming [event]?" For disapproval, see Qur'an, 49:12: "O you, who have believed, avoid much negative assumption. Indeed, some assumption is sin. And do not spy or backbite each other. Would one of you like to eat the flesh of his brother when dead? You would detest it. And fear Allāh; indeed, Allāh is Accepting of repentance and Merciful." For proof, see Qur'an, 30:50: "So observe the effects of the mercy of Allāh—how He gives life to the earth after its lifelessness. Indeed, that same one will give life to the dead, and He is over all things competent."

30. Qur'an, 88:1.

31. Qur'an, 67:8.

32. Qur'an, 50:1.

33. Qur'an, 78:7.

person, a poet, a geographer and a scientist. Furthermore, Nursi goes on to explain that an ordinary person would understand this verse literally, in terms of the mountains being pegged on the earth and giving benefits to people. A poet would see the mountains as pillars, which hold the massive tent of the sky. A geographer would perceive the mountains as the masts of a boat, which play essential roles in balancing and stabilizing the Earth. A scientist would read this verse in terms of the benefits of the mountains, which are the main source of water and air-cleansing. A natural philosopher would deduce a meaning whereby the Earth is the safety-valve on the internal tension of the Earth.[34]

Another verse Nursi cites is, "Have those who disbelieved not considered that the heavens and the earth were a joined entity, and We separated them and made from water every living thing? Then will they not believe?"[35] A scholar, Nursi claims, would read this verse as meaning that the Earth and the mountains are the artwork of a Glorious Maker. A modern philosopher understands how the Earth and the solar system are formed for a purpose by an all-knowing Creator.[36]

Also, Nursi argues that the verse "And the sun runs on course toward its stopping point. That is the determination of the Exalted in Might, the Knowing"[37] speaks to a scholar, an astronomer, a philosopher and a poet differently.

Having indicated numerous examples of the Qur'an's extraordinary comprehensiveness in terms of meaning, knowledge, the subject it puts forward, and concision, Nursi exclaims:

> Indeed, if the Qur'an's verses are considered carefully and fairly, it will be seen that they do not resemble a gradual chain of thought, following one or two aims, like other books. Rather, the Qur'an's manner is sudden and instantaneous; it is inspired on the moment; it has the mark that all its aspects which arrive together come independently from somewhere distant, a most serious and important discourse which comes singly and concisely.[38]

Nursi then moves on to his next argument regarding the Qur'an's miraculousness, that is, its reporting of future events.

34. Nursi, *The Words*, 174–75.
35. Qur'an, 21:30.
36. Nursi, *The Words*, 165.
37. Qur'an, 36:38.
38. Nursi, *The Words*, 165.

Reporting the Unseen (*Ikhbār-i Ghaybī*)

Any objective reader of the Qur'an can easily recognize that it reports the past and foretells future events. It informs its readers about the attributes of God, cosmic phenomena, the nature of Judgment Day, and life after death. Nursi considers the fact that the Prophet was an illiterate man, that there was little written culture and limited contact with the outside world. Yet, the Prophet reports many unseen matters with a great accuracy which is hard to explain.[39] The Qur'an mentions the names of and stories about some twenty-five previous messengers of God;[40] including Adam, who is believed to be the first man and the first prophet to have existed on earth. Some of the narrations are similar to, but not identical with, those in the Bible and the Torah. Nursi suggests that this kind of accurate reporting could only be the work of someone who has witnessed these events, which is impossible, since no one can live so long, or of someone who oversees and relates to everything. That could only be The Knower of the Unknown God.[41]

Regarding the news about the future in the Qur'an, Nursi notes few examples. It is therefore fairly easy to examine whether these represent just some remote guesses or whether they concern events that have actually happened.

Example 1: The Qur'an 30:1–2 tells us, "*Alīf, Lām, Mīm.* The Byzantines have been defeated."[42] Chapter 30 in the Qur'an is *Sūrat Al-Rūm* (The Romans), which was revealed in Mecca before 622 AD. Two of the superpowers at the time were the Roman Empire in the West and the Persian (Sassanid) Empire in the East. There were seven century-long wars between them from 92 BC to 628 AD. Although frontiers remained the same, it was a continuous conflict taking place over a long period of time. In 623 AD, the Persians conquered Syria, Palestine, Egypt and Rhodes, and entered Anatolia only a few years after the revelation of *Sūrat Al-Rūm*. What is more extraordinary is that, immediately after these verses, the Qur'an tells us: "In the nearest land. But they, after their defeat, will overcome. Within three to nine years. To Allāh belongs the command before and after. And that day the believers will rejoice."[43] In fact, the Persian victory was short-lived. In

39. Nursi, *The Letters*, 392–96.

40. See Appendix 5: Twenty-five prophets mentioned in Qur'an by name.

41. Nursi, *The Words*, 181.

42. This verse is given in the Sahih International English translation. The Yusuf Ali translation uses "The Roman Empire' rather than 'The Byzantine Empire." Historically, the latter is accepted as being the continuation of the former, hence there is no contradiction.

43. Qur'an, 30:1–2.

627 AD, the Roman commander Heraclius defeated the Persian army at Nineveh, and restored the True Cross to Jerusalem, after the Persians agreed to withdraw from all occupied territories.[44]

Example 2: Qur'an 48:27–28:

> Certainly has Allāh showed to his Messenger the vision in truth. You will surely enter *al-Masjid al-Ḥarām*, if Allāh wills, in safety, with your heads shaved and [hair] shortened, not fearing [anyone]. He knew what you did not know and has arranged before that a conquest near [at hand].

For Nursi, this appears to be a classic example of *Ikhbār-i Ghaybī* (news of the unknown). Indeed, when one looks more closely at the history of early Islam, one can clearly observe that, only few years after the revelation of this verse, the Prophet conquered the city of Mecca and the Sacred Mosque *(al-Masjid al-Ḥarām).*[45] The Qur'an, 5:67 also tells the Prophet, "O Messenger, announce that which has been revealed to you from your Lord, and if you do not, then you have not conveyed his message. And Allāh will protect you from the people. Indeed, Allāh does not guide the disbelieving people." In the latter part of this verse, there is a clear indication that the Prophet will not receive any harm from people. As a matter of fact, during his lifetime he escaped an assassination attempt in Mecca, fought one of the hardest battles in history in Badr and was wounded in the battle of Uḥud, yet no one could ever manage to do him any harm. He died in 632 AD in Medina in his bed, as a result of high fever.[46]

So far, we have seen some examples that Nursi cites of the Qur'an's news from the past and the future. The third type of information that the Qur'an imparts concerns what Nursi calls divine truths, cosmic truths, and matters of the Hereafter.[47] Nursi suggests that these represent the most im-

44. Ball, *Rome in the East: The Transformation of an Empire*, 106–14.

45. Some important dates of the Prophet Muhammad's life are;
571: He was born in Mecca.
610: He declared his prophethood.
622: He emigrated to Medina.
630: He conquered Mecca.
632: He died in Medina.
Also see, Appendix 8: Chronology of the Prophet Muḥammad

46. Lings, *Muhammad: His Life Based on the Earliest Sources*, 345–46.

47. For instance, the Qur'an reports about The Day of Judgement in [21:47]: And We place the scales of justice for the Day of Resurrection, so no soul will be treated unjustly at all. And if there is [even] the weight of a mustard seed, We will bring it forth. And sufficient are We as accountant.

And life after death in [4:13]: These are the limits [set by] Allāh, and whoever obeys Allāh and his Messenger will be admitted by him to gardens [in Paradise] under which

portant type of knowledge concerning the unseen; since no one could possible know about them. The pattern that emerges from Nursi's presentation is such that he tries to demonstrate that the Qur'an is very accurate in its reporting of past and future unseen events. Therefore, Nursi implies that the Qur'an's report of Divine truths and the nature of the Hereafter, though these could not be seen by naked eye, ought to be taken literally. In *The Words*, Nursi writes:

> The Qur'an's expositions of the Divine truths, and its explanations of the cosmos, which solve the talisman of the universe and riddle of creation, are the most important of its disclosures about the Unseen. For it is not reasonable to expect the human reason to discover those truths about the Unseen and follow them without deviating amid innumerable ways of misguidance. It is well-known that the most brilliant philosophers of mankind have been unable to solve the most insignificant of those matters by use of the reason.[48]

These examples of the first two types of reporting of the unseen (i.e., from the past and the future) to Nursi are very clear and verifiable, and the objective reader ought to be convinced about the truthfulness of the Qur'an. Nursi continues:

> For it is not reasonable to expect the human reason to discover those truths about the Unseen and follow them without deviating amid innumerable ways of misguidance. It is well known that the most brilliant philosophers of mankind have been unable to reach the most insignificant of those matters by use of the reason. Furthermore, it is after the Qur'an has explained those Divine truths and cosmic truths, which it points out, and after the heart has been cleansed and the soul purified, and after the spirit has advanced and the mind been perfected that the human mind affirms and accepts those truths.[49]

Nursi argues that the Qur'an speaks to its reader as if it is just being revealed now. In every century, its messages sound young and fresh. The Qur'an's orders and rules are always solid and permanent. They never change. But times, lifestyles, and the practices of mankind are ever changing. In order to build a functional society, the Qur'an asserts two rules,

---

rivers flow, abiding eternally therein; and that is the great attainment. And [3:12]: Say to those who disbelieve, "You will be overcome and gathered together to Hell, and wretched is the resting place."

48. Nursi, *The Words*, 182.

49. Ibid.

which, according to Nursi, have never been invalidated.[50] These rules are established in the Qur'an 2:43 and 2:275.

The Qur'an 2:43 orders: "And establish prayer and give zakat and bow with those who bow in worship and obedience." And the Qur'an 2:275 gives clear instructions about how to conduct business and trade, and explains:

> Those who consume interest cannot stand on the Day of Resurrection except as one stands who is being beaten by Satan into insanity. That is because they say, "Trade is just like interest." But Allāh has permitted trade and has forbidden interest. So whoever has received an admonition from his Lord and desists may have what is past, and his affair rests with Allāh. But whoever returns to dealing in interest or usury—those are the companions of the Fire; they will abide eternally therein.[51]

Here, we need to concentrate on the concepts of *zakāt*[52] (charity) and *ribā*[53] (charging interest, or usury). The absence of *zakāt* and the widespread practice of *ribā* are argued to be the root cause of almost every social problem in human history.[54] The Qur'an does not suggest complete, socialist-style equality between individuals. Instead, it encourages free trade and wealth building. However, in order to stabilize society, even the poorest must have their essential needs met. This, according to the Qur'an, has to be achieved by *zakāt*. *Zakāt* is essentially 2,5 percent of one's annual wealth, which is meant to be transferred to the poor of the community. If this were given, Nursi argues, the poor would show respect to the rich, not hatred as a result of jealousy. Moreover, the rich would not look down on the poor, since it would be their responsibility to share a certain amount of their wealth with them.[55] Nursi explains that, because of the lack of *zakāt*, the financial gap between the rich and poor widened to breaking point, which resulted in social clashes, wars and, eventually, revolutions in their extreme form.[56] One example of this is the communist revolution in Russia in the early twentieth century. The Communist regime took the extreme measure

50. Ibid., 183.

51. Qur'an, 2:275.

52. *Zakāt* is obligatory payment made annually under Islamic law on certain kinds of property about 2,5 percent and used for charitable and religious purposes. It is translated into English as "charity," which does not accurately represent the actual meaning.

53. *Ribā* is what we now call bank interest, which is the money paid regularly at a particular rate for the use of money lent, or for delaying the repayment of a debt.

54 See Elliott, *Usury: A Scriptural, Ethical and Economic View.*

55. Nursi, *The Words*, 163–64.

56. Ibid., 324.

of confiscating all personal property and distributing all the wealth generated equally. This eventually caused the collapse of the regime, since people did not have any personal motivation for productivity.[57] While this was the scene in Communist countries, the West took a complete opposite route, into capitalism. Capitalism effectively encouraged individuals to earn an unlimited amount of money and wealth. States had to set up unreasonable taxes[58] on these earnings, and largely failed to collect them. Unless taxes are collected forcibly, human nature is such that people would not share their money voluntarily if they had not got a strong faith in the cause. Similarly, *ribā* (usury) causes a great many social and financial problems in society.[59] These issues will be discussed in the next chapter, which focuses on "Morality and Conscience."

The Qur'an's Fluency, Coherence, and Harmony

Many linguists and experts in semantics have studied these characteristics of the Qur'an over the centuries.[60] Muslim scholars argue that there is a very clear coherence throughout the entire Qur'an considering the fact that it took some twenty years to complete its revelation.[61] In particular, most chapters were formed after separate groups of verses, which had been revealed on different occasions in order to deal with different matters.[62] Nursi claims that the fluency, coherence and harmony of the Qur'an represent further clear evidence of its divine source.[63] Nursi tries to demonstrate these aspects of the Qur'an in his *al-*ʿIshārāt-*ul I'jāz* (Signs of Miraculousness). The true appreciation of these aspects of the Qur'an, therefore, requires the

57. Lewis, *One Planet, Many Worlds*, 45.

58. For instance, the basic income tax in the UK in 2011 is 20 percent, higher income tax is 40 percent and the additional income tax is 45 percent. Value Added Tax (VAT) is 20 percent on most services and products.

59. For the lengthy argument, see O'Callaghan, *Usury, or Interest.*

60. For instance, Al-Jurjānī (d.1078) produced a list of books dedicated to demonstrating the linguistics and semantics of Qur'an. Some of his works are *'I'jaz al-Qur'an* (The inimitability of the Qur'an), *Kitab 'Aroud* (Poetic Structure), *Al-'Awamel al-Mi'ah* (The Hundred Elements), *Al-Miftāḥ* (The Key), *Shar'ḥ al-Fātiḥa fi Mujallad* (Explaining Al-*Fātiḥa* in a Volume), *Al-Jumal* (Sentences), *Asrar al-Balaghah* (The Secrets of Elucidation), and *Dalā'il al-I'jāz* (Intimations of Inimitability).

61. For instance, see El-Awa, *Textual Relations in the Quran.*

62. For instance, *Sūrah al-'Alaq* (The Clot) is Chapter 96 of the Qur'an, which has 19 verses in total and is located near the end of the Book. The first five verses of this chapter are actually the first-ever revelation to the Prophet. The remaining fourteen verses were revealed some time later, yet there is a perfect coherence within the whole chapter.

63. Nursi, *The Words*, 187–97.

full-length reading of the whole book, preferably in the original language, Arabic, since most of its beauty is easily lost in translation.

The Qur'anic Summations (*Faḍlaka*) and the Divine Names of God

For Nursi, the summations, which appear at the end of some verses of the Qur'an mentioning certain attributes of God, are also evidence of the uniqueness of the revelation. In these verses, the Qur'an presents to its readers certain reasonable and observable facts and challenges them to come up with an explanation should they deny the True Cause of the universe and everything it contains. Before we look at examples, it is worthwhile to highlight the themes of the Qur'an. According to Nursi, the Qur'an is set to prove *tawḥīd* (Oneness of God), *nubuwwah* (the prophethood), *ḥashr* (resurrection) and *'adālah* (justice). Similarly, Mawdūdī (1903–79) categorizes the themes into seven groups, as follows: [1] belief and conduct, [2] moral directives, [3] legal prescriptions, [4] exhortation and admonition, [5] censure and condemnation of evildoers, [6] warning to deniers, and [7] consolation and good cheer to those who suffer for God.[64] Now, let us see some examples that Nursi cites to demonstrate the context–attribute relations in the Qur'an, which in turn clarifies the attributes and characteristic of God, who is not simply the Creator, but possesses many other qualities such as being the Sustainer, the Judge, the Forbearer.[65]

Qur'an 2:29: "It is he who created for you all of that which is on the earth. Then he directed himself to the heaven [his being above all creation], and made them seven heavens, and he is knowing of all things."

Here, the Qur'an briefly tells us about the creation of the Earth and its contents and the creation of the atmosphere, other space, and all that there is in the universe. This requires immense knowledge and power. In the concluding phrase, instead of telling us "It is God who created everything," the passage tells us "He knows everything," which refers to his name '*al-'Alīm*' (The Knower of All). This verse is also a good example of the first of the four purposes of the Qur'an.

Nursi's second example comes in his analysis of Qur'an 10:31, which reads:

> Say, "Who provides for you from the heaven and the earth? Or who controls hearing and sight and who brings the living out of

64. See Maudoodi and Ansari, *Towards Understanding the Quran*.
65. See Appendix 2: Names and Attributes of God in Islam.

> the dead and brings the dead out of the living and who arranges [every] matter?" They will say, " Allāh," so say, "Then will you not fear him?[66]

Nursi's argues that there are four elements in this verse. The first element is the fact that the Earth and its natural events are acting in such a fashion that they are in excellent harmony and partnership in order to sustain life on Earth. The second element reminds the reader that there are certain organs (i.e., eyes, ears and hands, etc.) and senses (sight, sound, touch, taste, etc.) given to the organisms, especially human beings, to ensure that they can benefit from the Earth with maximum efficiency. In the third element, the fact of life and death is pointed out to the reader. The fourth element of this verse comes in the form of a question, which asks who could possibly manage all these interconnected and complicated affairs. Nursi, then, concludes that the first and the fourth elements entail *Allāh* (God), the second element entails *al-Rab* (The Sustaining Lord), and the third element entails *al-Ḥaqq* (The Truth).[67] Indeed, this verse is followed by "For that is Allāh, your Lord, the Truth. And what can be beyond truth except error? So how are you averted?".[68]

The Qur'an tells us the story of the prophet Joseph in Chapter 12. Revealed in Mecca, it consists of 111 verses which, for Nursi, display clear examples of the four themes mentioned above. Nursi takes the sixth verse to demonstrate the context–attribute relation of the Qur'an. The verse reads:

> And thus will your Lord choose you and teach you the interpretation of narratives and complete his favor upon you and upon the family of Jacob, as He completed it upon your fathers before, Abraham and Isaac. Indeed, your Lord is Knowing and Wise.[69]

For Nursi, this particular verse encompasses "the news of the unseen." First, it explains what had happened before the prophet Joseph, and then it tells what was going to happen (i.e., God should complete his favor to Joseph). The aspect of this verse which mentions all the favors of God to Joseph and his ancestors (i.e., Abraham, Isaac and Jacob) entails the name of *al-Rab* (The Sustaining Lord); the mention of the "interpretation of narratives" which is knowledge in general entails the name *al-ʿAlīm* (The Knower of All); and God's completion of his favors, which includes Joseph's being King of Egypt, entails the name *al-Ḥakīm* (The Perfectly Wise). A similar

66. Qur'an, 10:31.
67. Nursi, *The Words*, 188.
68. Qur'an, 10:32.
69. Qur'an, 12:6.

example is the Qur'anic verses 2:30–32,[70] which recount the story of the creation of Adam and the dialogue between God and the angels. After having taught Adam the names,[71] God turns to the angels and asks them to tell the names. In complete submission, the angels reply that they do not know anything other than what God teaches them. They admit and say, "You are *al-ʿAlīm* and *al-Ḥakīm*' (Knowing and Wise)."[72]

Also, Nursi points out some verses of *Sūrat al-Nūr*[73] in which the Qur'an talks about particular meteorological events and the origins of the living creatures. The verse concludes with the expression that God, who is the sole, powerful One above everything in the universe, is the cause behind all the phenomena mentioned.

The names *al-Ḥalīm* (The Forbearing) and *al-Ghafūr* (The Forgiver) represent the summary of *Sūrat al-'Isrā*.' The Qur'an [17:44] declares: "The seven heavens and the earth and whatever is in them exalt him. And there is not a thing except that it exalts [Allāh] by his praise, but you do

70. Qur'an, 2:30: And [mention, O Muḥammad], when your Lord said to the angels, "Indeed, I will make upon the earth a successive authority." They said, "Will You place upon it one who causes corruption therein and sheds blood, while we declare Your praise and sanctify You?" Allāh said, "Indeed, I know that which you do not know."

Qur'an, 2:31: And He taught Adam the names—all of them. Then He showed them to the angels and said, "Inform Me of the names of these, if you are truthful."

Qur'an, 2:32: They said, "Exalted are You; we have no knowledge except what You have taught us. Indeed, it is You who is the Knowing, the Wise."

71. Here, the word "names" implies "knowledge."

72. Qur'an, 23:12–14: And certainly did We create man from an extract of clay. Then We placed him as a sperm-drop in a firm lodging. Then We made the sperm-drop into a clinging clot, and We made the clot into a lump [of flesh], and We made [from] the lump, bones, and We covered the bones with flesh; then We developed him into another creation. So blessed is Allāh, the best of creators.

Qur'an, 7:54: Indeed, your Lord is Allāh, who created the heavens and earth in six days and then established himself above the Throne. He covers the night with the day, [another night] chasing it rapidly; and [He created] the sun, the moon, and the stars, subjected by His command. Unquestionably, His is the creation and the command; blessed is Allāh, Lord of the worlds.

73. Qur'an, 24:43: Do you not see that Allāh drives clouds? Then He brings them together, then He makes them into a mass, and you see the rain emerge from within it. And He sends down from the sky, mountains [of clouds] within which is hail, and He strikes with it whom He wills and averts it from whom He wills. The flash of its lightening almost takes away the eyesight.

Qur'an, 24:44: Allāh alternates the night and the day. Indeed in that is a lesson for those who have vision.

Qur'an, 24:45: Allāh has created every [living] creature from water. And of them are those that move on their bellies, and of them are those that walk on two legs, and of them are those that walk on four. Allāh creates what He wills. Indeed, Allāh is over all things competent.

not understand their [way of] exalting. Indeed, He is ever Forbearing and Forgiving." Prior to this particular verse, the Qur'an speaks about believers and deniers. It mentions the severe punishment awaiting disbelievers. At a point where hopes of salvation are about to be lost, the Qur'an tells us that God is Compassionate and Merciful; therefore, people should not despair but should work towards pleasing God by obeying his rules.

After a lengthy discussion and a long list of examples, Nursi remarks:

> . . . in the summaries at the conclusions of verses are numerous sprinklings of guidance and flashes of miraculousness. The greatest geniuses among the scholars of rhetoric have bitten their fingers in absolute wonder and admiration at these unique styles, and declared: "this is not the word of man."[74]

Considering the fact that the Prophet was allegedly an illiterate man who had never read any books in his life,[75] the Qur'an, for Nursi, clearly appears to be an outstanding book in every respect. In Nursi's opinion, the book has been "ever-young" since it first appeared in the seventh century AD. Nursi contends that the effective result the Qur'an has had in human social history over the last fourteen centuries is evidence of its miraculous nature.[76]

Philosophy Versus Qur'anic Wisdom

Throughout the *Risale-i Nur*, it is clear that Nursi is a fierce critic of materialist philosophy and of *'ilm al-kalām* equally.[77] According to Nursi, philosophy and the wisdom of the Qur'an differ in terms of their main points of view. To Nursi, philosophy fails spectacularly when faced with the wisdom of the Qur'an. Both philosophy and the Qur'an work towards explaining the nature and aim of the universe. According to Nursi, philosophy looks at the universe from a fixed point of view and sees the universe through

74. Nursi, *The Words*, 189.

75. To support this fact, Qur'an in Surat Al-`Ankabūt (The Spider) 29:48 reads: "And you did not recite before it any scripture, nor did you inscribe one with your right hand. Otherwise the falsifiers would have had cause for doubt."

76. Nursi, *The Words*, 197.

77. Here, it is important to note that Nursi mainly refers to the atheist philosophy, which tries to justify the universe without God. See Nursi, *The Flashes*, 643. Similarly, Nursi aims his criticisms at the *mutakallimūn* (the Muslim scholastics and philosophers) who accept the existence of God, but fail to understand and appreciate his attributes fully.

its "self-referential" meaning (*manā-i ismī*).[78] In an analogy, Nursi likens philosophy to a person who looks at the letters and words of a book without paying any attention to its meaning.[79] The account of philosophy is similar to the account of a person who looks into a garden through a peephole. Thus, his comprehension of that garden is limited to what the little hole allows him to see. The philosopher perceives the universe as a giant, mindless, lifeless entity where nature causes random creations, and planets, stars and heavenly bodies move about arbitrarily and mindlessly. If there is any apparent order in the universe, they believe that it is the product of pure chance.[80] When they see something beautiful, they say "How beautiful it is?" instead of appreciating it as an artwork of a Maker by saying "How beautifully it has been made?"[81]

In a total contrast, the Qur'an shows the "Other-indicative" meaning (*m'anā-i ḥarfī*)[82] of the universe. To Nursi, the Qur'an is the true expounder and interpreter of the universe. Unlike philosophy, which sees the letters and the words of a book without paying attention to their meaning, the Qur'an reads and explains the meaning of the text which those letters and words form. Philosophy without religion, Nursi writes, "is a sophistry divorced from reality and an insult to the universe."[83]

Nursi also compares philosophy with the wisdom of the Qur'an from the perspective of morality. He compares and contrasts the moral teachings of philosophy and those of the Qur'an. He argues that the Qur'an establishes

78. Two essential concepts define Nursi's philosophical standpoint. These are *m'anā-i ismī* (the apparent or direct meaning of things, self-referential meaning) and *m'anā-i ḥarfī* (the signifying or indirect meaning of things, other indicative meaning). These two original concepts can be explained with the following example. A tree is producing fruit. A person ascribing the qualities and production of the fruit to the tree is looking with *m'anā-i ismī* or the apparent or direct meaning of the fruit. A thinking person looking with *m'anā-i ḥarfī* will see that the fruit indicates there is something else causing the qualities and production of the fruit because the tree is so simple and the fruit is so complex and miraculous. Therefore, the first person sees only the mechanical cause–effect relationship in the nature, but the second person sees the effective work of the Creator on every object and every event. See Nursi, *Al-Mathnawi Al-Nuri*, 1297. And Nursi, *The Words*, 50, 211.

79. Nursi, *The Words*, 50.

80. See Chapter 3, for Nursi's arguments against the materialist and naturalist philosophy.

81. Nursi, *The Words*, 49.

82. Turner and Horkuç explain that Nursi's this particular twin concept of "self-referential" and "other-indicative" meanings represent the two diametrically opposite hermeneutical positions to man as "reader" of the cosmic narrative. See Turner and Horkuc, *Said Nursi*, 67–71.

83. Nursi, *The Words*, 50.

a list of very high moral codes thanks to its divine origin, whereas philosophy with its very limited insight fails to achieve the happiness of humankind. A person who takes the teachings of godless philosophy as a point of reference develops negative characteristics. Nursi calls such a person "a pharaoh" in the sense that he is known for his terrible qualities. These individuals became very stubborn since they were not open to listening to and understanding the truth revealed by God. They worship matter and wealth. For a little pleasure, they readily put up with great disgrace. They are usually very cruel and selfish. As opposed to the Qur'an, which teaches the worship and praise of the Creator, they worship Satan.[84]

Although these characteristics of godless philosophy are open to discussion and not fully verifiable, this is a common convention used in the Divine Texts.[85] Nursi's wording of his description of the unbelievers is similar to that of the Qur'an. Although it is the title given to ancient Egyptian rulers, the word "pharaoh" later became a synonym for disbeliever, since the pharaoh opposed the prophet Joseph. In addition to the Qur'anic inspirations, Nursi clearly refers to the experience people went through in the USSR, which was established on the basis of the philosophical teachings of Marx and Engels.[86]

In total contrast, Nursi cites all the positive qualities of the genuine followers of the Qur'an's teachings. They are humble, as they acknowledge the Most Powerful; and they are strong, as they take their strength from the Strongest. They do not worship matter or wealth; they worship the The Rich One (*al-Ghanī*) instead. They act only for the sake of their Lord.[87]

Nursi also condemns the teachings of what he terms "godless philosophy" on social matters in capitalist societies. For example, he explains that this philosophy encourages the gaining of wealth and power. This, inevitably, results in greed and in people acting unfairly for their own advantage. Competition and struggle become the purpose of life. Nursi writes:

Philosophy accepts force as its point of support in the life of society. It considers its aim to be benefits. The principle of its life it recognizes to be conflict. It holds the bond between communities to be racialism and negative nationalism. Its fruits are gratifying the appetites of the soul and increasing human needs. However, the mark of force is aggression. The mark of benefit—since they are insufficient for every desire—is jostling

84. Ibid.

85. The Bible refers to the atheist as "the fool." In a recent discussion in defense of atheism, the atheist complained about the tone of Bible, calling those who do not believe in God "fools." Similarly, the Qur'an describes unbelievers as ignorant and cruel.

86. Nursi, *The Words*, 50.

87. Ibid.

and tussling. While the mark of conflict is strife. And the mark of racialism—since it is nourished by devouring others—is aggression. It is for these reasons that it has negated the happiness of mankind.[88]

The Qur'an, on the other hand, promotes sharing, cooperation and virtuous behavior for the sake of God.[89] Nursi explains his Qur'anic position as follows:

> As for the Qur'anic wisdom, its point of support is truth instead of force. It takes virtue and God's pleasure as its aims in place of benefits. It takes the principle of mutual assistance as the principle of life in place of the principle of conflict. And it takes the ties of religion, class, and country to be the ties bonding communities. Its aim is to form a barrier against the lusts of the soul, urge the spirit to sublime matters, satisfy the high emotions, and urging man to the human perfections, make him a true human being. And the mark of the truth is accord. The mark of virtue is solidarity. The mark of mutual assistance is hastening to assist one another. The mark of religion is brotherhood and attraction. And the mark of reining in and tethering the soul and leaving the spirit free and urging it towards perfections is happiness in this world and the next.[90]

Nursi claims that racialism and destructive nationalism are another damaging result of godless philosophy. Nursi believes that these two are abused by selfish people and nations for their own benefit.[91] Here, there is a clear reference to the imperialist expansions of Western countries in the eighteenth and nineteenth centuries, as well as the USSR. These big and powerful nations swallowed, colonized, and assimilated smaller, less powerful nations all over the world. When a conflict of interest emerged, they fought among themselves. During their imperialist struggles, history recorded many cruel brutalities.[92] The Qur'an, however, endorses solidarity

88. Ibid.

89. Qur'an, 9:71: The believing men and believing women are allies of one another. They enjoin what is right and forbid what is wrong and establish prayer and give zakat and obey Allāh and his Messenger. Those—Allāh will have mercy upon them. Indeed, Allāh is Exalted in Might and Wise.

Qur'an, 28:54: Those will be given their reward twice for what they patiently endured and [because] they avert evil through good, and from what We have provided them they spend.

90. Nursi, *The Words*, 50.

91. Ibid.

92. American–Indian Wars (1622–1918). French–Indian Wars (1754–63), Inter-colonial wars involving the French, Spanish and Dutch, the Portuguese Colonial War (1961–74), and the British Indian Mutiny (1857–58) are just a few examples of colonial struggles.

between people on the basis that they live on the same land and believe in the same God. It declares:

> O mankind, indeed We have created you from male and female and made you peoples and tribes that you may know one another. Indeed, the most noble of you in the sight of Allāh is the most righteous of you. Indeed, Allāh is Knowing and Acquainted.[93]

What Nursi seems to be doing here is simply rewording and rephrasing the Qur'anic teachings on solidarity, comradeship, and fraternity. Although certain readers agree this particular view of materialist philosophy, the materialist philosophers think the opposite. They might easily claim that it is religion which causes bloodshed and terror. Putting aside these differences, what Nursi seems to try to achieve is that the Qur'an teaches higher values than any human intelligence could possibly achieve. Therefore, this particular scripture ought to have a divine origin, which itself is the proof of the existence of God. In order to strengthen his position on the Qur'an's being a divine scripture, Nursi turns to previously revealed scriptures, i.e., the Torah and the Gospels in anticipation of pulling further evidence.

Nursi on the Qur'an, the Gospels, and the Torah

Like all Muslim scholars, Nursi believes that the Bible and the Torah were genuine revelations, but that their messages have become partly corrupted over time and hence have lost their truthfulness. The Qur'an, according to Nursi, agrees with the preserved truths of the Torah and Bible, and corrects their corrupted points. He explains:

> Indeed, the All-Wise Qur'an mentions through the tongue of one whom everyone agreed was both unlettered and trustworthy the important events and significant facts concerning the prophets from the time of Adam till the Era of Bliss (time of Prophet Muḥammad) in a way which, confirmed by scriptures like the Torah and the Bible, tells of them with the greatest power and seriousness. It concurs with the points on which the former Books were agreed, and decides between them on the points over which they differed, pointing out the truth of the matter.[94]

93. Qur'an, 49:13.
94. Nursi, *The Words*, 181.

The Torah is accepted by Christianity as part of the Bible, comprising the first five books of the Old Testament.[95] Therefore, it is not inaccurate to make comparison between the Qur'an and the Bible and Torah combined. The Islamic creed asserts that all previous messengers and scripts were sent down to particular nations. For instance, the prophet Moses, the prophet Aaron and the prophet David were the guides of the children of Israel, prophethood was sent to a nation corresponding to modern Yemen, and the prophet Lūt was sent to the people of Samūd in modern Palestine. However, it is claimed that the Prophet Muḥammad and the Qur'an were sent for the *whole* of humankind, and that therefore their message ought to be universal. There are two verses in the Qur'an which are cited as evidence for this assumption. *Sūrat al-'Anbiyā'* (The Prophets) reads: "And We have not sent you, [O Muḥammad], except as a mercy to the worlds." [96] And *Sūrat al-Saba'* (Sheba) tells: "And We have not sent you except comprehensively to mankind as a bringer of good tidings and a warner. But most of the people do not know."[97] Also, Islamic doctrine claims that the line of prophethood ended with the Prophet Muḥammad, who is called "*khatama annabiyyeena*" (the last of the prophets). *Sūrat al-'Aḥzāb* (The Combined Forces) [33:40] declares: "Muḥammad is not the father of [any] one of your men, but [he is] the Messenger of Allāh and last of the prophets. And ever is Allāh, of all things, Knowing."[98] Therefore, the Prophet and the Qur'an have a very special position in the history of faiths.

The main Islamic justification for the revelation of the Qur'an is that parts of all previous messages sent by God had been altered by people.[99] Hence, the Qur'an states that God sent a newer, more correct version of his messages.[100] Among many messengers and their nations, perhaps Jesus

95. Coggins, *Introducing the Old Testament*, Chapter 1.

96. Qur'an, 21:107.

97. Qur'an, 21:107.

98. Qur'an, 33:40.

99. Qur'an, 3:71: O People of the Scripture, why do you confuse the truth with falsehood and conceal the truth while you know [it]?

Qur'an, 3:78: And indeed, there is among them a party who alter the Scripture with their tongues so you may think it is from the Scripture, but it is not from the Scripture. And they say, "This is from Allāh," but it is not from Allāh. And they speak untruth about Allāh while they know."

100. Qur'an, 5:48: And We have revealed to you, [O Muḥammad], the Book in truth, confirming that which preceded it of the Scripture and as a criterion over it. So judge between them by what Allāh has revealed and do not follow their inclinations away from what has come to you of the truth. To each of you We prescribed a law and a method. Had Allāh willed, He would have made you one nation [united in religion], but [He intended] to test you in what He has given you; so race to [all that is] good. To

and Moses are the best-known ones. Jesus was a Jew.[101] Since Judaism had been diverted from its original teaching, Jesus was sent to renew the faith. Similarly, he was replaced by the Prophet Muḥammad some six centuries later. Although the essential tenets of monotheism remain the same, a great many inventions (*bid'ah*) entered into the Bible; hence, God send another messenger to correct the distorted, wrong teachings of Christianity.[102] Islam and Christianity differ on several key points. For example, Christianity believes that Jesus was the Son of God, whereas Islam counters that He was a prophet only,[103] and strongly condemns those who claim Jesus to be the Son of God.[104] Also, the Qur'an explains that Jesus did not die on the cross, but was lifted into Heaven,[105] and that one of his disciples who resembled Jesus was killed instead of him.[106] Furthermore, Muslims believe that Jesus will return to the Earth to defeat the false messiah (*al-Masīḥ al-Dajjāl*), join forces with Islam, and then die.[107]

Nursi interprets the text of the *ḥadīth* (prophetic traditions and sayings) which reports "At the end of time, Jesus will come and act in accordance with the Sharia of the Prophet Muḥammad"[108] as requiring to be

---

Allāh is your return all together, and He will [then] inform you concerning that over which you used to differ.

101. Brown, *The Death of the Messiah, Vol. 1*, 964.

102. Qur'an, 18:4–5: And to warn those who say, "Allāh has taken a son." They have no knowledge of it, nor had their fathers. Grave is the word that comes out of their mouths; they speak not except a lie.

103. Qur'an, 5:39: Indeed, the example of Jesus to Allāh is like that of Adam. He created him from dust; then He said to him, "Be," and he was.

104. Qur'an, 5:17: They have certainly disbelieved who say that Allāh is Christ, the son of Mary. Say, "Then who could prevent Allāh at all if He had intended to destroy Christ, the son of Mary, or his mother or everyone on the earth?" And to Allāh belongs the dominion of the heavens and the earth and whatever is between them. He creates what He wills, and Allāh is over all things competent.

105. Qur'an, 3:55: Mention when Allāh said, "O Jesus, indeed I will take you and raise you to Myself and purify you from those who disbelieve and make those who follow you [in submission to Allāh alone] superior to those who disbelieve until the Day of Resurrection. Then to Me is your return, and I will judge between you concerning that in which you used to differ."

106. Qur'an, 4:157: And for their saying, "Indeed, we have killed the Messiah, Jesus, the son of Mary, the messenger of Allāh." And they did not kill him, nor did they crucify him; but [another] was made to resemble him to them. And indeed, those who differ over it are in doubt about it. They have no knowledge of it except the following of assumption. And they did not kill him, for certain."

107. Muslims believe these assumptions on the bases of the Prophet Muḥammad's sayings (*ḥadīth*) in *Bukhārī*, Maẓālim:31; Buyū':102, *Muslim*, Imān:242. 343 and *Ibn-i Majah*, Fitan: 33.

108. Khan, *Sahih Al-Bukhari*, Mazalim 31.

understood non-literally. He tells us that rather than Jesus coming back to life as a person and fulfilling what the above *ḥadīth* implies, his collective personality (i.e., the true teachings of Christianity) will cooperate with Islam to attack irreligion and atheism.[109]

Nursi moves on to compare the Books of the previous Messengers and the Qur'an. He claims that the Qur'an has the highest ranking among all the revelations since it reflects all the supreme attributes (*ism al-'āẓām*)[110] of God; hence it is called the Word of God (*kalām Allāh*), whereas all the other books are speeches, which have become evident through a particular regard, a minor title, through the partial manifestation of a particular Name, through a particular Dominicality, special sovereignty, or private mercy.[111]

Objections to the Arguments from Miracles

As we have seen, theologians, such as Nursi argue that the existence of prophets and the scriptures are proofs of the existence of a Deity. This is what constitutes the basis of "the argument from miracles" in philosophy. The theistic position is that God sends messengers to spread his word. He sometimes changes the course of nature in an extraordinary fashion (i.e., via miracles) in order to support his messengers. Some of the best-known miracles in theology are the prophet Moses parting the Red Sea and walking across to safety with the Israelites, Jesus healing the sick and raising people from the dead, and the Prophet Muḥammad splitting the moon with his finger and making water run through his fingers.[112] The bedrock of Nursi's theism, therefore, is partly the argument from miracles, as well as the teleological and moral arguments.[113] The main objection to this popular argu-

109. Nursi, *The Letters*, 347.

110. *Ism al-'āzām* literally means the greatest name of God. It is the name which contains the meanings of the entirety of the Most Beautiful Names an Attributes of Allāh. The Greatest Name means the most comprehensive Name among the Divine Names, which comprises the entirety of the Names. It is not known for sure which Name is the Greatest Name. The wisdom of keeping this Name secret is to encourage the remembrance of all Names with the probability that they might be the Greatest Name. According to Nursi the most possible six Names are *al-Fard* (The Single), *Al-Ḥayy* (Ever-Living), *Al-Qayyūm* (Self-Subsistent), *al-Ḥakīm* (Sapient), *al-'Adl* (All-Just), and *al-Quddūs* (Most Holy).

111. Nursi, *The Words*, 51.

112. Qur'an, 54:1: The Hour has come near, and the moon has split in two.
And Khan, *Sahih Al-Bukhari*, 32:46..

113. Although Nursi devotes separate arguments to prophethood and revelation, they are in fact part of the Argument from Miracle.

ment for the existence of God comes in the form of the scrutinizing of its credibility. Atheist philosophy tries to discredit the existence of miracles in order to disprove the existence of Deity. Arguments against miracles come in several broad categories.

Ontological Objections to Violation Miracles

The first category argues that violation miracles are impossible. The second category argues that miracles could never rationally be believed. Spinoza sets out to argue that miracles are impossible. He explains that the will of God is identical with the laws of nature. A miracle is a violation of the laws of nature. God's will is inviolable, and therefore miracles cannot happen.[114] Voltaire produces his own version of the rejection of miracles. In his *Philosophical Dictionary*, he writes:

> It is impossible a being infinitely wise (meaning God) can have made laws to violate them. He could not . . . derange the machine but with a view of making it work better; but it is evident that God, all-wise and omnipotent, originally made this immense machine, the universe, as good and perfect as He was able; if He saw that some imperfections would arise from the nature of matter, He provided for that in the beginning; and, accordingly, He will never change anything in it.[115]

Hume's ideas about miracles set the foundations of almost all atheist arguments. Hume does not try to prove that miracles do not happen or never could have happened. Instead, he tries to demonstrate that we have no good reason to believe that they happened. He rejects the concept of miracle. A miracle, by definition, is a violation of a law of nature, which is, by definition, a regularity about what happens, about how the universe functions. Consequently, if some events actually occur, no regularity which its occurrence infringes can really be a law of nature. So this event, however unusual and surprising, cannot after all be a miracle.[116] For instance, the universal law states that water cannot be turned into wine. Jesus is claimed to have turned water into wine. The conclusion is: the statement "Water cannot be turned into wine" is not a nature of law, *or* Jesus did not turn

114. Spinoza and Wernham, *The Political Works*, 123–28.

115. See Voltaire, *A Philosophical Dictionary*.

116. Hume, *Enquiries Concerning Human Understanding, and Concerning the Principles of Morals*, 115–16.

water into wine. John Stuart Mill gives a brief summary of what we have just attempted to explain. He writes:

> We cannot admit a proposition as a law of nature, and yet believe a fact in real contradiction to it. We must disbelieve the alleged fact, or believe we are mistaken in admitting the supposed law.[117]

So far, we have seen how the Humean argument develops around the ontological aspects of miracles. Now we turn to a more recent argument developed by Everitt, Dawkins and others.

Inexplicable Miracles

So far, we have seen that the theists built their argument from miracles on the basis of supernatural, or inexplicable incidents that have religious significance or have produced benefits, etc. Everitt argues that, on the basis of a lack of scientific explanation, certain events which were considered miraculous then do not constitute miracles now, simply because science can now explain them. For instance, it would have been seen as a miracle two centuries ago if someone had talked to another person on another continent. But now, developments in telecommunications and in radio and satellite technologies easily explain how this is done. Everitt elaborates on this, and writes:

> Given the occurrence of any event which we would find now baffling, and which we could not now explain in scientific terms, how could we know that future developments of science would not show it was explicable after all. For primitive people who first witnessed the solar eclipse, the event might have been utterly unprecedented and mysterious. Yet we now know it is fully explicable in scientific terms.[118]

Dawkins also dislikes the idea of calling scientifically inexplicable events miracles. For him, humankind should keep searching for scientific explanations for these phenomena.[119] For atheist philosophers, then, claiming that certain scientifically inexplicable events prove the existence of God is a very poor argument.

117. See Mill, *A System of Logic, Ratiocinative and Inductive*, 185.
118. Everitt, *The Non-Existence of God*, 124.
119. Dawkins, *The God Delusion*, 14.

Coincidence Miracles

Up to now, we have seen how skeptical philosophers objected to the occurrence of violation miracles and why they insist that what theists call miracle is not necessarily the work of God on the basis of its inexplicability. The third common skeptical view of miracle is that they may just be pure coincidence. R. F. Holland tells the story of the miraculous escape of a child from certain death. The child wanders on to a railway track, and there is a fast-approaching train whose driver cannot possibly see the child owing to a bend in the line. Just seconds before the train hits and kills the child, the train comes to a complete stop since the driver faints as a result of his heavy lunch. When he loses consciousness his hand ceases to exert pressure on the control lever; hence the auto-break system of the train is activated and stops the train.[120]

Everitt says that for the theist, this is an active act of God, a miracle, which proves there is a God. For the atheist, it is not a miracle because it is not a violation of a law of nature, and it is scientifically explicable. For this very reason, although it is called a miracle, it does not actually prove the existence of a supernatural being. It is entirely a matter of a chain of scientifically explicable events involving great coincidence.

Nursi's Approach to Miracles and His Critique of the Philosophers

Nursi considers miracles as God's alterations of some rules of the universe in order to support his messengers with their claim. With regards to incidents being inexplicable, Nursi does not go into a debate to argue whether an incident is explainable in terms of science or not. In Nursi's opinion, even if an incident is scientifically explainable, this does not disprove it as miracle. For instance, when Moses parted the Red Sea, there were certainly some physical rules applying. Science might be able explain how the mechanics of this miracle worked. There might have been certain electro-magnetic forces causing the partition of the sea. Or when considering Jesus' miracles, there might well be scientific explanations to them. However, for Nursi, what constitutes a miracle is the fact that these extraordinary events occurred upon the need or the request of God's messengers. Therefore Nursi puts three conditions to call an event "a miracle." It has to be performed by someone

120. Holland, "The Miraculous."

who is a prophet, it has to be completely extraordinary, and it has to be performed upon the need or the request of the prophet from God.[121]

All these arguments assume that a miracle is one single extraordinary event like the ones mentioned above. However, Nursi's exposition of the miraculousness of the Qur'an is very different from the critics' assumption of what constitutes a miracle. For instance, the continuous eloquence of the Qur'an is not a one-off argument from miracles. Nursi persistently tries to demonstrate how the Qur'an is written poetically without it losing any meaning throughout. Again, the critics' arguments fail to succeed when Nursi shows the reader the aspect of the Qur'an where extremely accurate and verifiable news is presented from the unseen future as well from not-yet-discovered scientific facts.[122] Modern critics of theism such as Mackie, Flew and Everitt do not produce any arguments against Nursi's expositions. They simply reformulate what has been said by previous philosophers such as Hume, Voltaire, and Copleston. This unique perspective of the argument from miracles to God's existence put forward by Nursi, one might argue, is still standing firm as it has not been refuted yet.

Problem of Inconsistent Revelations

One of the most popular arguments used to refute theism is the argument from the problem of inconsistent revelations. The upshot of this atheistic argument is this question; if there is only one God who sends messengers to mankind, why are there so many different versions of scriptures? In other words, why do the Torah, Bible, and the Qur'an tell us different stories and why do they all sound inconsistent with each other? Proponents of this argument say that this situation leads us to two different conclusions. Either there is no God and all these scriptures are the artificial works of men, or there are different gods whose guidance to humankind are different and false. Although this argument looks sound at first, for Nursi it is groundless. The formation of these three scriptures has already been mentioned in the previous part of this chapter. It is important, once again, to state that most Jews and Christians reject the Qur'an outright. Most of them assume that the Qur'an is a book written by Muḥammad. Hence, it is not helpful to go into the details of their arguments. Nursi holds a clear and strong Qur'anic ground against this particular argument of atheist philosophy. Nursi approaches this argument by putting a few historical facts. First and foremost is the fact that none of the Holy Books except for the Qur'an maintains its

121. Nursi, *The Letters*, 389.

122. See Harun Yahya's online resources at http://www.miraclesofthequran.com

original forms of revelation. The current versions of the Holy Books today are the works of different individuals. For instance, the Bible exits in several versions produced by different people.[123] Similarly, the Oral Torah consists of the traditional interpretations and amplifications handed down by word of mouth from generation to generation and now embodied in the Talmud and Midrash.[124] Blenkinsopp explains that the written books (Torah) were a product of the Babylonian exilic period (*c.*600 B CE) and that they were completed by the Persian period (*c.*400 B CE).[125]

Therefore, it would lead us into a wrong judgment to compare the current available versions of the Holy Books. Nursi's position is such that he believes that only the Qur'an is the genuine, truly preserved revelation; hence its words must be taken into account. The main message of God to mankind, Nursi articulates, has always been the same. It is *tawḥīd* (the Oneness of God), resurrection, justice, and the moral conduct of life. Therefore, for Nursi, the argument from inconsistent revelation is groundless and invalid. If the Bible and the Torah had been kept in their original forms, they would have been teaching exactly what the Qur'an teaches.

In other words, Nursi maintains a position whereby he argues that although all of the previous scriptures revealed by God to different messengers contain the same messages (i.e., the unity of God, resurrection, justice and the moral conduct of life), certain parts of these previous scriptures have not been kept in their original forms,[126] and therefore the Qur'an, the final revelation, was sent by God to agree with and strengthen the truly preserved parts of the previous scriptures and correct the corrupted parts.[127]

123. Some versions of the Bible: Septuagint—AD 250. Written in Greek. Vulgate—AD 400. First version of the Bible, canonized at the Council of Carthage in AD 400. Written in Latin. Luther's German Bible—AD 1534. King James Version—AD 1611. This is the most widely used version; however, it contains a large number of errors, since none of the writers had an adequate understanding of Hebrew. Revised Standard Version—AD 1952. Translation into American English that used the earliest possible text. New International Version—1960s–70s. This is a very good contemporary English version. Another good contemporary English version is the New King James Version (NKJV). Young's Literal Translation is as close to the original as one can get, translated by Robert Young in AD 1898.

124. Birnbaum, *A Book of Jewish Concepts*, 630.

125. Blenkinsopp, *Treasures Old and New*, 1.

126. Nursi's stand point on this is Qur'an, 2:79: So woe to those who write the "scripture" with their own hands, then say, "This is from Allāh," in order to exchange it for a small price. Woe to them for what their hands have written and woe to them for what they earn.

127. In *The Words*, Nursi writes: "Indeed, the All-Wise Qur'an mentions through the tongue of one whom everyone agreed was both unlettered and trustworthy the important events and significant facts concerning the prophets from the time of Adam till

Challenges to the Qur'an

Since its very first revelation, the Qur'an has always fascinated believers and disbelievers alike. The Arabic-speaking people, who acknowledge the eloquence of the Qur'an better than anyone else, have so far failed to take up the Qur'an's challenge, which is declared in *Sūrat al-Baqarah* (The Cow):

> And if you are in doubt about what We have sent down upon Our Servant [Muḥammad], then produce a surah the like thereof and call upon your witnesses other than Allāh, if you should be truthful."[128]

So far, the Qur'an has not been imitated nor have its contents been disproved successfully.

However, there are several rejectionist arguments attempting to refute Prophet Muḥammad and the Qur'an's authenticity from a historical point of view. Wagner encapsulates these as follows:

> Polytheistic Arabs from Arabia began to assert themselves in southern Palestine in the late 630s and through 640s, slowly taking control of Palestine, Syria and Egypt by 643. During the period 643–680, under Damascus-based Mu'awiyyah, coins were struck that reflect an indeterminate monotheism that could fit Jews, Christians and other monotheists. The first coins mentioning Muḥammad appear in 691. . . . By 720–750 biographies of the "traditional" Muḥammad appear. The first mention of "Book of Allah" appears in 752. Therefore, "Muḥammad is not a historical figure, and his biography is the product the 2nd century A.H. Muḥammad entered the official religion only ca. 71/690. The Qur'an is a late compilation; it was not canonized until the end of the 2nd century A.H, or perhaps early in the 3rd century. And Islam grew out of the need for Arab rulers to stabilize their new state. Later storytellers developed the traditions about Muḥammad the merchant from Mecca, using the name of a desert prophet named Mahmet who was linked to a Jewish-based Abrahamic messianic-apocalyptic monotheism.[129]

the Era of Bliss (i.e., the time of the Prophet Muḥammad), in a way which, confirmed by scriptures like the Torah and the Bible, tells of them with the greatest power and seriousness. It concurs with the points on which the former Books were agreed, and decides between them on the points over which they differed, pointing out the truth of the matter." See Nursi, *The Words*, 181.

128. Qur'an, 2:23.

129. Wagner, *Opening the Qur'an*, 426–27.

Cook and Crone attempt to refute the Qur'an on the basis of what they claim is a lack of archaeological evidence.[130] Wansbrough argues that the current body of the Qur'an came into existence long after the traditional account says it was revealed.[131] Cook and Crone claim that entire story of Muḥammad and the Qur'an is made up from Jewish tales. They argue that the Hagerens were disappointed by being rebuffed by the Jews and, after a period of positive relations with the Christians, decided to combine their religion of Abraham and Moses' Pentateuch with a version of Christian messianism–apocalypticism (minus Christology) to elaborate a full-scale religion of Abraham.[132] In the scenario they construct, Crone and Cook point out the geographical and personal parallels between Islam and Judaism. They explain that Muḥammad was a construction of the Hagerens to replace Moses, and that the Qur'an was the new and superior Pentateuch-Gospel that gave theological credibility to the new Arab state. Mecca was to replace Jerusalem, the Ka'bah became the Ismaelized Mount Moriah-Temple, Mount Hira was the new Sinai, *Jāhiliyyah* was the period of Egyptian bondage, the *Hijrah* was Exodus, the Medinan period was the shaping of the community in the wilderness, and the return to Mecca was the entry to the Promised Land.[133]

Nursi would have argued against this scenario by stating that none of these points actually refutes his argument that the Qur'an's is a miracle. This is simply a hypothetical reconstruction of the historical facts of Islam, Muḥammad and the Qur'an in parallel with the prior monotheistic religions. Whereas what Nursi demonstrates is the solid and testable qualities of the Qur'an.

Both Salman Rushdie and Taslima Nasrin follow a similar method to Cook and Crone's in order to disparage the Qur'an and Muḥammad. In *The Satanic Verses*,[134] a book listed as a fiction, Rushdie tells a story of a prophet, Mahound, establishing a new religion in *Jāhilī*. Rushdie tells the reader how Mahound's secretary, Salman, makes up verses none of which is noticed by Mahound. He also gives details of Mahound's despicable way of life and his sexuality. Again, Nursi would have argued that neither Rushdie's *Satanic Verses* nor Nasrin's views on Muḥammad and the Qur'an makes a credible theological or philosophical case against his argument.

130. Crone and Cook, *Hagarism*, 12–17.

131. John Wansbrough was not mainly interested in proving or disproving the authenticity of the Qur'an. He was mainly interested in how the Qur'an as a scripture emerged. See Wansbrough, *Quranic Studies*, xv.

132. Crone and Cook, *Hagarism*, 12–17.

133. Ibid., 3.

134. See Rushdie, *The Satanic Verses*.

Conclusion

This chapter has found out that Nursi takes the argument from miracles to a whole new level. Rather than following the classical argument that there is a Divine Scripture and hence there is Divinity, he goes to great lengths to convince his readers that the Qur'an ought to be a Divine Revelation owing to its miraculous properties such as eloquence, comprehensiveness, reporting the unseen, fluency, style, summarization, etc. He presents a list of testable characteristics of the Qur'an, which he believes furnish evidence of its divine origin. Reporting the unseen is perhaps the best testable aspect of the Qur'an. For Nursi, the skeptics ought to take all the news of the unseen mentioned in the Qur'an and crosscheck in the light of recorded history. This is clearly the first and the easiest way to refute the Qur'an should it be refutable. Nursi insists that there is no contradiction in the content of the Qur'an to raise suspicion about its divine origin. In addition to this, the fact that its verses almost always rhyme with each other can be always checked and confirmed. This, Nursi claims, is miracle itself since it is almost impossible to maintain a poetic writing without losing the consistency and integrity of a voluminous text.

The unique style of the Qur'an, for Nursi, is another miraculous aspect of it. It sounds like a poem, but is not poetry. It tells us very accurately about past events, but it is not a history book. It tells us about scientific facts, but it is not a science book. It reports the unseen future, but it is not a soothsaying book. It is very easy to the eyes and ears, but it is not a simple book. All these things, Nursi believes, could only be due to its divine origins. Therefore, Nursi concludes, miracles prove the existence of God; since the Qur'an is a miracle it is the evidence of the existence of God, who revealed this Book to his messenger, Muḥammad.

6

Morality and Conscience

Introduction

The moral argument is a small but possibly very powerful argument to prove the existence of God. Traces of this argument can be seen as early as in ancient Greek philosophy, in particular in the dilemma explored in Plato's *Euthyphro*, which we shall be examining in this chapter in greater detail. The moral arguments for the existence of God have been embraced by many theists, such as John Locke, John Hick, and Said Nursi. Nursi's version focuses mainly on conscience (*wijdān*) and human primordial nature (*fiṭrah*). William Lane Craig formulates this argument in a more systematic fashion in his debates with atheists.[1] There are some lively exchanges between the theist theologian William L. Craig and the evolutionary biologist Richard Dawkins which are worth noting in this chapter.

The focal point of this chapter is Nursi's approach to morality and conscience as proof of a Deity, and his response to atheistic arguments such as those concerning the problem of evil, the problem of Hell, the problem of free will, and the omnipotence paradox.

Popular Line of Thought

The argument from morality as a proof for a Deity comes in several different versions. The root of the current version in modern philosophy can arguably be attributed to Kant. Kant rejects all three previously mentioned

1. See God Debate II: Harris vs Craig (2011). Notre Dame College of Arts and Letters: The Henkels Lecturer Series, Center for Philosophy of Religion and Institute for Scholarship in the Liberal Arts.

arguments (that is, the cosmological argument, the ontological argument and the teleological argument). He rejects the cosmological argument since it is purely based on an indeterminate experience.[2] The ontological argument, according to Kant, is invalid because it is abstracted from all experience, and argues a *priori* from mere concepts.[3] And he rejects the teleological argument, since he believes that it rest upon the ontological argument which he thinks is already invalid.[4] However, Kant observes that it is a fact that people in all ages and at all times have always had a need to believe in a god. Shifting slightly into psychology from philosophy, he drew up a new argument for the existence of a god. This is rather a postulate than a proof. According to Kant, since God is a transcendent entity, his existence cannot be proven by pure or theoretical reasoning. Therefore, he removes the concept of God and religion in general from theoretical reason and places it in a new ground. He calls this new field the "ground of practical and moral reason."[5] He explains that people work towards their happiness in this life. This may be achieved by getting as close as possible to what he calls the *summum bonum* (the highest good). Now, there is a need for a Supreme Being with *intelligence* and *will*, who holds all the qualities and attributes of *summum bonum*, and it is He who sets the standards of the *summum bonum*.[6] In his article "*The Existence of God as a Postulate of Practical Reason*," Kant concludes:

> . . . therefore the supreme cause of nature, which must be presupposed as a condition of the *summum bonum*, is a being which is the cause of nature by *intelligence* and *will*, consequently its author, that is God.[7]

This claim clearly makes Kant a deist; since he accepts the necessity of the existence of a Supreme Lawgiver from whom morality and happiness could be obtained.

One of the most prominent modern advocates of the moral argument, William Lane Craig, formulates the argument as follows:

2. Kant, *Critique of Practical Reason*, 493.
3. Ibid., 569.
4. Ibid., 615.
5. Ibid., 117.
6. Ibid., 580.
7. Ibid.

> If God does not exist, objective moral values and duties do not exist. Since objective moral values and duties do exist, therefore God exists.[8]

According to Craig, this is a simple, straightforward proof of the God's existence. The two premises of Craig's argument could not be rejected even by evolutionist atheists. The postulate of the existence of moral values and duties is widely accepted by almost everybody. Atheists generally argue that there have to be moral values and duties to control our lives, but that morality does not require a moral lawgiver. They claim that one can be an atheist, yet hold high moral values.[9] The problem here, it is argued, is that moral values without the Highest Law Giver become subjective, that is, they differ from people to people and from society to society.[10] However, the moral values that originated from God are objective: hence they do not change in time or place. The key concept here is the "objective/subjective" distinction. Atheists do not reject moral values and obligations—they simply claim that they exist according to the opinion of an individual. Therefore, the moral values of an atheist are always "subjective." On this basis, an atheist should not confront a burglar who breaks into his house and steals his possessions since stealing is not wrong for the burglar. This simple scenario arguably creates a dilemma for any atheist. Some theists would claim that if there is no God, there is no objective right or wrong.[11] Therefore, an atheist cannot judge anyone on the basis of any wrongdoing. Richard Dawkins has faced a similar dilemma recently. When the Enron executive Jeff Skilling claimed that Dawkins' *The Selfish Gene* is his favorite book since it advocates evolutionist atheism, which claims that all people are animals and that there is no right or wrong, just pitiless indifference, in order to justify his action, Dawkins got furious.[12] Craig believes that although Dawkins denies

8. For Craig's works, see his website at http://www.reasonablefaith.org.

9. Harris, *The Moral Landscape*. And Sam Harris, "Ten Myths and Ten Truths about Atheism" at http://www.samharris.org/site/full_text/10-myths-and-10-truths-about-atheism1, last accessed on 14 December 2013

10. For instance, marriage is regarded as a sacred union between men and women in most societies. However, in some Arctic communities, visitors are encouraged to have intercourse with the host women to bear children with what they believe to be "fresh blood."

11. Craig holds this position in almost all his speeches and debates with atheists. For instance, see Craig, Flew, and Wallace, *Does God Exist?* 11.

12. For the full report and analysis of former Enron CEO Jeff Skilling's defense, see Eric Michael Johnson review in the 24 September 2009 issue of *Seed* magazine at http://www.emory.edu/LIVING_LINKS/empathy/Reviewfiles/Seed.html

the existence of God, he is regularly in conflict with himself since he always tries to hold the higher moral ground.[13]

Perhaps the moral argument is the hardest to refute for an atheist. Similarly, to Dawkins, Everitt seems to struggle handling this argument. The theist position on morality is that God is the creator of human beings; therefore, we humans owe him special duties. These duties are formulated by religions and display similar characteristics, such as worship, praying, fasting, giving to charity, etc. God is the life-giver and the maintainer of the universe. Life is the greatest gift that God gives us. Therefore, it is our duty to return his favor. Everitt makes an attempt to refute this theist position. In *The non-existence of God*, he writes:

> . . . the very idea of life being a gift is incoherent. If A is to make a gift to B, then both A and B must exist. So if the gift is meant to be the gift of life, to whom is the gift made? Either we exist already, in which case we already have what the gift is supposed to give us; or we do not yet exist, in which case there is no recipient for the alleged gift. Either way, the thought that life is a gift makes no sense.[14]

Nursi would have argued against Everitt's claim, since he does not believe in creation *ex nihilo* as Everitt implies. Nursi argues that man existed in God's knowledge.[15] This argument of Everitt's is very poor, even for an ordinary intelligence. We did not exist physically at all until our parents came together and started the parental biological process. The apparent cause of our coming into existence is our parents. But they are just the cause, not the creator. In other words, the Creator willed our existence and by means of our parents He granted us the gift of existence. One can make a promise of a gift to an unborn child. Similarly, God can obviously make a promise of a gift to his not-yet-come-into-existence subject, and this gift could easily be the gift of life and health.

Everitt also claims that if such a God exists, He deserves resentment rather than gratitude considering the existence of pain and the sufferings inflicted on his creatures.[16] This argument of Everitt's is generally recognized in philosophy as the Problem of Evil, which is the focus later in this chapter, where the Nursian approach is discussed.

13. See Craig's lectures at http://www.reasonablefaith.org

14. See Everitt, *The Non-Existence of God*, 130.

15. Nursi explains this around the concepts of *imām-ı mubīn* (the clear record) and *kitāb-ı mubīn* (the clear book) and *lavh-ı mahv wa isbāt* (the Tablet of Appearance and Dissolution) in Nursi, *The Letters*, 363–64.

16. Everitt, *The Non-Existence of God*, 130.

Again, perhaps we should answer the best argument of secular intelligence with Nursi's point of view.[17] Clearly, from a Nursian perspective, what is missing from secular minds of such as Everitt's, Flew's, and Dawkins' is the fact that the cosmos has an unseen component, which ontologically precedes the phenomenal world (i.e., the realm of existence before us). The secular minds simply start their analysis from the birth, or at best from the parental union. The Islamic position on this matter is as follows. God[18] created souls and asked them "Am I not your Lord?," They all confirmed him being their Lord.[19] Since that moment, God gave them the gift of physical existence in this world. In this sense, Islamic thought concerning this particular aspect of morality is extremely compatible with the popular line of thought. Indeed, Muslims would argue that God created our souls, then our bodies with all their faculties, and sent us down to Earth. Therefore, we all owe him gratitude, which is following the moral values and duties He established in this world.

Kant's argument shows some parallels with those of Aquinas.' In the fourth of The Five Ways, Aquinas explains:

> There is a gradation to be found in things: some are better or worse than others. Predications of degree require reference to the "uttermost" case (e.g., a thing is said to be hotter according as it more nearly resembles that which is hottest). The maximum in any genus is the cause of all in that genus. Therefore there must also be something, which is to all beings the cause of their being, goodness, and every other perfection; and this we call God.[20]

Among the critics of the moral argument, Sigmund Freud stands out noticeably, since he is not a philosopher but a psychologist. Freud made

17. Nursi repeatedly mentions the reasons of man's creation in *Risale-i Nur*. He explains that this life of ours is the second of three phases of our existence. The first phase is the pre-Earth phase, which is the universe of the souls. This current phase is the second phase, where we wear our physical bodies and are subjected to a test, i.e., the test of obedience to God's orders and instructions given in the Holy Revelations through his Messengers. And the final phase of existence is the life in the Hereafter, where the souls will be either rewarded for their good practice in the world by means of Paradise or punished in Hell as a result of their bad behavior in the world. See *The Words*, at 44–48, 132–42, 241–46 and 315–16

18. Here God means the God of Islam, i.e., *Allāh*.

19. Qur'an, 7:171: And mention when your Lord took from the children of Adam—from their loins—their descendants and made them testify of themselves, saying to them, "Am I not your Lord?" They said, "Yes, we have testified." This—lest you should say on the day of Resurrection, "Indeed, we were of this unaware."

20. See Aquinas, *Summa Theologica*, 14.

an attempt to explain the source of inspiration of objective moral values. He claims that there is no need for a Deity to underpin Kantian morality. According to Freud, there are three parts of the human psyche. These are id, ego and super-ego. It is the third part, i.e., super-ego, which is the moral component of the psyche. Therefore, all moral decisions and judgements are made within the human psyche, not set by a Deity.[21] Daniel C. Dennett, like Freud, makes an attempt to explain consciousness, which is meant to be the source of morality. According to Dennett, consciousness is all about brain mechanics. It is the product of the random, algorithmic process of Darwinian natural selection.[22] Dennett goes to great length to explain consciousness in terms of how brain mechanics work.[23] Indeed, even the theists agree with Dennett's cognitive explanation; however, for theists, it is neither a satisfactory explanation nor a proof of the non-existence of God.

Human Conscience (*Wijdān-i Bashar*) as an Evidence to God's Existence

Similar to Aquinas's Five Ways, Nursi's argument for the existence of God is fourfold. The fourth way of demonstrating that there is a Creator and Sustainer of life and the universe, according to Nursi, is the argument from primordial nature (*fiṭrat-i zī shuʿūr*) or conscience (*wijdān*).[24] With regard to the issue of *fiṭrah* (human primordial nature), Nursi's claim is that in a more general sense, all living things have certain natural tendencies, which he calls *shariʿat-i fiṭriya*. For example, a seed tends to germinate and grow into a plant in order to give fruit. Wherever it falls, it seeks moisture and light and pushes hard to root into the ground. An egg has a natural tendency to incubate and hatch into a new life. Even non-living things have their natural tendencies, such as water expanding as it gets below zero at the expense of breaking its steel container. These natural events occur not as a result of intelligent thinking on the part of the plants, animals and matter. But, in Nursi's opinion, as part of the nature's laws and instincts stemming from the Lawgiver, the creator of the universe.[25]

Turning our attention from the universe to human, Nursi, like other Muslim scholars before him, explains that there are more than the

21. See Freud, *The Ego and the Id*, 51.

22. See Dennett, *Darwin's Dangerous Idea: Evolution and the Meanings of Life.*

23. Dennett dedicates an entire book to explain this. See Dennett, *Consciousness Explained.*

24. See Nursi, *Al-Mathnawi Al-Nuri*, 1368.

25. See Chapter 3: Nursi on the Design Argument.

commonly known five senses[26] in every person as well as many other living things. Shifting into human psychology, Nursi explains that the sixth sense is the sense of direction or orientation (*ḥiss-i sāiqah*) and the seventh is the sense of motivation or desire to do things (*ḥiss-i shāiqah*).[27] *Ḥiss-i sāiqah,* Nursi argues, almost always points us into the right direction. When we follow our instincts (i.e., our sense of direction), we are rarely disappointed. For example, our instincts tell us to help out someone in need even though there is no material reward. We all feel compassion in our heart when we see an injured animal or a crying child. This is due to what Nursi calls the sense of direction (*ḥiss-i sāiqah*), and the non-material reward of any positive behaviour as a result of this sense is what he calls sense of satisfaction or motivation (*ḥiss-i shāiqah*). These two senses, he claims, never lie and never guide us into any wrong.[28] It is clear for Nursi that these two senses are the source of all good behavior. In his *al-Mathnawī al-Nūriyah*, Nursi writes:

> . . . human instinct (*fiṭrah*) and human conscience (*wijdān*) are two essential truths without which mankind would turn into immoral, despicable creatures. However, the order and harmony in the universe rejects this possibility.[29]

Nursi, in line with mainstream theism, places God at the center of morality. For him, God is the source of all positive behavior and good conduct. Rejecting the existence and ever-present authority of the Creator would make the atheist a self-denier. His attitude would not actually change the fact that the universe and everything it contains are created, controlled, and maintained by Almighty God. Nursi describes the unbeliever as an ostrich.[30]

26. These five senses are: hearing, sight, touch, smell and taste.

27. See Nursi, *Al-Mathnawi Al-Nuri*, 1371. Some of the other subtle faculties Nursi mentions in *The Flashes* at 641 are conscience, nerves, emotions, intellect, desires, power of animal appetites, power of anger, heart, spirit, inner heart, sense of premonition, and various motive and appetitive powers.

28. One possible example of this physiological phenomenon is that of Oskar Schindler's act during the Nazi Holocaust in Austria. In a well-presented Hollywood production, the world has watched a German businessman setting up a fake establishment and employing Jewish prisoners in order to save their lives. Clearly, there was no material gain for Schindler in this act; on the contrary, he exposed himself to Nazi wrath and risked his own life. His instincts simply told him that letting innocent women and children getting killed is wrong. Nursi would have argued that Schindler's instincts (*ḥiss-i sāiqah*) directed him to an act of righteousness at the cost of risking his own life. The reward he got was personal satisfaction for doing what is instantly and naturally right, i.e., his sense of satisfaction (*ḥiss-i shāiqah*).

29. Nursi, *Al-Mathnawi Al-Nuri*, 1371.

30. Nursi, *The Rays*, 964.

The myth suggests that ostriches bury their heads in sand when faced a danger. Their poor intelligence actually makes them think that if they cannot see the enemy, the enemy cannot see them either.[31] Yet, Nursi argues this is not the case. Those who bury their heads in the sand, or close their eyes to the sun, do not make the sun non-existent; they simply turn their own world into darkness.[32]

Human psychology is such that even though the mind may reject the existence of a Deity, conscience never forgets his presence.[33] *Wijdān*, Nursi asserts, is where the visible universe and the unknown universe meet. In other words, *wijdān* is a tool to detect or feel what cannot be detected or felt by means of five common senses.

All previous arguments for the existence of God, discussed in this study, start off with intellect (*aql*). *Aql* is only one of the many tools that can help one attaining the knowledge of God. Some of the others, identified by Nursi, are *ḥads* (intuition), *ilhām* (inspiration), *mayalān* (tendency), *ishtiyāq* (desire), and *ashq-ı ilāhi* (divine love).

Table 1: Four Constituents of Conscience and Their Purpose

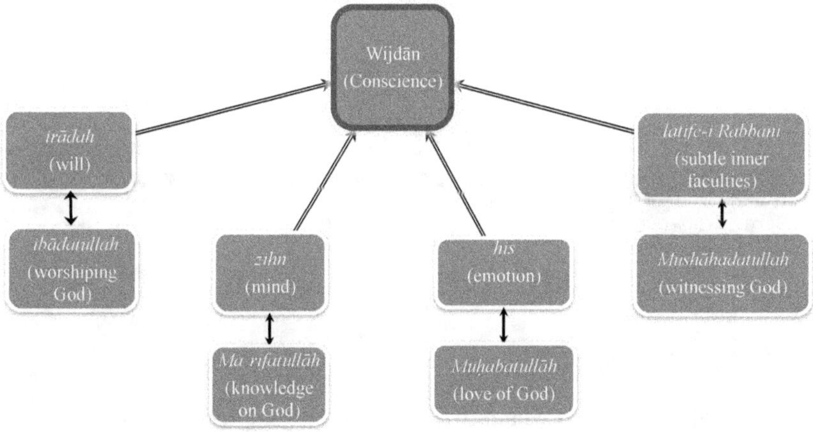

31. Here, it is important to clarify that, according to the American Ostrich Association, ostriches do not actually bury their heads. It is a complete myth. However, Nursi is more interested in making his point through the ostrich analogy, even though the behavior is not scientifically accurate.

32. Nursi, *The Rays*, 905.

33. Nursi, *Al-Mathnawi Al-Nuri*, 1371.

Nursi claims that not only *aql* but also *wijdān* could assist one into understanding that there is God. *Wijdān*, according to Nursi, has four elements. These are will (*irāda*), mind (*zihin*), emotion (*his*), and the subtle inner faculties (*latīfe-i Rabbaniye*). These four elements of *wijdān* cannot be justified within the norms of the material world. Furthermore, he maintains that *wijdān* has two windows that open into accepting God. These windows are *istinād* (stand point) and *istimdāt* (source of help). *Wijdān* and soul both attract (*jazba*) are attracted to (*injizāb*) as magnet and iron dusts. Every soul needs a point to lean against in order to be stay up and needs some sort of source for help since he or she is incapable of meeting all his or her personal, physical and spiritual needs. Nursi suggests that leaning point (*istinād*) and source of help (*istimdāt)* is God.

Table 2: Some ways to attain the knowledge on God based on *al-Mathnawī al-Nuriya*

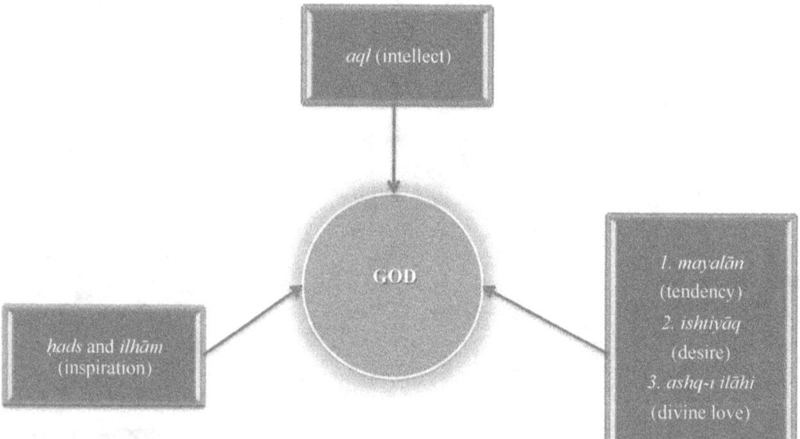

In an analogy presented in *The Words*,[34] Nursi tells the story of two servants. One was given ten pieces of gold, and the other was given 1,000 pieces of gold along with a note. The first servant goes to a shop and buys a dress with the ten pieces of gold. The second servant goes to the same shop and spends all 1,000 gold pieces on a similar dress, without reading the note given to him by his master. Obviously, Nursi remarks that the second

34. This particular analogy appears twice in *The Words*. See Nursi, *The Words*, 47 and 139.

servant, who received much more money than the first, was not meant to squander all this money on something really cheap. He should have read the note given to him by his master to understand what he was meant to spend the money on.

Nursi explains that the first ten pieces of gold are the tools, skills, and intelligence given to all animals. The one thousand gold pieces are the skills, tools and intelligence given to man. The little note represents the messages that God sent to humankind. Nursi concludes that human beings must read the note before spending the capital given to them. In other words, mankind is meant to read and understand the scriptures revealed through God's prophets.

Dilemma of the Secular Thought with Regard to Morality and Conscience

The atheist position so far has always been concerned with accepting or not accepting a Deity. Atheists such as Flew, Everitt, and Mackie comfortably make their case against theistic arguments, sometimes on philosophical, sometimes on logical, and sometimes on scientific grounds. Their denial does not put them in a very awkward position. However, the moral argument has been formulated in such a fashion that deniers of it often find themselves in a completely unjustified position.

Sartre claims that the existence of God is not essential to conduct good behavior. In *Existentialism and Humanism*, he writes, "It is nowhere written that 'the good' exists, that one must be honest, or must not lie"[35]

To Sartre and to many atheists, the way out of this moral dilemma seems to be the refuge of existentialist humanism. Existentialism, which is embraced both by atheists like Sartre himself and by devout religious theists like Kierkegaard, became more popular after World War II.[36] The upshot of Sartre's philosophy is that everyone is responsible for his or her own life. You choose where you want to be. Freedom and personal choice are the essence of Sartre's philosophy. Here comes the problem of subjectivity. The theist position on morality is that all moral laws come only from the Highest Lawgiver (i.e., God). This makes the set of duties and obligations "objective." However, atheists, it is argued, can only rely on their own subjective judgment, which results in many different sets of moral values.[37]

35. Sartre, *Existentialism and Humanism*, 33–34.

36. For the religious existentialism, see Stewart, *Kierkegaard and Existentialism*.

37. See Craig, Flew, and Wallace, *Does God Exist?*

For example, one individual might see his happiness in the destruction of what he sees as "problem people," as in the case of Nazi Germany. Or, as in the context of Stalin's USSR, the communist regime is the ultimate authority which all citizens have to respect and fear. The problem of subjectivity creates happiness for a small group of people at the expense of the sufferings of much larger groups. It is well-documented that Stalin confiscated the land and property of millions of people in order to create common happiness for the entire country, a move which did not necessarily achieve its objective. The core problem was that the losers did not accept the ruling Communist Party as the source of moral authority. This resulted in resistance and consequent bloodshed. The recent history of the world is full of similar horror stories. In a BBC documentary entitled *The Gathering*, a rabbi tells how the Ten Commandments were reversed during the Holocaust: "You shall murder," "You shall steal," "You shall commit adultery."[38]

For the theist, the strength of his or her argument derives from the fact that the source of all moral codes is God. Hence they are objective and universal.

It is argued that the systems, which were based on Marxism (i.e., subjective moral values and duties), have all failed. Citizens were expected to fear the police and follow the laws. Nursi explains that the state then has to put one policeman in order to control one individual. He claims that believing in God can do better than a thousand policemen. In *The Rays*, Nursi writes:

> So I say: Religion does not consist only of belief; its second half is righteous action. Is fear of imprisonment or being seen by a government detective sufficient to deter those who commit numerous grievous sins which poison society, like murder, adultery, theft, gambling, and drinking. If that was so, there would have to be a policeman or detective stationed permanently in every house, or at everyone's side even, so that obdurate souls would restrain themselves from those filthy acts. Whereas, in respect of good deeds and belief, the *Risale-i Nur* places a permanent immaterial "prohibitor" next to everyone. It easily saves them from bad deeds by recalling the prison of Hell and Divine wrath.[39]

Theists would argue that, where there is a high level of belief, there is less crime. Aymaz reported that during his travels in Sudan, he came across

38. The holocaust documentary is accessible through BBC archive at: http://www.bbc.co.uk/archive/holocaust/5103.shtml

39. Nursi, *The Rays*, 994.

extremely poor Christian communities where, despite extreme poverty, there was absolutely no theft as it was against the community's religious belief.[40] However, the claim is quickly rejected by the atheist camp. In *Breaking The Spell*, Dennett gives some US statistics from which it is evident that the US prison population proportionally represents the public faith profile.[41] This, according to Dennett, disproves the argument that religion is a source of good behavior.

Atheists' Challenge to Nursi

The main conflict between the atheist and the theist as regards morality is that both parties claim that they have better morality as a result of their faith. The theist claims that God, the ultimate moral authority, is the moral compass for humanity. The atheist claims that there is no need for a moral compass (i.e., God or religion). Morality is not God-given but inherent in human beings.[42] In *God is Not Great*, Hitchens, a prominent atheist, asked how evil behavior such as suicide bombings and circumcision (or FGM) could be reconciled with an all-good, all-loving and compassionate God. Hitchens argues, and this is the most common atheist challenge to the theist, that either what the theist calls God is a made-up concept or that He is not good but evil Himself. The question can be narrowed down to this: "Which has done more evil—atheism or religion?"

Nursi counters by telling us that God created the good and the apparent evil.[43] He then left humans to choose between them. Choosing the good might be hard, but would result in eternal happiness in Paradise. On the contrary, doing evil is easy, but would result in punishment in Hell.[44]

The theists claim that the grim results of atheist regimes in terms of the pain and suffering of innocent human beings imply that the absence of God means no morality. The atheists tell us about the crimes committed against humanity by so-called religious people to imply that religion is evil itself. It has been a long-standing debate and therefore it is worth a closer examination.

First of all, theists may argue that not all religious people behave according to their religion. For example, while Stalin was an atheist but a

40. Abdullah Aymaz, Interview. Frankfurt. January 11, 2011.

41. See Dennett, *Breaking the Spell: Religion as a Natural Phenomenon*, 279.

42. Sharpton, A. vs. Hitchens, C. debate on Morality, (7/5/2007), New York Public Library, FORA.tv

43. See Chapter 6 for The Problem of Evil

44. Nursi, *The Letters*, 365.

tyrannical dictator with the blood of millions on his hands, so was Saddam Hussein, who was supposed to be a religious person. There are many more examples of these types of religion versus non-religion atrocities. Nursi indicates that the conducting of the evil act is evil, rather than the act itself.[45] It is the person who is responsible for his own behavior. Secondly, what Hitchens highlights in his argument is not necessarily sourced from religion. For example, suicide bombings were first used by Dutch soldiers in 1661 in a war in Taiwan to avoid capture. The Prussian soldier Karl Klinke blew himself up in order to open a hole in Danish fortifications in 1864. Kamikaze dives were very common kinds of suicide mission among Japanese pilots in World War II. Recently, Tamil Tigers, Hamas, the PKK and the militia in Iraq used this method of warfare.[46] This act of desperation has been implemented by many as a last resort. It is remarkable to see that there is a wide range of diversity of faiths among these groups. For instance, Hamas is considered to be an Islamist group, whereas PKK holds a Marxist/Leninist ideology. So, here we see personal desperation rather than a mainstream religious teaching in action. It is also fair to note that some of these suicide bombers derive some of their motivations from religious leaders. However, speaking from the Muslim point of view, there is no hard evidence for the legitimacy of this type of suicide action from the two main sources of Islam, namely the Qur'an and the tradition of the Prophet Muḥammad (*sunnah*). So, few Muslim scholars authorize this kind of act, as opposed to the great majority who clearly condemn them.[47] Those who promotes suicide missions among Muslims, such as Zarein Ahmadzay,[48] base their argument on Qur'an 9:111, *Sūrat al-Tawbah* (The Repentance), which reads:

> Indeed, Allāh has purchased from the believers their lives and their properties in exchange for that they will have Paradise. They fight in the cause of Allāh, so they kill and are killed. It is a true promise binding upon him in the Torah and the Gospel and the Qur'ān. And who is truer to his covenant than Allāh? So rejoice in your transaction which you have contracted. And it is that which is the great attainment.[49]

45. Ibid.

46. Greenberger, *Suicide Bombers*, 4–12.

47. One example of a modern Muslim scholar who considers suicide attacks a legitimate means of defense is Al-Qaradawi. See Abdelhadi, M. (2004), *BBC World News Profile of Sheikh Yusuf Qaradawi*. BBC News. http://news.bbc.co.uk/1/hi/uk/3874893.stm

48. The terrorist who plotted a suicide attack on the New York subway. See the *New York Times*, 23 April 2010 at http://www.nypost.com/p/news/local/zarein_ahmedzay_statement_when_he_ECm9fYgzMCuq9JTvBApBjN

49. Qur'an, 9:111.

Opposing scholars, such as Fethullah Gülen, on the other hand, raise their argument from Qur'an 2:195, *Sūrat al-Baqarah* (The Cow):

> And spend in the way of Allāh and do not throw [yourselves] with your [own] hands into destruction [by refraining]. And do good; indeed, Allāh loves the doers of good.[50]

It is clear from these two positions that the holy texts are open to interpretation. Socio- political situations can easily affect the outcome of these interpretations. Gülen, who is among the second group of scholars, writes, "religion does not approve of the killing of people in order to attain a goal."[51] Therefore, it is incorrect to conclude, as Hitchens does, that religion is the source of evil on the basis of a judgment of the acts of certain groups of people. Perhaps one needs to explore the correct ways of understanding Holy Scripture, and thereby understand the true meaning of it.

The second most common challenge to the theist concerns the act of circumcision. Here, Jews, Muslims, and some Orthodox Churches in Africa are targeted equally, as it is religiously obligatory to carry out male circumcision. Hitchens portrays this ritual as a cruelty to children. He also claims that the act of circumcision is in conflict with the design argument, since it implies imperfection in creation.[52] Theists would argue that the imperfection part of his argument is fairly simple to refute. Humans instinctively work towards their personal comfort. For example, we dress up in winter to be protected from cold, or wear a hat in summer to avoid the damaging effects of the sunlight. We trim our hair, cut our nails or wash frequently to stay healthy. The act of circumcision is similar to one of the practices just mentioned. Although it is not ordered anywhere in the Qur'an, the Prophet Muḥammad carried out circumcision and advised his followers to do the same. Therefore, the word *sunnah* (prophet Muḥammad's tradition) is widely used in the Islamic world to describe circumcision. It is essentially owing to its medical benefits that circumcision has been carried out all around the world for centuries. There is evidence of ancient Egyptians carrying out circumcision not on religious but on health grounds. It is a well-known medical fact that circumcision helps to reduce many diseases, including urinary tract infection[53] and HIV.[54] Hitchens' argument is therefore invalid on the

50. Qur'an, 2:195.

51. Gülen, *Terror and Suicide Attacks*, 5.

52. Sharpton vs. Hitchens debate on Morality, (7/5/2007), New York Public Library, FORA.tv

53. Huang, Craig J. "Problems of the Foreskin and Glans Penis" (abstract). *Clinical Pediatric Emergency Medicine* 10.1 (2009) 56–59.

54. Krieger, "Male Circumcision and HIV Infection Risk," *World Journal of Urology*

grounds that not every painful act is immoral, provided that there are benefits entailed. Bathing babies is usually uncomfortable for them. However, it is medically advised by professionals to bathe babies to avoid hygiene-related diseases. The theist could then argue that Hitchens needs to argue against the bathing of babies, as this causes discomfort for them. Nursi sets out a general rule of judgment in similar situations. He writes:

> The lesser evil is acceptable for the greater good. If an evil which will lead to a greater good is abandoned so that a lesser evil should not be, a greater evil will then have been perpetrated.[55]

On the issue of female genital mutilation (FGM), Hitchens seems to be either confused or ill-informed. This is mainly a cultural practice, not the obligation of any monotheistic religion. Hence, it is not considered in this study.

Resurrection and Life After Death (*Ḥashr*)

Morality, with or without God, requires justice. If justice is not accomplished, injustice and consequent suffering become rampant. A torturer in a USSR prison famously told his political prisoner that he would get away with whatever he might do to him since he was not answerable to anyone in this life, and there is no afterlife anyway. Ivan Fyodorovitch in Dostoyevsky's *The Brothers Karamazov* implies that "if there is no God, everything is permitted."[56]

Nursi places great importance on the concept of resurrection (*ḥashr*), as it is one of the major requirements of a God who, by definition, holds the ultimate best qualities, one of which is being just. He argues that resurrection after life is the only logical explanation of the apparent injustice in life. He argues that a just God ought to provide his subjects with justice. Since this justice is not apparent here in this life, Nursi claims that it is left to the

---

(2011).

55. Nursi, *The Letters*, 365.

56. The actual quote is: "Ivan Fyodorovich added in parenthesis that the whole natural law lies in that faith, and that if you were to destroy in mankind the belief in immortality, not only love but every living force maintaining the life of the world would at once be dried up. Moreover, nothing then would be immoral, everything would be lawful, even cannibalism. That's not all. He ended by asserting that for every individual, like ourselves, who does not believe in God or immortality, the moral law of nature must immediately be changed into the exact contrary of the former religious law, and that egoism, even to crime, must become not only lawful but even recognized as the inevitable, the most rational, even honorable outcome of his position." See Dostoyevsky and Garnett, *The Brothers Karamazov*, 134–35.

Hereafter. In his works, Nursi refers to God as the Absolute Just (*ʿĀdil-i Muṭlaq*), and it is in his nature to give justice to his subjects eventually. The atheist point of view highlights the unfairness and lack of justice in this life to demean God. Either there is no God, or He is not capable of providing justice. A few popular examples of this are people with certain disabilities, apparent cruelty in the animal kingdom, and the unfair treatment of innocent people such as the victims of the Holocaust or of Pol Pot.

Nursi believes that a logical demonstration of the existence of and necessity for a life after death (i.e., resurrection) decisively proves God's existence and "breaks the backbone of atheism."[57]

The argument, where Nursi sets off to prove the logical necessity of resurrection (*ḥashr*) and life after death (*akhirah*), is based on a fairly easy-to-understand analogy via which he prefers to get his message across throughout the *Risale-i Nur*.[58] Two travelers, one righteous and one a skeptic, reach a country with perfect order. They witness an apparent freedom and lack of instant punishment for any offence committed in that country. Then the philosophical dialogue begins between these two imaginary characters. In this dialogue, the righteous man represents the theist/religious point of view (i.e., Nursi's own) and the skeptic represents the atheist point of view:

The atheist: There are a lot of goods and property lying about, there does not seem to be anyone guarding them. So I shall help myself with whatever I fancy.

The theist: I do not think all this wonderfully made country and its contents are unsupervised. There must be a Ruler and an Owner of all this property.

The atheist: I cannot see a Ruler; therefore I do not believe his existence. Prove me of his existence.

Nursi, then, speaks to the heart (conscience) and mind (intelligence) of his readers, and presents his case in a very logical fashion.

First: The order and design requires an order-giver and a designer. There is no possibility of it coming into existence as result of random change. Fred Hoyle's Boeing 747 example (also known as "the junk yard tornado") is a well-known one. Asprin is a common popular medicine which consists of a certain percentage of certain chemical, organic and synthetic substances. If someone were to claim that Aspirin came into existence as a result of some random result of a maverick wind which spilt these chemicals and

57. Şahiner, *Bilinmeyen Taraflariyla Bediüzzaman Said Nursi: Kronolojik Hayati*, 298–99.

58. Despite its massive philosophical worth, Nursi initially wrote this work in Barla, a small village, for the local people, who did not have a high level of education in 1926.

mixed them in exact proportions, this would be completely unfeasible to any intelligent mind, let alone the exact conditions (i.e., temperature, pressure and light) happening by chance. Therefore, this perfect universe is the work of God who, by definition, has to be just. The lack of instant justice in this life could only imply that the Lord of the universe postpones it to a further time and place. That is *akhirah* (life after death).

Second: The care and compassion evident in this world imply a Carer and the Compassionate. The example given of this is the excellent maintenance and care of all living things in this world. The Maker of this universe is compassionate, generous, and has great dignity. All these qualities require the rewarding of the righteous and the punishment of wrongdoers. Since this does not seem to happen here, it means it will happen later elsewhere, that is, on the Day of Judgement and in the Hereafter.

Third: All the wealth of this Earth is a small sample of the riches of its Owner. He displays some of them here in this world, retaining the originals elsewhere. Those who follow his moral codes in this life ought to be rewarded, and those who show disregard for his moral orders ought to be punished. This could only be achieved by resurrection. His subjects will be rewarded or punished according to their conduct in this world.

Fourth: Justice requires pre-notifications of rules and laws. When entering a new country, travelers are informed about lawful and unlawful acts. For example, we are well-informed beforehand about the country's legal requirements regarding speed limits, use of drugs and liquor, etc. They come either in the form of a written document, or a person explaining them. Similarly, the laws of this life are given to mankind in the form of holy scriptures and explained by the prophets. The Lord of the Universe is fair and would not punish anyone without prior notification. Therefore, the existence of the Books, i.e., the Gospels, the Torah, and the Qur'an, and of the prophets, i.e., Moses, Jesus and Muḥammad, is the indication of a Deity, the Day of Judgment and the Hereafter.

In addition to these four points, Nursi presents one more piece of evidence from the Qur'an. *Sūrat al-Rūm* (The Romans), 30:50 reads:

> So observe the effects of the mercy of Allah—how He gives life to the earth after its lifelessness. Indeed, that [same one] will give life to the dead, and He is over all things competent.[59]

Therefore, Nursi concludes that even though there is no visible imminent justice in this life; all these arguments prove the existence of a Ruler

59. Qur'an, 30:50.

and the existence of a great court whereby the evildoers are to be judged and punished accordingly.

The Euthyphro Dilemma

Whenever the subject of God or morality is discussed, there is one issue which always sits at the heart of the debate, that is, Plato's Euthyphro dilemma. The gist of the problem is this: In *The Life of Socrates*, Plato tells us that Socrates' prosecution for not being pious. Socrates meets Euthyphro, who is at the porch of the King Archon prosecuting his father for killing a servant, who is also accused of a murder. Socrates asks Euthyphro, who poses as a moral expert: "Is what is pious loved by God because it is pious, or is it pious because it is loved?"[60] In other words, "Does God command the good because it is good by its own nature, or is it good because it is commanded by God?" This is one of the most popular arguments against the divine command theory, which holds that morality is essentially doing God's will.

In the field of modern philosophy and religion, there is a specific defense against this argument from the Christian point of view. However, I shall by pass these arguments and focus on Nursi's point of view on this issue. I deliberately avoid using the term "Islamic point of view," since this dilemma has not been addressed identically within Islam by *kalām* scholars. There is a clear conflict between the *Mu'tazila* way of interpretation and Nursi's own, which is essentially the mainstream Sunni view.[61] On the issue of what is good and why, the *Mu'tazila* school of thought says:

> Actions and things for which a person is responsible are either, of themselves and in regard to the hereafter, good, and because of that good they were commanded, or they are bad, and because they are bad they were prohibited. That means, from the point of view of reality and the hereafter, the good and bad in things is dependent on the things themselves, and the Divine command and prohibition follows this.[62]

This point of view is completely opposed by Nursi. In *The Words*, he writes:

> Almighty God orders a thing, and then it becomes good. He prohibits a thing, and then it becomes bad. That is, goodness becomes existent through command, and badness through

60. Plato, *Euthyphro*, 9A–11B

61. See Footnote 43 in Chapter 1 for The Schools of Thoughts in Islam.

62. Nursi, *The Words*, 113.

> prohibition. They look to the awareness of the one who performs the action, and are established according to that. And this good and bad is not in the apparent face and that which looks to this world, but in the face that looks to the hereafter.[63]

The crucial point in Nursi's argument is the fact that moral judgments of goodness and wickedness cannot be based on worldly criteria. In other words, what is good or bad can only be judged according to their results regarding the Hereafter. For example, Muslims, as well as the followers of some other religions, are enjoined to fast. The Islamic version of fasting is essentially abstaining from food, drink and sexual relations. The moral judgment on fasting is this: fasting is hard, since it causes extreme hunger and dehydration. There are some medical and social benefits in it. These worldly benefits are irrelevant. Fasting is good because it was ordered by God.

Another example is giving to charity. It is hard, because the act of giving to charity takes from one's wealth and reduces one's assets. There are worldly social and physiological benefits in giving to charity, but they are irrelevant. Giving to charity is good because it is ordered by God.

Farming pigs is easy and very profitable. They reproduce quickly and produce a lot of meat, which has worldly benefits in fighting poverty and famine. Despite these benefits, this act is bad, simply because it is prohibited by God. The same argument goes for intoxicating liquors. Ingesting alcohol might well help people to become cheerful. But drinking is bad simply because God willed so.

It is indeed true that secular minds might find it very hard to digest this type of interpretation. For them, people are mere machines; there is no God, no resurrection, no Hereafter, no morality.[64] If achieving a task requires certain tools, and one lacks any of them, one is destined to fail. Nursi believes since atheists reject the certain components of life and existence, they find it very difficult to understand basic moral issues, and get bogged down in a basic dilemma like the Euthyphro dilemma.

The Problem of Evil, Calamities and Tribulations

One of the paramount arguments of the atheists against the existence of God is the problem of evil. Beginning with Epicurus of the ancient Greece, John Stuart Mill, David Hume, Sam Harris, and almost every atheist claim

63. Ibid.

64. For instance see Dawkins, *The God Delusion*. In this book, evolutionary biologist Prof Richard Dawkins argues that man is not much different from animals.

that the existence of evil conflicts with the existence of God. Hence, if there is a God, evil should not exist. Alternatively, if there is evil, it means there is no God. This issue has been tackled by many natural theologians for centuries. Nursi's approach to this challenge is follows. Nursi declares that 'the creation of evil is not evil itself. Conducting evil actions is evil.'[65] What appears to be harsh and bad on the face of things might actually be beneficial and good in the end. Therefore, we have to look at the end-result to see the benefits of an action. For instance, war seems to be very negative and bad at first glance. In reality, wars are fought to avoid bigger troubles such as invasions, imprisonment or death. Lesser evil is acceptable for a greater good.[66] If a nation evades wars and does not defend itself in order to avoid a lesser evil, it will almost certainly end up facing a bigger evil of losing property, land, and freedom. Therefore, it is wrong to imply that war is a bad thing. It is essential to compare the current required action and the possible consequences of avoidance.

Another example Nursi gives is the surgical removal of necrotic body tissues. At first, cutting and removing tissues from body seems very unpleasant, and disturbing. But it is a medical fact that necrotic tissues have to be removed from the body in order to avoid further, bigger damage.[67] What initially seems to be evil is not evil after all.

Rain and fire are another example. They are beneficial overall and good for mankind. If someone does not take precautions before rain comes and receive harm from it, he cannot claim that rain is bad. Or, if he puts his hand in the fire and burns himself, this does not mean fire is evil. Probably, it is more accurate to conclude that rain or fire is bad for this particular individual on this particular occasion as a result of his wrong action.

Two aphorisms highlight Nursi's dismissal of the problem of evil. These are, "The creation of evil is not evil, the desire for or inclination towards evil, rather, is evil," and "The lesser evil is acceptable for the greater good."[68]

Having negated the argument, Nursi goes on to attract our attention to another benefit of the existence of evil. In physics, contrasting qualities give us measurement, for example hot and cold, fast and slow, heavy and light. Similarly, in physiology, happy and sad, optimist and pessimist, good and bad are all measured and understood by their opposites. In other word,

65. Nursi, *The Letters*, 365.

66. Ibid.

67. Necrosis is the death of body tissue. It occurs when there is not enough blood flowing to the tissue. Necrosis is not reversible. When substantial areas of tissue die owing to a lack of blood supply, the condition is called gangrene. Unless surgically removed, gangrene spreads to the other tissues.

68. Nursi, *The Letters*, 365.

if there were no bad, there would be no point of reference from which to measure good, and so on. Everything is known by its opposite. Life in this world, Nursi argues, is all about trial and examination. If there had been no competition brought about through the existence of evil, there would have been no difference between people. Evil people would have been equal to good people. Since the creation of evil points to greater, universal results, it is false to assume that its existence is bad.

Further to the problem of evil, Nursi also explains why people have no right to complain about the calamities and tribulations they face in life. Having established the existence and authority of God, Nursi seeks answers to these questions through the attributes of God. He reminds us that the sovereignty is his. He holds sway over his possessions as He wishes. For example, a skilled, rich tailor employs you as a model in return of a wage and the dress he makes. As part of the position you have, you are required to move around, stand up or sit down. The tailor wishes to make different applications in order to fashion the dress. Would you have a right to complain about this situation, considering the fact that you are a paid model? Similarly, Nursi reminds us that this life and body were given to us by the All-Glorious Maker without us paying anything for them. Therefore, He has got every right to manipulate his property in the way he wishes. Secondly, producing calamities and inflicting tribulations is the way by which God reveals his attributes.[69] For example, the name *al-Munʿim* (The Nourisher) requires hunger, *al-Fattāḥ* (The Opener) requires stress and depression, *al-Ghanī* (The Rich One) requires poverty, *al-Salām* (The Source of Peace) requires distress, *al-Walī* (The Protecting Friend) requires insecurity, and so on. This approach to the problem of calamity and tribulation is quite original to Western philosophy, but not to *kalām*.

The Problem of Hell

The theist standpoint on justice is that evildoers will be punished in Hell for their bad deeds here on earth. There is an almost parallel concept of Paradise and Hell in every monotheistic religion, with only slight differences. The fact is that anyone who believes in the existence of God also believes in the existence of the Hereafter, and consequently in Heaven and Hell.

The problem emerges from the fact that there is a God who is, by definition, omnipotent, omniscient and omnibenevolent, who possesses a place of eternal punishment. The omnibenevolent character of God clearly

69. See Appendix 2 for the 99 names and attributes of God in Islam.

contradicts the existence of Hell. How can someone be all-loving and punisher at the same time?

One of the most comprehensive studies on the problem of Hell was carried out by Jonathan Kvanvig. Kvanvig, a Christian theist, describes the Christian point of view on Hell, using the term "strong view of Hell." His strong view of Hell consists of four elements. These are:

1. The Anti-Universalism Thesis: Some persons are consigned to Hell;
2. The Existence Thesis: Hell is a place where people exist, if they are consigned there;
3. The No Escape Thesis: There is no possibility of leaving Hell and nothing one can do, change, or become in order to get out of Hell, once one is consigned there; and
4. The Retribution Thesis: The justification for Hell is retributive in nature, Hell being constituted to mete out punishment to those whose earthly lives and behavior warrant it.[70]

Since Western philosophy develops mainly around the dominant Western faith of Christianity, most atheist arguments are based on Kvanvig's Christian description of Hell. Although the concept of Hell exists among all monotheistic religions, there are certainly differences between the above-mentioned four aspects of Hell and the Islamic description of it.

The Qur'an mentions Hell in more than thirty different places.[71] Hell is used as an ultimate deterrent for evil. In *Sūrat Hūd*, God vows, "But the word of your Lord is to be fulfilled that, 'I will surely fill Hell with jinn and men all together.'"[72] There is a slight addition to the Sahih Translation in Yildirim's version, where he translates "fill Hell with *deserving* jinn and men . . . ."[73] Yildirim's translation is better in terms of showing the consistency of justice and Hell. God clearly promises to punish those who deserve Hell. The Qur'an threatens those who refuse to follow the divine instructions, thereby falling into sin. In terms of moral objectivity, the Islamic description of sin seems very feasible. There is not much room to object to the sins described in the Qur'an.[74] The chief of these sins is the associating of God with others (*shirk*). The Qur'an tells, in *Sūrat al-Mulk* (The Sovereignty) [67:6], of

70. Kvanvig, *The Problem of Hell*, 25.

71. On balance, the Qur'an mentions Heaven (Paradise) in more than seventy places, that is, twice the mentions of Hell. The Qur'an, therefore, seems to first encourage good deeds by showing the ultimate reward, and then threatens with the punishment.

72. Qur'an, 11:119.

73. See Yıldırım, *Kur'an-I Hakim Ve Meali*, 234.

74. See Appendix 6: Major Sins in Islam.

the destination of disbelievers (*mushrikūn*), "And for those who disbelieved in their Lord is the punishment of Hell, and wretched is the destination."[75]

Nursi argues that the existence of Hell does not contradict the benevolence of God. On the contrary: the non-existence of Hell or the ultimate court of justice is contradictory to the qualities of God.

The Justice ('Adālah)

The first Nursian argument for the necessity of Hell is on the grounds of justice and fairness. Nursi asks his readers to imagine a mini-civilized society where the system runs perfectly, there is no crime and, therefore, no system of punishment. A criminal comes into this particular community and commits some serious crimes, totally disregarding the rules and laws everyone else abides by. The governor of this community has two options following the arrest of this criminal. The first is that he acts with the utmost love and compassion, and thinks that punishment of this individual runs counter to his loving nature. He then releases this criminal back into the community. Is this act right? How about the victims of the crimes? This is not an ethical dilemma. To Nursi, the answer is fairly straightforward. It is the duty of the governor to fulfill justice, protect the rights of the righteous, and punish the criminals. The truth from this metaphor is that life on earth is governed by God, and it is his duty to look after his servants. He had to realize a place of punishment (i.e., Hell); even he did not have it in the first place.

The Deterrent

When people complain about the fear that Hell generates, Nursi tells what God intends with the creation of Hell.

> The Divine Mercy says to the fearful man: Come to me! Enter the door of repentance, then the existence of Hell will not frighten you, but make known completely the pleasures of Paradise, and avenge you and all creatures whose rights have been transgressed, and give you enjoyment.[76]

Therefore, God encourages people to use their intelligence to avoid committing wrong and to do righteous acts. The existence of Hell also promotes self-control. People fear the heavy hand of the Judicial System and stay

75. Qur'an, 67:6.

76. Nursi, *The Rays*, 965.

within what the law permits. We all know that if we exceed the speed limit we are penalized, or that if we steal we will be caught and sent to prison. Prison exists not principally for punishing people, but in order to encourage lawful behavior. Similarly, Hell does not exist principally for punishing wrongdoers; rather, it exists to help people stop committing unlawful acts.

Repentance (Tawbah)

According to Nursi, another aspect of Hell is the establishment of the position of men and God. The fear of Hell helps people to approach God and seek help and refuge. God is clearly more forgiving than punishing. God created men having the nature of committing sins. However, his ultimate purpose is to make them understand that He is most powerful and that they are most needy and humble. The Qur'an begins almost all its one hundred and fourteen verses with the name of Allah, who is *al-Raḥmān* (the most beneficent) and *al-Raḥīm* (the most compassionate), and it tells us repeatedly that God is most Forgiving (*al-Ghafūr*). All He wants is for people to think about and understand the meaning of life and the universe. *Sūrat Āli 'Imrān* (Family of Imran) reads, "Who remember Allāh while standing or sitting or lying on their sides and give thought to the creation of the heavens and the earth, saying, 'Our Lord, You did not create this aimlessly; exalted are You above such a thing; then protect us from the punishment of the Fire.'"[77]

The Contrast

Atheists argue that if God is all-loving, He should not punish anyone; on the contrary, He should place all his subjects in Paradise. According to Nursi, this argument is flawed. Every entity is measured against its opposite. In *The Rays*, Nursi explains:

> . . . the confrontation and interpenetration of good and evil in the universe, and pain and pleasure, light and darkness, heat and cold, beauty and ugliness, and guidance and misguidance are for a vast instance of wisdom. For if there was no evil, good would not be known. If there were no pain, pleasure would not be understood. Light without darkness would lack all importance. The degrees of heat are realized through cold. Through ugliness, a single instance of beauty becomes a thousand in-stances, and thousands of varying degrees of beauty come into existence. If

77. Qur'an, 3:191.

> there were no Hell, many of the pleasures of Paradise would remain concealed. By analogy with these, in one respect everything may be known through its opposite and a single truth produce numerous shoots and become numerous truths.[78]

In short, according to Nursi, the existence of Hell is not only fair but also essential to reveal the true beauty of Paradise, the ultimate reward of good morality.

In the light of the above arguments, Nursi's justification of the existence of Hell is reasonably in line with Kvanvig's fourth aspect of the strong view of Hell.[79] Retribution is the essential requirement of justice. God does not send people to Hell; instead, people choose to go there. The Qur'an explains the position of God on the Day of Judgement (*yawm al qiyāmah*). It is similar to the position of a judge sitting in a courthouse. The accused are brought in front of him, and he examines the evidence. If the evidence proves the criminality, he sends them to prison. Otherwise, he just releases them. In order to fulfill the justice He promised, God tells sinners "But stand apart today, you criminals,"[80] and to the righteous He says: "Peace be upon you; you have become pure; so enter it to abide eternally therein . . . ."[81]

The third element of Kvanvig's description[82] is also in line with Nursi's views. Our limited time of life on earth earns people either an eternal, pleasurable stay in Paradise or suffering in Hell. There is only one condition of eternal punishment, which is disbelief of God (*shirk*). The Islamic position on this issue is that if people die in belief with a great many sins, they are first sent to Hell to pay for their sins. Then, they will be sent to Paradise eventually. In *Sūrat al-Baqara* (The Cow), the Qur'an tells us: "Yes, whoever earns evil and his sin has encompassed him—those are the companions of the Fire; they will abide therein eternally. But they who believe and do righteous deeds—those are the companions of Paradise; they will abide therein eternally."[83]

Here, the dilemma of justice emerges. How can boundless torment in an endless Hell in return for limited sins in a limited life be justice?[84] An av-

78. Nursi, *The Rays*, 967.

79. 4. The Retribution Thesis: The justification for Hell is retributive in nature, Hell being constituted in order to mete out punishment to those whose earthly lives and behavior warrant it.

80. Qur'an, 36:59.

81. Qur'an, 39:73.

82. The No Escape thesis: there is no possibility of leaving Hell and nothing one can do, change, or become in order to get out of Hell, once one is consigned there.

83. Qur'an, 2:81–82.

84. Nursi, *The Flashes*, 625.

erage person lives about eighty years. If we remove the period of childhood and very old age, he effectively lives about sixty years. He might well have committed sins in his life, but God tells us that the disbeliever will stay in Hell-fire forever as a result of his action during this sixty years. This for the atheist surely does not sound fair.

There are two aspects of this claim. The first is that, as mentioned previously, sinners who believe in God suffer in Hell for a limited time until they are cleansed of their sins. The people who are mentioned in the verses above and in the question are the disbelievers. They are the ones who reject the existence of God, and therefore his authority. They also disregard the value of every single creature in the universe. Nursi explains that this kind of rejection and disregard is worse than murdering every creature. In a simple mathematical analogy, he explains that a single murder of a man results in some twenty-four years of prison despite the fact that the act of murder takes only a few seconds. The logic convinces us that the punishment of a crime, which takes only a few seconds, could last many years. On this basis, unbelief and misguidance are an infinite crime, and transgression against innumerable rights, and therefore deserve an infinite punishment.[85]

Free Will Versus Determinism

One of the objections to punishment in Hell as retribution is the argument of predestination (*qadar*), or determinism. Predestination, which has been a very well debated issue in theology over the centuries, suggests that God created everything, including men, his mind and all his actions. For example, a murderer can argue that it was written in his destiny that he would adopt the act of killing. He claims that it was not his fault, but it was his destiny. Determinists also have the same defense. The doctrine of determinism claims that all events, including the actions of people, are determined as a product of a physical cause–effect chain. Therefore, people cannot be held morally responsible for their actions. Determinists receive a great deal of help from science. Newton's Laws of Motion[86] have been the Holy Grail

85. Ibid.

86. Newton's first law states that every object will remain at rest or in uniform motion in a straight line unless compelled to change its state by the action of an external force. This is normally taken as the definition of inertia. The key point here is that if there is no net force acting on an object (if all the external forces cancel each other out), the object will maintain a constant velocity. If that velocity is zero, then the object remains at rest. If an external force is applied, the velocity will change because of the force.

The second law explains how the velocity of an object changes when it is subjected

of the determinist argument. Newton suggests that the universe is a clock which was wound up millions of years ago, and has been ticking ever since. In other words, everything which is going to happen has already been determined. Einstein believed that there is no room for randomness in the universe; everything is pre-planned and the universe is like a clock working on a mechanical system explained by Newton. He famously said "God does not play dice"; in other words, everything is part of a determined destiny.[87] Dawkins, along with Dennett, Harris, and Hitchens, who are known as the four horsemen of the "New Atheism," embraces the idea of determinism. According to these evolutionary atheists, man is just a machine or animal with a slightly better evolved intelligence. Although they claim to be moral individuals, they reject morality as a product of consciousness. To them, behavior cannot be chosen; they are just the products of some biochemical cognitive activities in the brain. Although some determinists, like Dennett, accept the compatibility of determinism with free will, radical atheists place themselves in an awkward position on the issue of morality. If all the actions we take are the product of Newtonian mechanics, how can anyone be held responsible for his actions?

The determinists seem to narrow down their vision by looking solely at biochemical activities in the brain. Their view suggests that IBM's Deeper Blue and Kasparov[88] are very similar machines, although the former is an electronically pre-programmed computer which simply checks millions of possible options and selects the optimum one while the latter is a biochemical organism possessing emotions, senses, mind and conscience.

---

to an external force. The law defines a force to be equal to change in momentum (mass times velocity) per change in time. Newton also developed the calculus of mathematics, and the "changes" expressed in the second law are most accurately defined in differential forms. (Calculus can also be used to determine the velocity and location variations experienced by an object subjected to an external force.) For an object with a constant mass m, the second law states that the force F is the product of an object's mass and its acceleration a:

$$F = m.\, a$$

For an external applied force, the change in velocity depends on the mass of the object. A force will cause a change in velocity; and likewise, a change in velocity will generate a force. The equation works both ways.

The third law states that for every action (force) in nature there is an equal and opposite reaction. In other words, if object A exerts a force on object B, then object B also exerts an equal force on object A.

87. For Einstein's views on religion, see Haught, *2000 Years of Disbelief*, 239–41.

88. Garry Kasparov (1963–), Azerbaijani chess player; born Gary Weinstein. In 1985, at the age of twenty-two, he defeated Anatoly Karpov to become the youngest-ever world chess champion. In 1997, he was beaten in a match with the IBM computer Deeper Blue, a loss that did not affect his world championship title.

The first blow to mechanistic determinism came from Heisenberg, with his Uncertainty Principle.[89] The advent of modern physics (i.e., quantum theory) has changed a great many of the conceptions of classical physics. While classical physics argues the standard universal mechanics formulated by Galileo, Kepler, and Newton, modern physics discovered that not everything is as it seems. The Uncertainty Principle states that it is impossible to know both the exact position and the exact velocity of an object at the same time. However, the effect is tiny and so is only noticeable on a subatomic scale. Leaving the physical and neurological aspect of destiny (*qadar*) and free will (*juz'ī irāda*, or *juz'ī ikhtiyārī*), Nursi brings a fresh approach to the concept. He maintains his position that this life is a place of testing, the result of which will lead people either to Paradise or to Hell. God is the ultimate Governor of the Universe; however, He leaves people with free choice. In *The Words*, Nursi writes:

> . . . a believer attributes everything to Almighty God, even his actions and self, till finally the power of choice confronts him and he is not saved from obligation and responsibility. It [*juz'ī irāda*] tells him: "You are responsible and under obligation." Then, so that he does not become proud due to the good things and perfections which issue from him, Divine Determining (*qadar*) confronts him, saying: "Know your limits; the one who does them is not you." Yes, Divine Determining and the power of choice are at the final degrees of belief and Islam; the former has entered among the matters of belief to save the soul from pride, and latter, to save it from lack of responsibility.[90]

This implies that the final decision is taken by man and that the physical consequences, as well as the action itself, are created by God. For example, a child sits on his father's shoulders. He is incapable of climbing up a hill, but capable of asking his father to take him up to the mountaintop. His father has the strength and carries him to the summit, where the child gets cold and gets sick. So the child cannot blame anyone other than himself, since he chose to be taken there himself. He cannot take pride in reaching the summit, since it was his father who took him there. Similarly, man chooses his way between the good and the bad. Either way, God creates whatever man chooses. If bad comes from his decision, he can only blame himself. If good

89. Werner Heisenberg (1901–76) was a German physicist who helped to formulate quantum mechanics at the beginning of the twentieth century. He first presented the *Heisenberg Uncertainty Principle* in February 1927 in a letter to Wolfgang Pauli, and then published it later that year.

90. Nursi, *The Words*, 204.

comes out of his decision, he cannot take pride of it, because it was God who created the goodness.[91]

Acknowledging the Newtonian theory of cause and effect, Nursi objects to the *Jabrī* and *Mu'tazilite* point of view on divine determining. The Qur'an says:

> Say, never will we be struck except by what Allah has decreed for us; he is our protector. And upon Allah let the believers rely.[92]

In other words, everything has already been determined by God. Whatever he planned comes into existence when the time comes.

For example: a man gets shot with a gun by a gunman, and dies. The *Jabrī* school of thought says: "If the gunman had not fired the gun, the man still would have died"—that is, God is so powerful that He would have created the effect even without the necessary cause. Meanwhile the *Mu'tazilite* school of thought says: "If he had not fired it, he would not have died"—that is, God is completely dependent on the laws of classical physics: no cause means no effect. Dismissing both these views, Nursi explains that we do not know whether, if the gunman had not fired the gun, the man would have died.[93]

In short, according to Nursi, man is morally responsible for and answerable for his actions. God is the creator of the actions and their results. With his eternal divine knowledge, He knows what your choice will be. But it is you who make the final decision with your free will.

Problem of Theological Non-Cognitivism

Having presented his four ways of arguing for the existence of God, Nursi now faces one more challenge from the atheists, that is, the problem of theological non-cognitivism.

Theological non-cognitivism is another atheistic argument which states that the term "god" is unverifiable and cognitively meaningless. Michael Martin proposes one version of this particular argument in his *Atheism: A Philosophical Justification*.[94] Perhaps a less elegant yet more striking question comes from an ordinary atheist. He says, "If there is a god, why does he not

91. Ibid., 206.

92. Qur'an, 9:51.

93. Nursi, *The Words*, 206.

94. See Part I of Martin, *Atheism: A Philosophical Justification*. Also his extended essay of *Positive Atheism and the Meaninglessness of Theism*, 1999 Michael Martin at http://www.infidels.org/library/modern/michael_martin/meaningless.html

make himself seen to me and speak to me directly? Why is he confusing me with all these scriptures and messengers?" To address this question, the following Nursian analogy may be helpful. Imagine that two students are preparing to sit the same examination. The first revises all the topics thoroughly and works hard towards the examination. The second student is given the set of questions which are going to be asked in the exam. On the day, they are given the questions. The first student sets down what he learned by his own hard work. The second student just copies the answers to the questions he has already been given. The result of this exam is inevitably to the advantage of the second student at the cost of total unfairness to the first student. Nursi's logic in the *Risale-i Nur* helps us understand that the element of test (*sirr-i taklīf*) is essential in life. Therefore, the difference between good and evil can become apparent. The simple, straightforward Nursian answer to this atheist claim is this. Man is different from the animals and angels. He is exposed to test, since the purpose of the intelligence given to him requires so. The animals and angels have steady levels in front of God, since they are not tested. The overall purpose of the creation of human beings with intelligence is that they investigate and find out the right way even though they are not given any books or messengers.[95] However, God is fair and He always sends humankind a guide. To Nursi, then, the intelligence and material given to humankind is sufficient for it to attain to the existence of God without him revealing and speaking to individuals.[96]

However, Nursi takes his argument further, and explains that prophets and scriptures (i.e., God's speaking to humankind through the tools of prophets and revelation) are complementary pieces of the jigsaw puzzle that enable mankind to fully understand life and the universe. In *The Words*, Nursi likens this universe to a well-decorated, glamorous, artistic palace wherein the Creator exhibits his arts. Nursi also likens the prophets to the guides of this art exhibition, so that the visitors (i.e., human beings) can understand the true meanings of everything they see in this exhibition. Nursi then elucidates the purpose of this universe through the mouth of the prophet:

95. Ibn Tufayl's work *Hayy ibn Yaqzan* is a good example of this self-investigation into the existence of a Maker. Ibn-i Tufayl creates a fictitious infant, resembling Robinson Crusoe, called Hayy in a deserted Pacific Ocean island. The infant has been fed and brought up by a female deer. When he reaches adulthood, Hayy questions the life and universe and successfully and convincingly concludes that there has to be a Maker. See Nursi, *Hutbe-I Şamiye*, 206.

96. See Chapter 3: The teleological (design) argument, whereby Nursi claims that human intellect is a sufficient tool for understanding the existence of a Deity.

> By making this palace and displaying these things, our lord, who is the king of the palace, wants to make himself known to you. You therefore should recognize him and try to get to know him. And with these adornments he wants to make himself loved by you. Also, he shows his love for you through these bounties that you see, so you should love him too by obeying him. And through these bounties and gifts which are to be seen he shows his compassion and kindness for you, so you should show your respect for him by offering thanks. And through these works of his perfection he wants to display his transcendent beauty to you, so you should show your eagerness to see him and gain his regard. And through placing a particular stamp and special seal and an inimitable signet on every one of these adorned works of art that you see, He wants to show that everything is particular to him, and is the work of his own hand, and that he is single and unique and independent and removed. You therefore should recognize that he is single and alone, and without peer or like or match, and accept that he is such.[97]

In other words, Nursi claims that God created human beings as different from animals, plants and angels in order to put them to test (*sirr-i taklīf*), to see how each individual perceives him, and how he is reflected on every individual's mirror.[98]

Moral Nihilism and a Comparison between the Skeptics and Nursi

The eighteenth century saw a great change in European art, science, philosophy and many other fields thanks to the Enlightenment movement. The focal point of the intellectual enlightenment was to mobilize positive reason to reform society. The church was seen as one of the main obstacles to intellectual progress. Therefore, its influence had to be reduced. While doing this, intellectuals ventured into unexplored fields in order to solve society's problems. The idea of atheism began to flourish. The misconduct of the church led many philosophers into thinking without a God. One of the key figures of the nineteenth century was Schopenhauer. He removed the idea of God from men's lives, which inevitably pushed him to the doorstep of nihilism. Schopenhauer's pessimism about life and the world influenced too many

97. Nursi, *The Words*, 44.
98. Nursi, *The Letters*, 365.

other intellectuals, such as Wagner and Nietzsche.[99] When the concept of and faith in God and resurrection are removed, men find it extremely hard to justify morality and find meaning in life. If we do not believe anything, what is there to motivate us, what is there to give us values and duties, or, in other words, what is the point of life? Schopenhauer describes life as an "unpleasant business".[100] He rejected God outright, writing:

> Behind everything, there is not a God but the groundless and motiveless primordial urge to live, for which, however, we should not use "negative conceptions, void of content," such as "absolutes," "infinites" and "supersensibles"—all really amounting to "cloud-cuckoo-town."[101]

It is clear in his writings that he was one of the leading pessimists of his time. He sees man as a guideless being thrown into infinite space and infinite time, without any firm, absolute where and when.[102] To Schopenhauer, life is death from the very beginning, clamped down between fulfilled desires and boredom. Man is left with nothing but misery and the fear of death.[103]

Although Schopenhauer's godless philosophy pushes people towards a pessimistic worldview, and hence depression, it became a substitute for religion.[104] Nietzsche admits, "it was atheism that led him to Schopenhauer."[105] Nietzsche's rejection of God and God-based morality seems to be more a question of his physiological life-trauma than a new philosophical discovery. He was born into a very religious Christian family, and was nicknamed "little pastor" owing to his deep knowledge of Christianity at an early age. Nihilism, which is by definition the outright rejection of any authority, is associated with Nietzsche. He tells us the story of a madman who lit up a lantern in bright daylight and proclaimed the death of God. However, there needs to be solutions to the problems generated by killing God. His death is a great collapse. Desolate emptiness: the sea drunk up. A living space without prospect: the horizon wiped away. Unfathomable nothingness: the Earth unchained from the sun. For man himself, a desperate, aimless fall, which must tear him apart. The chaos of nihilism opens further apart. Is there still up or down? Are we not straying as through an infinite nothing?

99. Küng, *Does God Exist?* 356.

100. Ibid., 359.

101. Schopenhauer, *The World as Will and Representation*, 377.

102. Ibid.

103. Ibid.

104. Küng, *Does God Exist?* 357.

105. Nietzsche, *On the Genealogy of Morals*, 279.

Do we not feel the breath of empty space? Has it not become colder? Is not night continually closing in on us?[106]

Belief in God, Nursi argues, gives meaning to man's life and becomes a source of purpose and morality. Nursi bases his arguments on the completely opposing view to nihilism. Like Schopenhauer, Nursi talks about primordial urge which only necessitates the existence of a deity. Nursi argues that among all creatures living on the planet, mankind is the only one who has got intelligence and conscience to think about the purpose of existence. In other words, mankind is the only species who has got morality and conscience. There are two possible answers to these questions. One is the version of the secular thinkers and philosophers who have tried to explain existence and the universe with the absence of God. The other version is that of Nursi's, which is the explanation involving God (i.e., the theist version).

Loren Eiseley, who wrote as part of personal contemplation, once said that man is the cosmic orphan. He is the only creature in the universe who asks, why?[107] That is to say, he has got no owner, no minder or no carer. He is the accidental by-product of matter, time and chance. The materialist/atheist version of existence comes with its own problems. Rather than solving them, it creates more of them. There are three possible outcome of this view. First, life has no ultimate purpose. It is a total nothingness, and it is destined to perish. Existentialists, such as Sartre and Camus, reveal the dark side of this view. Camus describes man as like a rolling boulder. In his novel *The Stranger*, he emphasizes the fact that life has no meaning.[108] Sartre describes man as being "like a boat without a rudder."[109] In one of Beckett's plays, the audience is shown an empty stage with lots of rubbish for thirty seconds and the curtains are closed. Beckett wants to tell the audience that life is exactly like the empty, messy stage he has just shown.

The second outcome is that "life has no ultimate value." As Dostoevsky tells his readers, "if there is no God, if there is no mortality, everything is permitted."[110] In this view, there is absolutely no difference between Stalin and Mother Teresa. There is no difference between the good and the evil. This is where one needs to touch the necessity of God's existence in order to have objective moral rights and wrongs. Without God, whose values do we accept? Is it those presented by Hitler, or by Jesus? Sartre believes that there

106. Nietzsche, *Fröchliche Wissenschaft III*, 127

107. '*The Cosmic Orphan*' An essay by Loren Eiseley (1907–77), available at http://www.unz.org/Pub/SaturdayRev-1974feb23-00016, last accessed on December 21, 2013

108. Camus, *The Stranger*.

109. Sartre and Cumming, *The Philosophy of Jean-Paul Sartre*.

110. Dostoyevsky, *The Brothers Karamazov*, 134–35.

is no right or wrong. They are bare, valueless facts of existence. Is there any difference between the set of values where there exist brotherhood, love, equality, respect and self-sacrifice and the set where there exist war, oppression, crime, brutality and so on? If there is no God, there are no moral values of any of the qualities above. If there is no God, no resurrection, no afterlife, mankind is absolutely no different in value to the carnivores. We are all born, eat, drink, sleep, reproduce, and die. Once we complete our biological purpose, we all become fertilizers. There is no value in learning, teaching, working, giving to charity, and helping others, if the final destination is under the ground. According to the atheists, there are, of course, the values of working, wealth, and building the earth. But they are just part of a struggle of survival. Atheism gives us two options: either commit suicide or face the absurdity of life bravely and live on. Camus asks himself "Is it really worth living?" and he answers, "Recognize the absurdity and live in love," which is completely contradictory. Sartre advises us: "Let's pretend the universe has meaning." But it hasn't. How is it possible to live life consistently, if there are no sets of objective moral values? In *The Brothers Karamazov* and *Crime and Punishment*, Dostoyevsky demonstrates that man cannot live without morality. We have already seen in the Nazi and Stalinist rules what kind of life awaits us should we remove God.

Nursi tells us the complete opposite. There is God, the Creator and the Sustainer of the universe. Thanks to him, there are universal moral values and duties. Divine commandments constitute moral values. Life has a meaning and a purpose. Mankind has been created in the image of God; hence we have completely different qualities from those of other creatures. The purpose of life in this world is merely to earn a permanent life in the Hereafter. If a person fulfills God's moral duties, he will be rewarded with eternal life in Paradise. If one follows the teachings of the Devil, he will be punished in Hell-fire. Nursi also tells us that man is different from the animals, in the sense that he has got conscience, which causes him anguish should he do evil. Nursi believes he succeeds where the secular atheists fail.

Out of these two possible views (i.e., the atheist's and Nursi's), one is more inclined towards Nursi's. His views do not only make strong philosophical sense, but also give a great physiological advantage. Nursi implies that those who observe the secular atheist view are more likely to despair. Statistics shows that one of the main causes of death for young people in the USA is suicide.[111] If there is no God, there is no reason for morality. This

111. American Foundation of Suicide Prevention at http://www.afsp.org/understanding-suicide/facts-and-figures, last accessed December 23, 2013

idea eventually leads its followers to nihilism, the consequences of which are not particularly cheerful.

Nursi's view, on the other hand, motivates individuals to live life according to the divine values, which are undoubtedly objective for everyone, even for atheists. The ultimate purpose of life is not to gather an infinite amount of money and wealth, but to help others. Death is not the end of life but the gate opening into permanent life. For every small good deed in this life, there is a reward. And for every small bad deed, there is punishment.

Blaise Pascal tells us that, out of theism and atheism, logic tells us to choose theism. He says, "We have nothing to lose, but infinity to gain."[112] Much in line with Pascal, Nursi resonates Hikam Ata'iyya who asked, "What does he who finds God lose? And what does he who loses him find?."[113] Nursi then remarks, "the person who finds him finds everything, while the person who fails to find him, can find nothing. If he does find something, it will only bring him trouble."[114]

Conclusion

This chapter has outlined the basis of moral arguments in general and Nursi's version in particular. The idea of the necessity of God's existence expressed for the first time by Kant as a source of *summum bonum*, the highest good. Elaborating around two new terms, Kant argues that theoretical reason cannot prove the existence of God. Practical reasoning, on the other hand, can help one into believing in God since it is about what to do in life. To Kant, individuals need to endeavor after the highest good which is simply possible in this world only on the supposition of a supreme cause of nature. Therefore it is morally necessary to assume the existence of God.

Craig, similar to Kant, claims that there are objective moral values and duties which ought to be generated owing to the supreme moral giver, that is God. Theists, in all Abrahamic religions, assert that God is essential in order to give humanity objective validity and act as the overriding authority.

Nursi's argument comes in two versions. Nursi's first version of the moral argument is based on human conscience which he describes as primordial nature of human beings. To Nursi, one can and should find out that there is God simply based on the intelligence and senses given to him. Further to what is already out there, Nursi introduces some new terminology such as the sense of direction or orientation (*ḥiss-i sāiqah*) and the sense

112. Pascal, *Pensées*, Part III, Note 233.

113. Ibn 'Ata'illah al-Iskandari, *Sharh al-Hikam al-'Ata'iyya*, 208.

114. Nursi, *The Letters*, 357.

of motivation or desire to do things (*ḥiss-i shāiqah*). Constructing his arguments on these two terms, he posits that the sources of these senses could only be the Supreme Maker of the universe.

Nursi's second version of the moral argument, one might argue, comes in the form of arguing for the existence of life after death. Nursi seems to be at pains with demonstrating how the lack of full justice in this life is actually an indication of the continuation of this life in a different format elsewhere.

The analysis of Nursi's *Risale-i Nur* reveals that there is very little mention of human conscience as an evidence of God compared to his other arguments. However, great many sections of his work seem to be dedicated rather to defend the theistic position against various skeptic attacts. For instance, the contradiction between a loving God and the existence of evil and Hell, question of free will and determinism are some of the issues he tackles in his writings. Nursi seems to be at pains with reconciling God and the existence of evil, calamities, tribulations and Hell. To him, these counter arguments are not a contradiction with the concept of God, they are, on the contrary, evidence of his necessity.

7

Analysis and Conclusion

This book has examined the life and philosophy of one of the most influential twentieth-century Islamic scholars, Bediüzzaman Saïd Nursi, in order to examine his methods of arguing for the existence of God. Although Nursi never considered himself a philosopher and did not intend to write his *Risale-i Nur* (Epistles of Light), as a philosophical work, the arguments he developed in his writings deserve to be examined among those produced by major philosophers. In this sense one could consider Nursi as a modern day *mutakallim*.

Nursi believed that human happiness here in this life, as well as in the Hereafter, depends on belief in God. He insisted in his 1909 Court-Marshal Defense that Plato's ideal *Republic* could be achieved only through the teachings of the Qur'an—in other words, via a strong belief in the unity and oneness of God. Nursi always believed that the meaning of life and of human existence could only be understood through the Qur'anic injunctions and prophetic teachings. According to Nursi, the true believer could acquire such strength, thanks to his belief in God, that he could challenge all that the universe could ever throw at him. He partly demonstrated this strength in his eighty-three-year-long life largely spent in wars, in prisoner of war camps, in exile, and in prisons. Failure to attain the true knowledge of God (*ma'rifatullāh*) could potentially drive people into despair, depression, and enormous mental and spiritual suffering.

Upon close scrutiny, Said Nursi's six-thousand-page-long *Risale-i Nur*, consisting of around twenty volumes, reveals that there are four distinctive arguments that Nursi develops in order to defend his version of theism. These four arguments (*barāhin*, single *burhān*) are the argument from the universe, which is similar to a version of the teleological argument (*kitāb-ı kabīr-i kāināt*); the prophethood argument (*nubuwwah*); the argument from revelation or scriptures (*waḥy*); and the argument from human conscience or primordial nature (*wijdān* or *fiṭrat-i bashar*). Although none of these arguments is completely new in philosophy *per se*, Nursi elegantly elaborates these four themes to build a four-legged structure upon which he attempts to locate the existence of God as an indestructible idea.

One may consider these four Nursian arguments as part of theistic tradition. In other words, those who to defend Abrahamic theism from an Islamic or monotheistic point of view may employ these four Nursian arguments. In this respect, at least two of these arguments (the teleological and moral arguments) could be employed not only by Muslims but also by Christians and Jews.

Although Nursi never considered these arguments individually and independently from each other, for the sake of their systematic analysis in this book they have been studied individually in separate chapters.

Having reviewed the historical background of atheism and theism in Chapter 1, and Said Nursi's life and discourse in Chapter 2, I analyzed the first of Nursi's four ways of arguing for the existence of God, namely the "great book of the universe" (*kitāb-ı kabīr-i kāināt*), in Chapter 3. The great book of the universe, Nursi argues, when read reveals the existence of its intelligent, all-powerful and magnificent designer. This particular argument is essentially what the ancient Greeks called the teleological argument, or modern philosophy's argument from design. Although Nursi, rather differently from other philosophers, calls it "the book of the universe," the theme he builds up is similar to that constructed by his predecessors: the universe and everything it contains demonstrate purposefulness, which in turn can only imply the existence of an intelligent Maker. On every occasion on which Nursi defends this argument, his analogy of a "king and his kingdom" appears consistently. The upshot of this Nursian metaphor is that the universe is ultimately the kingdom of God, where He designs, creates and maintains his art in order to be seen and appreciated by humankind, whom He has blessed with reason and intellect.

The book-of-the-universe argument, for Nursi, is a sufficient tool wherewith the human intellect can detect that there is an intelligent maker and maintainer of this world, life and cosmos in a wider sense, even without the tools of the prophetic teachings or the scriptures.

Clearly, Nursi's use of the design argument occurs most frequently throughout his *Risale-i Nur*, not only because he primarily targets the average citizen, who does not necessarily hold any deep philosophical or scientific knowledge but also he imitates the method of the Qur'an. Like William Paley, Said Nursi tells the ordinary reader (or listener in some cases) that a book requires the existence of an author to write it, a needle requires the existence of a needle-making craftsman to manufacture it, and similarly, this universe requires a Maker with infinite power, knowledge and intellect to design, create and sustain it. For Nursi, therefore, anyone with a little intelligence can be convinced by the design argument that nothing can come into existence by itself, by nature or by chance, three atheistic viewpoints which Nursi always seems to be at pains to refute.

Nursi not only argues for the validity of his version of the design argument, but also tries to refute the counter-arguments of the atheists. In *The Flashes*, he tries to demolish the three possible atheist proposals regarding the origin of creation. The postulates Nursi tries to refute are: things create themselves (*tashakkala bi nafsihi*); nature creates things (*iqtaẓathu al-ṭabīʿah*); and causes create things (*aʿwjadathu al-asbāb*).

In the bulk of the *Risale-i Nur*, Nursi targets, without mentioning the names, the philosophy of Ludwig Büchner's materialism, Auguste Comte's positivism and Charles Darwin's evolutionism. This appears nowhere more evidently than in his *Tabiat Risalesi* (Treaties on Nature), where Nursi tackles the above-mentioned three main atheistic proposals for the origins of existence in the cosmos. He meticulously tries to refute the idea that science, logic and reason could possibly accept that natural causes create life without the interference or control of an intelligent being. This is partly what Darwin proposed as an explanation of the origins of life, and it has been embraced by many atheists, such as Bertrand Russell, Charles Darwin, Richard Dawkins, and Daniel C. Dennett.

For Nursi, ascribing the power of reason and intellect to mindless nature, causes and elements forming organisms is so absurd that were it so, all these entities ought to be cleverer than man. He tells the atheist that his propositions require "the ear of his donkey has to be clever than himself."

The imagery and metaphors used by Nursi in his "New Said" works such as; *The Words*, *The Letters*, *The Flashes* and *The Rays*, as well as in his transitional work *Al-Mathnawī al-Nūriyah*, reflect the influence the Qur'an had upon him. As Nursi indicated on countless occasions, he took full guidance from the Qur'an and did not study anything other than it during his transitional life and the 'New Said' Era. This had a significant impact on his method of expressing his views. For Nursi, metaphors are the philosophy of the common people or like binoculars which bring further truth closer to people's comprehension.

Another possible reason Nursi used this particular method could be the context in which Nursi wrote these pieces. The main body of the *Risale-i Nur*, that is, the first five books listed above, were written during Nursi's various Anatolian exiles, which started in Barla in 1926 and continued in Eskişehir, Kastamonu, Denizli, Emirdağ, Afyon and Isparta. During this period, Nursi's first audience consisted of a few ordinary villagers of Barla. Therefore, Nursi might have been trying to speak to their hearts and minds using simple, universal and easy-to-understand analogies such as gardens, trees, seeds, plants, animals, etc.

As his influence grew, Nursi began to gain new followers from various walks of life, including members of the Army. In addition to this, having nearly forty years of war experience, Nursi's audience were well aware of matters of war and the military. Hence, military analogies started to appear in Nursi's writings.

The originality of Nursi's design argument is that rather than connecting the artifact to a necessary designer, or as Paley puts, the watch requires the watchmaker, Nursi connects the artefact to a designer with certain characteristics. He, then, draws a picture of the Designer who has *al-asma al-husna*, in other words, he demonstrates the God described in the Qur'an. This is what makes Nursi different from almost every other philosopher.

Having built his theism from the ground up, Nursi proceeds from his "argument from the book of the universe" to his second argument for the existence of God, that is, the institution of prophethood (*nubuwwah*), which was the focus of Chapter 4. Nursi suggests that the universe is like a palace built by God, who in turn wanted the secret of it to be understood better by mankind by means of explainers (i.e., the prophets). Without the prophets (*anbiyā*) and the revelations given to the prophets (*waḥy*), Nursi asserts, mankind could, possibly, come to the conclusion that there is a Deity who creates and sustains the universe, but he could neither understand his qualities in full nor know what He really expects from humankind. This argument is expressed in certain parts of the *Risale-i Nur* by means of an analogy, where Nursi tells his readers that the visitor to a palace could guess that the property has an owner, but would not know the exact characteristics of that person or what he expects from his visitors without a guide or guidebook. Here, Nursi clearly refers to the prophets when he talks about "guides," and to revelation or the scriptures when he talks about guidebooks.

Two types of tool become highly visible as Nursi argues for the authenticity of all prophets, especially the prophet Muḥammad, in the *Risale-i Nur*. Indeed, Nursi explains that the personal religious experiences (argument from religious experience, or ARE) of these individuals, supported by miracles (arguments from miracles) shown to them by God, ought to be accepted as genuine.

According to Nursi, all prophets (*anbiyā*) and their books (*kutub*), including the prophet Muḥammad and the Qur'an, have been sent by God to guide humanity to the truth. Therefore, the Nursian position implies that all prophets prior to prophet Muḥammad, no matter where, when, and to whom they were sent, essentially tried to spread the same message, that is, the unity of God (*tawḥīd*), the authenticity of their and previous prophets' prophethood (*nubuwwah*), and life after death and resurrection (*ḥashr*).

By way of a defense of the prophets' religious experiences, the prophet Muḥammad's in particular, Nursi applies a set of tests very similar to Richard Swinburne's in order to investigate whether or not their experiences were genuine. He draws attention to the fact that, other than through minor mishaps, none of the prophets had ever been proven unreliable. They have always been truthful, trustworthy and consistent. Therefore, Nursi suggests, all prophets ought to pass Swinburne's first test, the "reliability test."

Swinburne's second test, namely "whether or not the claimant is under the influence of intoxicants," is applied to the prophet Muḥammad, only to reveal that he never used alcohol or drugs in his life. Therefore, there is no possibility of his being under the influence of intoxicants that could invalidate his claims.

The third test, "testing the physical conditions to have accurate perception," is also applied. Although Nursi argues that there is no reason to doubt the prophet Muḥammad's religious experience in terms of his having misperceptions or hallucinations, the atheist camp disagrees with him. Freud, for instance, makes a psychological analysis of Muḥammad's having been an orphan for years prior to his claiming of religious experience, and implies that he was having hallucinations. Thus, according to Freud and the atheists, Muḥammad's religious claims are false. Patricia Crone and Michael Cook reconstruct Muḥammad's life story and religious experience (the Qur'an and Islam in general) as a cheaper copy of previous religious lives and experiences such as those of Jesus or Moses, drawing parallels between the Islamic narration and the other religious narrations.

However, the claims put forward by skeptics such as Freud, Cook, and Crone are dismissed outright in the *Risale-i Nur*. Nursi claims that Muḥammad is either a deceitful master-charlatan or a genuine prophet of God. Since, according to Nursi, none can prove that he was a lying, cheating impostor who benefited from his status, he ought to be seen and accepted as the last true prophet of God. Indeed, Nursi underlines the fact that the historical records indicate that the prophet Muḥammad showed the utmost integrity throughout his life, did not change his lifestyle for the better, and even suffered hardship because of his claims.

Proving Muḥammad's prophethood, according to Nursi, also automatically proves the prophethood of his predecessors such as Abraham, Moses and Jesus, since Muḥammad clearly indicates that he is the last in a chain of prophets (*khāṭam al-anbiyā*) starting with Adam.

The novel aspect of Nursi's prophethood argument is that it is not only based on the miracles of Prophet Muḥammad but also based on the tests set to verify the claimants authenticity. There is no account that Nursi were aware of William James's work on the ARE, yet his approach to prophethood is considerably new in the world of philosophy. This might well be due to the fact that until Nursi's time not many people so openly criticized Prophet Muhammad. Nursi's argument to defend Prophet Muhammad's prophethood is unprecedented not because of Nursi being an outstanding scholar but because of the fact that he was one of the earliest defenders of the critics.

The concepts of prophethood and revelation or scripture are so closely knitted together that it is impossible to separate them. In the *Risale-i Nur*, these two are presented as two supporting legs of the same argument. For Nursi, Muḥammad is obsolete without the Qur'an, and so is the Qur'an without Muḥammad. A guide needs a guidebook to learn from in order to teach others. The Nursian explanation of the Muḥammad–Qur'an duo is such that Muḥammad never made up anything from his own mind: he was given the Qur'an to learn and to teach from.

Throughout the *Risale-i Nur*, Nursi tries to establish a logical link between the apparent design and the designer; message and the messenger. That is to say, the universe requires the existence of God which requires the Qur'an which requires Prophet Muḥammad. Nursi, on two separate occasions, likens men to the servant who was given one thousand gold pieces and sent shopping with a little note given by his master as opposed to the other living things, especially animals who were given only ten pieces of gold without a note. Clearly, the little note given to men indicates the scriptures, particularly the Qur'an.

The challenge faced by Nursi at this point is how to prove that the note given to mankind (i.e., the scriptures, and the Qur'an in particular) is genuine. This challenge leads Nursi to his third argument for the existence of God, which is the argument from revelations or scriptures (*waḥy*), the Qur'an in particular, which was examined in Chapter 5. This Nursian approach to the revelations and scriptures is unique, in the sense that not many theologians have ever developed a methodology regarding this subject, as Nursi did. What Nursi does in the *Risale-i Nur* is that he closely scrutinizes whether the Qur'an is the work of Muḥammad or a true revelation from God (*waḥy-i ilāhi*). Nursi systematically examines the properties of the Qur'an to refute the thesis that it represents the poetic writings of Muḥammad. Certain aspects of the Qur'an, Nursi asserts, could not possibly be the work of an illiterate shepherd turned merchant like Muḥammad. For instance, characteristics such as excellence in eloquence, coherence, harmony and comprehensiveness could not possibly have been attained by

Muḥammad. Nursi explains that although Muḥammad was a very honest, trustworthy and reliable person, he was not a poet who was able to produce a work of poetry like the Qur'an, where he could maintain superhuman eloquence in telling stories from the past, and report the unseen from the future without any inaccuracy, discrepancy or wearisomeness. Besides, the verbal traditions concerning the prophet Muḥammad (*aḥādith*) reported in volumes such as al-Bukhāri, al-Muslim and Abū Dawūd demonstrate that, in his day-to-day conversations, he spoke ordinary Arabic, which is completely different from the speech of the Qur'an. Therefore, Nursi suggests that the Qur'an is the word of a different speaker (i.e., God) revealed to Muḥammad, who in turn spoke it to people.

Nursi's systematic exposition of the Qur'an's miraculousness in terms of eloquence, comprehensiveness and reporting of the unseen is his method of paving the way for the Qur'an's description of the nature of God, death, and life after death. Nursi implies that the irrefutable, wondrous and verifiable aspects of the Qur'an oblige its readers to believe what it says about those other matters which cannot possibly be known by humankind or be verified by anyone other than God himself. For instance, the Qur'an tells us about the Day of Judgment (*al-qiyāmah*), resurrection (*ḥashr*), and a rewarding life after death in Paradise (*al-jannah*), or retribution in Hell (*jahannam*). Nursi claims that, since parts of what the Qur'an says about the past and the future have been verified, what it says about other matters, such as the ones mentioned above, must be true too.

The predecessors of Nursi used the verses of the Qur'an to demonstrate that there is God. However, Nursi scrutinizes the Qur'an in order to demonstrate that it is not the work of man but work of Deity. In this regard, Nursi's approach to Qur'an as an evidence for God's existence is rather unprecedented.

The fourth argument Nursi puts forward for the existence of God, which was discussed in Chapter 6, is that of human conscience or primordial nature (*wijdān* or *fiṭrat-i bashar*). Man, according to Nursi, is a small-scale mirror of God and his attributes. If there had been no prophets or scriptures, man would still have been able to discover that there is a deity who possesses much greater power and intellect than himself.

To explain how human conscience (*wijdān-i bashar*) proves the existence of God, Nursi introduces five senses that have never been acknowledged by materialist scientists in Chapter 5. In *al-Mathnawī al-Nūriyah*, Nursi gives brief particulars of these new five senses. On top of sight, hearing, taste, smell and touch he adds *quwwa-i shā'iqah* (sense of enthusiasm or longing for the truth), *quwwa-i sāiqah* (sense of drive or attraction towards the truth), *ḥiss-i qabl al-wuqū* (sense of forefeeling in the heart), *ruyā-i ṣādiqah* (genuine dreams), and *kashf-i ṣaḥīḥ* (genuine spiritual discovery). If mind (*ʿaql*) forgets God, Nursi claims, human conscience, which consists of the further five senses mentioned above, never forgets God. Nursi explains that no senses in humans are without a corresponding entity. For instance, humans cannot develop a taste for something non-existent. Similarly, the sense of enthusiasm (*shāiqah*) and sense of drive (*sāiqah*) require some entity towards which humans are attracted or driven. This entity, for Nursi, is God.

Another tool for achieving understanding of God is "the human I" (*anā*), as Nursi calls it. This tool is extremely useful, yet also extremely dangerous. Nursi explains that *anā* is given to man in order for him to attain belief in the existence of God with his attributes, in comparison to his own limited power and intelligence. In Nursi's words, *anā* is the key given by God to man so that he can unlock the hidden secrets or talisman of the universe (*ṭılsım-ı kāināt*). However, it might dangerously lead man into materialist atheism as well. When man considers himself intelligent and powerful, he imputes certain godly attributes to himself. When he fails to attain certain high targets, he realizes that he is not actually fully capable. Hence, Nursi concludes, man understands that there ought to be someone much greater than him in terms of power and intellect, and that is God.

Arguably, Nursi's Treatise on Self (*Anā Risalesi*) in *The Words* is the epicenter of his thought, where his unique philosophy of life, universe, and God can be seen clearly. Nursi builds his theism on three concepts. These are "the human I" (*anā*), "the self-referential meaning" (*mʿanā-i ismī*) and "the other-indicative meaning" (*mʿanā-i ḥarfī)* of life and the universe.

Using the tool of "the human I" (anā), which Nursi describes as "a unit of measurement to know the attributes and functions of the Deity," man is meant to read life and the universe through the spectacles of their "other-indicative meaning" (i.e., *mʿanā-i ḥarfī*). For instance, you look at a flower and say "How beautiful it is!." This is seeing through the flower's self-referential meaning. If you look at the same flower and say "How beautifully it has been made!" this is seeing it through its other-indicative meaning. For Nursi, everything has these two meanings. Man is meant to read everything, including his *anā*, through the other-indicative meaning, without rejecting the self-referential meaning.

Failure to use the tool of *anā* properly by ignoring the other-indicative meaning of things, Nursi argues, leads man into materialist atheism. In other words, as was discussed in Chapter 3, man has to impute power and intellect to powerless and mindless objects in order to explain their existence. To counter this atheistic point of view, Nursi builds his philosophy on the linguistic deconstruction of the terms "self-referential meaning" (*mʿanā-i ismī*) and "other-indicative meaning" (*mʿanā-i ḥarfī*).

The great book of the universe, Nursi explains, consists of an infinite number of letters which express the meanings of life and the cosmos. The letters (*ḥurūf*, single *ḥarf*) of this book are the individual readings of the "other-indicative meanings" of infinite creations. None of these letters has a full meaning (*mʿanā*) on its own other than its self-referential meaning. Their meaning emerges fully, provided they are read through their "other-indicative meanings."

Point of view (*naẓar*) and intention (*niyyah*) are two additional concepts employed by Nursi. *Naẓar*, how one looks at things, is the tool which directly affects one's perception of the universe. For instance, if one looks at scavengers consuming a carcass of a dead animal, depending on one's point of view (*naẓar*) one might conclude either that a gross act is taking place or that a beautiful cleaning-up operation is under way. Similarly, man's intention, or *niyyah*, affects the output of his actions. For example, if a horseman puts a post in the ground, to which to tie up his horse, and leaves it there for the benefit of other horsemen, but someone trips over it and gets hurt, he would still get the reward rather than blame, thanks to his initial good intention. Therefore, Nursi thinks *naẓar* and *niyyah* change the nature of things and actions. For that, man will always be rewarded in the eyes of God as long as he sees, thinks and acts through pragmatic *naẓar* and *niyyah*.

The arguments for the existence of God propounded by some ancient Greek and early Muslim philosophers (*falāsifūn*) have also been examined in this book. There are parallels between Nursi's arguments and these philosophers' in respect of the teleological and moral arguments. Undoubtedly, Nursi had been inspired by the ancients such as Socrates and Plato, who are mentioned repeatedly throughout the *Risale-i Nur*. Nursi seems to hold these philosophers in high regard and believe that they attained a certain level of knowledge of God (*maʿrifatullāh*).

Nursi argues that, among many routes leading man to the knowledge of God, the route of philosophy is the hardest one. In an analogy, Nursi likens this route to digging a tunnel underground to go from point A to point B. This route, he says, is the riskiest one, where many bright minds have failed to reach *maʿrifatullāh* (knowledge of God) and have fallen into the arms of atheism or disbelief (*kufr*). For Nursi, Aristotle, and some Muslim philosophers influenced by Aristotle such as Al-Fārābī and Ibn Sina, misjudged the nature and truth about *anā* and fell into a fatal error.

Although Nursi is at ease with the cosmological and moral arguments developed by these philosophers, he is highly critical of their level of true knowledge of God. For Nursi, great minds such as Al-Fārābī's and Ibn Sina's could only reach the level of belief of an ordinary believer. One potential explanation of this Nursian judgment could be that they seriously focused on philosophy, but ignored the tools of prophethood (*nubuwwah*) and holy revelation (*waḥy-i ilāhi*). An ordinary believer who follows the prophetic and Qur'anic teachings might not necessarily have the cosmological and philosophical knowledge attained by Al-Fārābī and Ibn Sina, yet he might well be more aware of the nature and the will of God thanks to the teachings of the prophet and the Qur'an.

Nursi continues his criticism of the route of philosophy as a means of attaining true *tawḥīd* (oneness of God), especially the one adopted by the *Mu'tazilah* such as al-Kindī. There is no question about the *Mu'tazilah's* belief in the existence of God; however, Nursi raises concerns over their interpretations of God's attributes. For instance, he fiercely criticizes the *Mu'tazilah's* for their claim that man is fully responsible for his actions since man is the creator of his actions. For Nursi, this approach grossly undermines God's continuous creation principle whereby God is believed to be the ultimate creator of the output of man's free will.

In other words, the route of philosophy, which only relies on knowledge and reasoning (*'aql*), is almost always insufficient for attaining true understanding of the reality of the existence and nature of God. Nursi explains the hardship these philosophers faced in their "travel through an underground tunnel," where many philosophers such as Plato, Aristotle, Al-Fārābī and Ibn Sina were stranded and got lost. Nursi reports that he briefly travelled via the route of philosophy in the Old Said period, only to face the destiny of his predecessors. He explains that a light, symbolizing the Qur'an, was given to him so that he could find the exit from that dark tunnel and come back into the light.

Another obvious difference between Muslim philosophers such as Ibn Sina and Al-Fārābī and Said Nursi concerns the level of attainment required to understand God (*ma'rifatullāh*). According to Nursi, *kalām* scholars could at best reach level three on the seven-level Nursian scale of *ma'rifatullāh*. Nursi explains that the stages of *ma'rifatullāh* are *asar* (the output of an act), *fi'il* (the act), *fā'il* (the one who acts), *ism* (the name of the actor), *ṣifat* (the attributes of the actor), *shuūn* (the various work of the actor), and finally *Dhāt* (the Actor, God or Allāh).

According to Nursi, *kalām* arguments developed by Ibn Sina, Al-Fārābī and the like started off from the output of an act (*asar*), which is the universe, and the observable acts (*fi'il*). They therefore draw the conclusion that these arguments require someone (*fā'il*) who carries out these acts. This person, for *kalām* scholars, must be the Prime Mover, Unmoved

Mover or First Cause. In other words, *kalām* scholars base their argument on "contingency and createdness" (*ḥudūth* and *imkān*); hence they only reach to the existence of a Necessary Being (*Wājib-al wujūd*). However, in order to attain full knowledge of the *Dhāt* of this deity, one needs to move to steps four, five and six on the scale. For Nursi, these steps are only taken thanks to the help of prophethood and revelations. In Nursi's mind, what makes his arguments in the *Risale-i Nur* superior to the ones developed by the *kalām* scholars is the fact that the *Risale-i Nur* helps one to complete this seven-step climb to attain true knowledge of *Dhāt* (God) or *ma'rifatullāh* (true knowledge of God).

Nursi clearly constructs his philosophy not only on reason and knowledge (*'aql*), like the *kalām* scholars, but also on heart (*qalb*) and on the Qur'anic teachings (*waḥy*), like the Sufis. For Nursi, neither the route of *qalb* and *waḥy* adopted by the Sufis nor the route of *'aql* used by *kalām* scholars is sufficient on its own. This is why Nursi claims that neither philosophers nor Sufis are on the right path. If reason and knowledge (*'aql*) form one wing and heart and revelation (*qalb* and *waḥy*) the other, getting airborne without having them both would be an extremely hard task.

It appears it the chronology of Nursi that he initially used *wijdān* argument in the Old Said period. Especially brief appearance of *wijdān* can be seen in his 1911 Damascus Sermon. Few years later, *wijdān* argument reappears in *al-Mathnawi al-Nuri* again but extremely briefly. All in all, the *Risale-i Nur* dedicates only a few pages to elaborate around *wijdān* as opposed to many hundreds for the other three arguments especially the teleological argument. The Second Said period sees not *wijdān* argument but mainly the teleological argument. The reason, one might argue, could be that the transition from The Ottoman Empire into the new secular Turkish Republic necessitated the use of intellect and reason rather than spiritual elements. It appears that Nursi delicately avoided *wijdān* argument in the secular period in order to avoid being discredited outright on the basis that he, unlike the defenders of the new regime, invokes unverifiable elements.

It could be argued that Nursi systematically tries to merge reason and knowledge (*'aql*) with heart and revelation (*qalb* and *waḥy*) in his *Risale-i Nur*. He starts off with the teleological argument, which speaks directly to the mind, explaining that science, knowledge and reasoning could not possibly accept creation through natural forces, self-creation or pure luck alone. They require the existence of an Intelligent Creator. However, reason and knowledge could at best reach the conclusion that there must be a deity, without knowing his true nature and wishes. This is when Nursi brings forward his second and third arguments, that is, prophethood (*nubuwwah*) and revelation (*waḥy*). For Nursi, these two are essential for understanding what kind of being this Deity is and what exactly He expects from humankind.

Unlike most *kalām* scholars, Al-Ghazzālī seems to have achieved this mind–heart balance. Hence, Nursi regards him highly and respects his authority. As was discussed in Chapter 1, Al-Ghazzālī, a dominant character who also appears in Nursi's work in opposition to other Muslim philosophers such as Al-Fārābī and Ibn Sina, was more a mystic than a philosopher. Perhaps one reason Nursi considers himself more in alliance with Al-Ghazzālī might be their common hostility towards the *Mu'tazilah* school of thought. Al-Ghazālī followed the *Ash'arite* school of thought, as did Nursi. Therefore, their views on God's essence and attributes are very similar.

Although Nursi seems to have inspired many Muslim scholars, especially in Turkey, there is no strong evidence of his influence on modern Western intellectuals. In terms of methodology, however, Nursi's way of arguing for his version of theism looks similar to the methods of Richard Swinburne and William L. Craig.

Swinburne, a contemporary academic and Christian apologist, works on Christian theism. In line with Thomas Aquinas's, his theism is not greatly different from the Nursian version of Islamic theism exposed in the *Risale-i Nur*. Although Swinburne employs almost all known theistic arguments, he specializes in the argument from religious experience (ARE) and the arguments from miracles. As was discussed in Chapter 4, the authenticity test of a religious experience developed by Swinburne seems to have been applied by Nursi in his *Risale-i Nur* many years prior to Swinburne's introduction of it.

Craig takes a more proactive route to preach his theism, using similar arguments to Nursi's. As opposed to Nursi's text-based teaching, Craig's is more speech-plus-text-oriented. For instance, in his academic debates, the cosmological argument, especially the *kalām* cosmological argument, is the argument Craig employs the most. His moral argument, though not identical to Nursi's, is probably his second most common argument. On the use of prophethood and revelation Nursi and Craig differ. Nursi dedicates the bulk of his writings to try to prove the authenticity of the prophet Muḥammad and the Qur'an, whereas Craig refers to Jesus and the Bible a great deal without trying to prove their authenticity.

Alvin Plantinga, another influential Professor of Christian theology, differs from Nursi in terms of the theistic argument he focuses on. Among other Christian apologists such as Charles Hartshorne and Norman Malcolm, Plantinga is mainly interested in a modern version of St Anselm's ontological argument, which he tries to develop into a "modal logic" version. In spite of being the first line of defense for Abrahamic theism, the ontological argument is almost completely ignored by Nursi, perhaps because he is more of a scholar who wishes to deal with verifiable theories.

Despite a traditional rivalry between Jews, Christians and Muslims, Nursi does not try to underline the differences, but rather highlights the common ground that all Abrahamic religions hold. That is to say, Nursi is keen on forming a common front with Jews, Christians, and Muslims to defend Abrahamic theism and reduce the damage caused by aggressive atheism. Although he occasionally displays distaste for the aggressive, imperialist behavior of the Christian West, especially during World War I, he later makes it clear that the Abrahamic religions need to join forces to defend the oneness (*tawḥīd*) of God.

In this sense, Nursi's three arguments—the teleological, the prophethood-based and the moral—are, it may be argued, easily transferable to the Jewish and Christian contexts. However, the Nursian defense of the revelation of the Qur'an to the prophet Muḥammad is difficult to transfer to the Old and New Testaments.

Said Nursi's four ways of arguing for the existence of God are clearly not original in light of the history of theism. Yet, in bringing them together to form a fool proof, fourfold argument and in constructing thereby a unique theism from the ground up, Nursi shows that he is another shield for the defense of Abrahamic theism.

Appendices

Appendix 1: Chronology and Diagram of the Risale-i Nur Collection

1A. Chronology of the Risale-i Nur Collection

1877	Saïd Nursi was born
1892	Nicknamed '*Bediüzzaman*' (wonder of the ages)
1911	*Hutbe-i Şamiye*, (Damascus Sermon) *Muḥākamāt* (Reasoning) published
1913	*Mûnāẓarāt* (Debates) published
1916	He began writing *al-Isharat al-I'jāz* (Signs of Miraculousness)
1919–21	Small treaties *Tuluât, Sunūhat, Lemaāt, Ishārāt* and *Hutuvat-i Sitte* written
1920–21	Collapse of the Ottoman Empire, emergence of Republic of Turkey. Beginning of New Said Era.
1923	*al-Mathnawī al-'Arabī al-Nūrī* (Epitomes of Light) translated into Turkish.
1926	Writing of *Risale-i Nur* begun in exile in Barla.
1926–29	*The Words*
1929–32	*The Letters*
1932–34	*The Flashes*
1936–40	Majority of *The Rays* written.
1948	Writing of *Risale-i Nur* completed.
1950	First democratically elected government came to power. Beginning of The Third Said Era.
1956	*Risale-i Nur* is printed in Latin alphabet.
1960	Saïd Nursi dies.

1B. Diagram of the Risale-i Nur Collection

The Words *(Sözler)*			
1st Word			
.			
.			
.			
33rd Word >>becomes	The Letters *(Mektūbat)*		
	1st Letter		
	.		
	.		
	.		
	27th Letter >>becomes	Barla-Kastamonu and Emirdağ Lâhikası	
	.		
	.		
	30th Letter >>becomes	Al-Ishārāt al-I'jāz (Signs of Miraculousness)	
	31st Letter >>becomes	The Flashes *(Lem'alar)*	
	.	1st Flash	
	33rd Letter	.	
		.	
		.	
		31st Flash >>becomes	The Rays *(Şualar)*
		.	1st Ray
		33rd Flash (al-Mathnawī al-Nūriyah)	.
			.
			.
			15th Ray

Appendix 2: Names and Attributes of God in Islam

Names in Transliterations	Meaning	Names in Transliterations	Meaning
Allāh	*The God.* The only one Almighty. He alone is worthy of worship.	*Al-Mubdī*	*The Originator.* He who creates all creatures initially without matter or model.
Al-'Adl	*The Just.* He who is Equitable.	*Al-Mughnī*	*The Enricher.* The Sufficer.
Al-Ākhir	*The Last.*	*Al-Muhaymin*	*The Guardian.* He who watches over and protects all things. (Helper in Peril)
al-'Afuw	*The Pardoner.* He who pardons all who sincerely repents.	*Al-Muḥsī*	*The Appraiser.* He who knows the number of every single thing in existence, even to infinity.
al-'Alīm	*The Knower of All.* He who has full knowledge of all things.	*al-Mu'īd*	*The Restorer.* He who recreates His creatures after He has annihilated them.
al-Aḥad	*The One.* The only one.	*al-Muʿizz*	*The Bestower of Honours.* He who confers honor and dignity.
al-Awwal	*The First.*	*al-Mujīb*	*The Responder to Prayer.* He who grants the wishes who appeals to him.
al-' Azīz	*The Mighty and Strong.*	*al-Munʿīm*	*The Nourisher.* He who gives every creature its sustenance.
al-' Azīm	*The Magnificent.* The Most High. He who is Most Splendid.	*al-Muqaddim*	*The Expediter.* He who brings forward whatever He wills (Forewarner).
al-Badī'	*The Incomparable.* He who is without model or match, and who brings into being worlds of amazing wonder.	*al-Muqsīt*	*The Equitable One.* He who does everything with proper balance and harmony.

Names in Transliterations	Meaning	Names in Transliterations	Meaning
al-Bā'ith	*The Resurrector.* He who brings the dead to life, and raises them from their tombs.	*al-Muqtadir*	*The Creator of All Power.* He who disposes at His will even of the strongest and mightiest of His creatures.
al-Bāqī	*The Everlasting One.* Eternal (in the future).	*al-Mumīt*	*The Taker of Life.* He who creates the death of a living creature.
al-Bāri'	*The Maker of Order* (Skilled Worker). O Evolver who created all things so that each whole and its parts are in perfect conformity and harmony.	*al-Muntaqīm*	*The Avenger.* He who justly inflicts upon wrongdoers the punishment they deserve.
al-Barr	Source of all Goodness. He who treats His servants tolerantly, and whose goodness and kindness are very great indeed.	*al-Muṣawwir*	*The Shaper of Beauty.* He who designs all things, giving each its particular form and character (Sculptor).
al-Baṣīr	*The All-Seeing.* To those who invoke this Name one hundred times between the obligatory and customary prayers in Friday congregation, Allah grants esteem in the eyes of others.	*al-Muta'āli*	*The Supreme One.* He is exalted in every respect, far beyond anything the mind could possibly attribute to His creatures.
al-Bāsiṭ	*The Reliever* (Uncloser). He who releases, letting things expand.	*al-Mutakabbir*	*The Majestic.* He who demonstrates His greatness in all things and in all ways.
al-Bāṭin	*The Hidden One.* He who is hidden, concealed.	*al-Mudhill*	*The Humiliator.* He who degrades and abases.
al-Dhārr	*The Distresser.* The Creator of the Harmful. He who creates things that cause pain and injury.	*An-Nāfi'*	*The Creator of Good.* He who creates things that yields advantages and benefit.
al-Fattāh	*The Opener.* He who opens the solution to all problems and makes things easy.	*al-Nūr*	*The Light.* He who gives light to all the worlds, who illuminates the faces, minds and hearts of His servants.

Names in Transliterations	Meaning	Names in Transliterations	Meaning
al-Ghaffār	*The Forgiving.* He who is always ready to forgive.	*al-Qābiḍ*	*The Constrictor.* He who constricts and restricts.
al-Ghafūr	*The Forgiver* and Hider of Faults.	*al-Qādir*	*The All-Powerful.* He who is Able to do what He wills as He wills (Providence).
al-Ghanī	*The Rich One.* He who is infinitely rich and completely Independent.	*al-Qahhār*	*The Subduer.* He who dominates all things, and prevails upon them to do whatever He wills (Dominant).
al-Hādī	*The Guide.* He who provides guidance.	*al-Qawī*	*The Most Strong.* The Possessor of All Strength.
al-Ḥāfiẓ	*The Preserver.* He who guards all creatures in every detail.	*al-Qayyūm*	*The Self-Existing One.* He who maintains the heavens, the earth, and everything that exists.
al-Ḥayy	*The Ever Living One.* The living who knows all things and whose strength is sufficient for everything.	*al-Quddūs*	*The Pure One.* He who is free from all errors.
al-Ḥakīm	*The Perfectly Wise.* He whose every command and action is pure wisdom.	*al-Rāfi'*	*The Exalter.* He who raises up.
al-Ḥakam	*The Judge.* He who judges and makes right prevails.	*al-Raḥīm*	*The All Compassionate.* He who acts with extreme kindness.
al-'Aliyyu	*The Highest.* The Exalted.	*al-Raḥmān*	*The All Merciful.* He who wills goodness and mercy for all His creatures.
al-Ḥalīm	*The Forbearing.* He who is Most Clement.	*al-Raqīb*	*The Watchful One.*
al-Ḥamīd	*The Praiseworthy.* All praise belongs to Him, and who alone do the tongues of all creation laud.	*al-Rashīd*	*The Righteous Teacher.* He who moves all things in accordance with His eternal plan, bringing them without error and with order and wisdom to their ultimate destiny (Unerring).

Names in Transliterations	Meaning	Names in Transliterations	Meaning
al-Ḥaqq	*The Truth.* He who's being endures unchangingly.	*al-Ra'ūf*	*The Kind.* He who is very compassionate (Indulgent).
al-Ḥasīb	*The Accounter.* He who knows every detail.	*al-Razzāq*	*The Sustainer.* He who provides all things useful to His creatures.
al-Jabbār	*The Compelling.* He who repairs all broken thing, and completes that which is incomplete.	*as-Ṣabūr*	*The Patient One.* He who is characterized by infinite patience.
al-Jalīl	*The Glorious.* He who is Lord of Majesty and Grandeur.	*al-Salām*	*The Source of Peace.* He who frees His servants from all danger.
al-Jāmi'	*The Gatherer.* He who brings together what He wills, when He wills, where He wills.	*al-Ṣamad*	*The Eternal.* He who is the only recourse for the ending of need and the removal of affliction.
al-Kabīr	*The Greatest.* He who supremely great.	*al-Samī'u*	*The Hearer of All.* Allah takes care of all the needs of those who invoke this glorious Name one hundred times.
al-Karīm	*The Generous.* He whose generosity is most abundant.	*al-Shāhid*	*The Witness.* He who is present everywhere and observes all things.
al-Khabīr	*The All Aware.* He who has the knowledge of inner and most secret aspects of all things.	*al-Shakūr*	*The Rewarder of Thankfulness.* He who gratefully rewards good deeds (Appreciator).
al-Khāfiḍ	*The Abaser.* He who brings down, diminishes.	*al-Tawwāb*	*The Acceptor to Repentance.* He who is ever ready to accept repentance and to forgive sins (Relenting).
al-Khāliq	*The Creator.* He who brings from non-being into being, creating all things in such a way that He determines their existence and the conditions and events they are to experience.	*al-Wakīl*	*The Trustee/ Guardian.* He who manages the affairs of those who duly commit them to His charge, and who looks after them better than they could themselves.

Names in Transliterations	Meaning	Names in Transliterations	Meaning
al-Laṭīf	*The Subtle One.* He who knows the minutest subtleties of all things.	*al-Wālī*	*The Protecting Friend.* He who is a nearest friend to His good servants.
al-Majīd	*The Majestic One.* He whose glory is most great and most high.	*al-Wahhāb*	*The Giver of All.* He who constantly bestows blessings of every kind.
al-Majīd	*The Glorious.* He, whose dignity and glory are most great, and whose generosity and munificence are bountiful.	*al-Wāḥid*	*The Unique.* He who is Single, absolutely without partner or equal in His Essence, Attributes, Actions, Names and Decrees.
al-Mālik	*The Absolute Ruler.* The Ruler of the entire universe (King of Kings).	*al-Wājid*	*The Finder.* He who finds what He wishes when He wishes (Perceiving).
Mālik-ul-Mulk	*The Owner of All.* The King of the Kingdom.	*al-Wadūd*	*The Loving One.* He who loves His good servants, and bestows his compassion upon them.
al-Māni'	*The Preventer of Harm.* The Withholder.	*Al-Wālī*	*The Governor.* The Protecting Friend. He who administers this vast universe and all its passing phenomena.
al-Mu'min	*The Inspirer of Faith.* He who awakes the light of faith in our hearts.	*al-Wās'i*	*The All Comprehending.* He who has limitless capacity and abundance.
al-Matīn	*The Firm.* He who is very steadfast.	*al-Wārith*	*The Inheritor of All.* He who is the Real Owner of all riches.
Al-Muhyi	*The Giver of Life.* He who confers life, gives vitality, revives.	*Az-Zāhir*	*The Manifest One.* He who is Evident.
al-Mu'akhkhir	*The Delayer.* He who sets back or delays whatever He wills.	*Zul-Jalāli-Wal-Ikrām*	*The Lord of Majesty and Bounty.* He who possesses both greatness and gracious magnanimity.

Appendix 3: Elements in the Human Body

Percentage of Body Weight	Element	Usage
65%	Oxygen	This element is obviously the most important element in the human body. Oxygen atoms are present in water, which is the compound most common in the body, and other compounds that make up tissues. It is also found in the blood and lungs owing to respiration.
18.6%	Carbon	Carbon is found in every organic molecule in the body, as well as the waste product of respiration (carbon dioxide). It is typically ingested in food that is eaten.
9.7%	Hydrogen	Hydrogen is found in all water molecules in the body as well as many other compounds making up the various tissues.
3.2%	Nitrogen	Nitrogen is very common in proteins and organic compounds. It is also present in the lungs owing to its abundance in the atmosphere.
1.8%	Calcium	Calcium is a primary component of the skeletal system, including the teeth. It is also found in the nervous system, muscles, and the blood.
1.0%	Phosphorus	This element is common in the bones and teeth, as well as nucleic acids.
0.4%	Potassium	Potassium is found in the muscles, nerves, and certain tissues.
0.2%	Sodium	Sodium is excreted in sweat, but is also found in muscles and nerves.
0.2%	Chlorine	Chlorine is present in the skin and facilitates water absorption by the cells.
0.06%	Magnesium	Magnesium serves as a cofactor for various enzymes in the body.
0.04%	Sulphur	Sulphur is present in many amino acids and proteins.
0.007%	Iron	Iron is found mostly in the blood since it facilitates the transportation of oxygen.
0.0002%	Iodine	Iodine is found in certain hormones in the thyroid gland.

Source: ***Lenntech BV***
Rotterdamseweg 402 M 2629 HH Delft, The Netherlands

Appendix 4: Marriages of the Prophet Muḥammad (571-632) in Chronological Order

	Name of wife	Wife's age	Muḥammad's age	Date	Notes
1	Khādījah b. al-Khuwaylid	40	25	595 CE	Marriage lasted 25 years until her death. She gave birth to 6 children: Abd Allāh (M), Qāsim (M), Zaynab (F), Ruqiyyah (F), Fāṭimah (F), and Umm Kulthūm (F)
2	Sawdah b. Zamʿah	53 or 55	53	623 CE	She was the only wife for three years
3	ʿĀishah b. Abī Bakr	7 to 13 or 17 (Disputed)	53	623 CE	Only virgin wife
4	Ḥafṣah b. ʿUmar	20	55	625 CE	She was a widow
5	Zaynab b. Khuzayma	50	56	625-626 CE	She died within eight months of marriage owing to illness
6	Hind b. Abī Umayya (Umm Salamah)	65	56	626 CE	Married after the death of Zaynab. Umm Salamah had 3 children from her previous marriage
7	Rayḥānah b. Zayd	?	56	626 CE	She was a Jew from Bani Qurayzah tribe
8	Zaynab b. Jaḥsh	34	56	626 CE	She was a widow
9	Juwayriyya b. Ḥārith	20	58	628 CE	She was captured as a slave, freed and married to Muḥammad
10	Ṣafiyyah b. Ḥuyay Ibn Akhtab	20	58	629 CE	She was a Jew captured from Bani Nadīr
11	Ramlah b. Abī Sufyān (Umm Ḥabībah)	55	58	629 CE	She was the daughter of the leader of Quraysh tribe in Mecca

	Name of wife	Wife's age	Muḥammad's age	Date	Notes
12	Māriyah al-Qibṭiyyah	?	57	628 CE	Gift from Byzantine ruler Muqawqis. Mother of Ibrāhim who died during infancy.
13	Maymūna b. al-Ḥārith	36	60	630	She had two children from her previous marriage.

Owing to differences between the Islamic and Gregorian calendars, some ages and dates are estimates.

Source: M. Lings, *Muḥammad: His Life Based on the Earliest Sources* (New York: Inner Traditions International, 1983).

Appendix 5: The Names and Characteristics of the Prophets Mentioned in the Qur'ān

Qur'ān, 4:163–165

163: Lo! We inspire thee (Muḥammad) as We inspired Noah and the prophets after him, as We inspired Abraham and Ishmael and Isaac and Jacob and the tribes, and Jesus and Job and Jonah and Aaron and Solomon, and as we imparted unto David the Psalms;

164: And messengers We have mentioned unto thee before and messengers We have not mentioned unto thee; and Allah spake directly unto Moses;

165 Messengers of good cheer and off warning, in order that mankind might have no argument against Allah after the messengers. Allah was ever Mighty, Wise.

Qur'ān, 6:84–86

84: And We bestowed upon him Isaac and Jacob; each of them We guided; and Noah did We guide aforetime; and of his seed (We guided) David and Solomon and Job and Joseph and Moses and Aaron. Thus do We reward the good.

85: And Zachariah and John and Jesus and Elias. Each one (of them) was of the righteous.

86: And Ishmael and Elisha and Jonah and Lot. Each one of them did We prefer above (Our) creatures,

Qur'ān, 21:85–88

85: And (mention) Ishmael, and Idris (Enoch), and Dhul-Kifl (Ezekiel). All were of the steadfast.

86: And We brought them in unto Our mercy. Lo! they are among the righteous.

87: And (mention) Dhun Nun (Jonah), when he went off in anger and deemed that We had no power over him, but he cried out in the darkness, saying: There is no God save Thee. Be Thou glorified! I have been a wrong-doer.
88: Then We heard his prayer and saved him from the anguish. Thus We save believers.

Qur'ān, 7:73

And to (the tribe of) Thamud (We sent) their brother Salih. He said: O my people! Serve Allah. Ye have no other God save Him. A wonder from your Lord hath come unto you. Lo! this is the camel of Allah, a token unto you; so let her feed in Allah's earth, and touch her not with hurt lest painful torment seize you.

Qur'ān, 26:123–125

123: (The tribe of) Aad denied the messengers (of Allah),
124: When their brother Hud said unto them: Will ye not ward off (evil)?
125: Lo! I am a faithful messenger unto you,

Qur'ān, 7:85

To the Madyan people We sent Shu'aib one of their own brethren: he said: "O my people! worship Allah; Ye have no other god but Him. Now hath come unto you a clear (sign) from your Lord! Give just measure and weight nor withhold from the people the things that are their due; and do no mischief on the earth after it has been set in order: that will be best for you if ye have faith.

Appendix 6: Major Sins (*Al-Kaba'ir*) in Islam deduced from the Qur'an and the Hadīth

1. Associating partners with Allāh (*Shirk*)
2. Committing murder (Qur'an, 25:68)
3. Performing Sorcery (Qur'an, 2:102)
4. Not performing the Prayers (Qur'an, 19:59)
5. Withholding *Zakah* (Charity) (Qur'an, 3:180)
6. Breaking the fast of Ramadān or not fasting in that month without a valid excuse
7. Not performing the pilgrimage when one has the ability to do so
8. Disobeying one's parents (Qur'an, 17:23)
9. Cutting off the ties of relationships (Qur'an, 47:22)
10. Committing adultery or fornication (Qur'an, 17:30)
11. Committing sodomy
12. Taking or paying interest (Qur'an, 2:275)
13. Devouring the wealth of orphans (Qur'an, 4:10)
14. Forging statements concerning Allāh or forging *hadīth* (Qur'an, 39:60)
15. Fleeing from battle (Qur'an, 8:16)
16. Wrongdoing, deception or oppression on the part of the ruler (Qur'an, 26:42)
17. Being arrogant, boastful or vain (Qur'an, 16:23)
18. Giving false testimony (Qur'an, 25:72)
19. Drinking alcoholic beverages (Qur'an, 5:90)
20. Gambling (Qur'an, 5:90)
21. Slandering innocent women (Qur'an, 24:23)
22. Misappropriating something from booty (Qur'an, 3:161)
23. Stealing (Qur'an, 5:38)
24. Committing highway robbery (Qur'an, 5:33)

25. Making a false oath
26. Committing oppression (Qur'an, 26:277)
27. Levying illegal taxes
28. Consuming forbidden wealth or taking it by any means (Qur'an, 2:188)
29. Committing suicide (Qur'an, 4:29)
30. Being a perpetual liar (Qur'an, 3:61)
31. Ruling by laws other than the laws of Islam (Qur'an, 5:44)
32. Engaging in bribery (Qur'an, 2:188)
33. Women appearing like men and vice versa
34. Being a *dayyouth* (A *dayyouth* is one who approves of the indecency of his womenfolk and who is void of jealousy, or the pimp who facilitates indecency between two people.)
35. Marrying for the purpose of making a woman allowable for another (Qur'an, 2)
36. Not keeping clean from the remains of urine
37. Acting for show (Qur'an, 107:4–6)
38. Acquiring knowledge only for worldly gain or concealing knowledge (Qur'an, 2:160)
39. Breaching trusts (Qur'an, 8:27)
40. Reminding people of one's kindness (Qur'an, 2:27)
41. Denying predestination (Qur'an, 54:49)
42. Eavesdropping on other's private conversation (Qur'an, 54:12)
43. Spreading harmful tales (Qur'an, 54:10)
44. Cursing others
45. Not fulfilling one's promises
46. Believing in what soothsayers and astrologers say
47. A wife being rebellious to her husband (Qur'an, 4:34)
48. Putting pictures of beings with souls on clothing, curtains, rocks and any other items
49. Striking oneself, wailing, tearing one's clothing, pulling one's hair and similar deeds as a form of mourning
50. Committing injustice (Qur'an, 42:42)

51. Being overbearing or taking advantage of the weak, slaves, wives or animals
52. Harming neighbours
53. Harming and abusing Muslims (Qur'an, 33:58)
54. Wearing one's clothes too long (i.e., below the ankles)
55. Harming the slaves of Allāh
56. Men wearing silk and gold
57. The running away of a slave
58. Sacrificing animals for other than Allāh
59. Claiming that somebody is one's father while the claimant knows it is not true
60. Arguing or quarrelling for show and not seeking the truth
61. Not allowing excess water to flow to others
62. Not measuring weights properly (Qur'an, 83:1–3)
63. Thinking that one is safe from Allāh's planning (Qur'an, 7:99)
64. Eating carrion, blood or pork meat (Qur'an, 6:145)
65. Not praying in the congregation and praying by oneself without a valid excuse
66. Continually not performing the Friday prayers and congregational prayers without any valid excuse
67. Harming others by manipulating one's bequests (Qur'an, 4:12)
68. Being deceitful or deceptive (Qur'an, 35:43)
69. Spying on Muslims and pointing out their secrets (Qur'an, 68:11)
70. Abusing or reviling anyone about the Companions of the Prophet Muḥammad

Appendix 7: Nursi's Exposition of The Qur'an's Miraculousness

(Outline of The Twenty-fifth Word)

Evidence Group I:

First Ray: This is the eloquence of the Qur'an (*balāghah*)

1.a. by means of poetic eloquence

First: There is a wonderful eloquence and purity of style in the Qur'an's word-order (*jazālah*)

Second: This is the wonderful eloquence in its meaning. (*ma'nà*)

Third: This is the wonderful uniqueness of its style (*'uslūb*)

Fourth: This is the wonderful eloquence in its wording; that is, in the words employed (*faṣāḥah*)

Fifth: This is the excellence in its manner of exposition; that is to say, the superiority, conciseness, and grandeur. (*barāah*)

i. eloquence in encouragement and urging (*targhīb wa tashwīq*)

ii. eloquence in deterring and threatening (*tarhīb wa takdīr*)

iii. eloquence in praising (*madḥ*)

iv. eloquence in censure and restraint (*dhamm wa zajr*)

v. eloquence proof and demonstration (*ithbāt*)

vi. eloquence in guidance (*irshād*)

vii. eloquence in making understood and silencing in argument (*ifhām wa ilzām*)

Second Ray: This is the Qur'an's extraordinary comprehensiveness (*jāmi' iyyah*)

a. the comprehensiveness in the words (*lafẓ*)

b. the extraordinary comprehensiveness in its meaning (*ma'nà*)

c. the extraordinary comprehensiveness in its knowledge (*' ilm*)

d. the extraordinary comprehensiveness of the subjects it puts forward (*mabāḥis*)

e. the wonderful comprehensiveness of the Qur'an's style and conciseness. (*'uslūb*)

Third Ray: These are the Qur'an's [a] giving news of the Unseen (*ikhbār-i ghaybī*), [b] preserving its youth in every age (*shabābah*), and [c] being appropriate to every level of person (*muwāfakah*).

a.i. its telling about the past, one part of the Unseen

a.ii. its giving news of the future

a. iii. its giving news of the Divine truths, cosmic truths, and the matters of the hereafter

b.i. the Qur'an's youth

c.i. It is as though the All-Wise Qur'an is every century turned directly towards all the classes of humanity, and addresses each particularly

Evidence Group II:

1. Qur'an's pleasant fluency (*salāsah*), a superior correctness, a firm mutual solidarity (*tasānud*), and compact proportionateness (*tanāsub*), powerful co-operation between the sentences and parts (*ta' āwun*), and an elevated harmony between the verses and their aims (*tajāwub*).
2. Its unique style in the summaries and Most Beautiful Divine Names, which it shows at the ends of its verses (*fadhlakah*)

Evidence Group III.

1. Its Miraculous Expositions (*'ijāz*)
2. Its superiority of its wisdom over the human philosophy
3. Its degree of the wisdom and scienc—before Qur'anic wisdom—of the purified scholars, the saints, and the enlightened among philosophers

Source: Risale-i Nur Külliyatı, and eRisale.com

Appendix 8: Chronology of the Prophet Muḥammad's Life

Time Line of Some Important Events in the Prophet Muḥammad's Life

570 C.E. Muḥammad is born in Mecca

595 C.E. Muḥammad marries Khadija, who later becomes the first Muslim

610 C.E. Muḥammad receives what he comes to believe is his first visitation from the angel Gabriel and revelation from Allāh

613 C.E. Muḥammad begins preaching Islam publicly in Mecca

615 C.E. Friction with the Quraysh causes some Muslims to leave Arabia for Abyssinia

619 C.E. Khadija dies

620 C.E. The Night Journey (*Isrā wa al-Mi'rāj)* Prophet Muḥammad is carried from Mecca to Jerusalem and then travels to the heavens and meets the previous prophets (Adam, Noah, Abraham, Moses, Jesus, etc).

622 C.E. The *Hijra*: Muḥammad and the Muslims flee from Mecca to Medina

624 C.E. The *Nakhla* raid. These raids were not solely designed to exact revenge from the people who had rejected the Prophet who had arisen among them. They served a key economic purpose, keeping the Muslim movement solvent.

624 C.E. The Battle of Badr: the Muslims overcome great odds to defeat the pagan Meccans

624 C.E. Muḥammad and the Muslims besiege the Jewish Qaynuqa tribe and exile them from Medina

625 C.E. The Battle of Uhud: the pagan Meccans defeat the Muslims

625 C.E. Siege and exile from Medina of the Jewish Nadir tribe

627 C.E. The Battle of the Trench: the Jewish Qurayzah tribe betrays Muḥammad

627 C.E. The Execution the males of the Qurayzah tribe and enslaves the women and children by Sa'd Ibn Mutab

628 C.E. Muḥammad concludes the Treaty of Hudaybiyya with the pagan Meccans

628 C.E. Prophet Muḥammad and the Muslims besiege the Khaybar oasis and exile the Jews from it.

630 C.E. Muḥammad and the Muslims conquer Mecca

630 C.E. The Muslims prevail in the Battle of Hunayn and conquer Ta'if; Muḥammad becomes the ruler of Arabia

631 C.E. The Arabian tribes remaining outside Islamic rule accept Islam

631 C.E. the expedition to Tabuk

632 C.E. Muḥammad dies in Medina on June 8, 632 CE

Sources:

1. Martin Lings, *Muhammad: His Life Based on the Earliest Sources* (New York: Inner Traditions International, 1983).

and

2. Reşit Haylamaz, *Gönül tahtımızın eşsiz sultanı: Efendimiz (sallallahu aleyhi ve sellem)* (Istanbul: Muştu, 2008).

Appendix 9: Nursi's Exposition of the Miracles of the Prophet Muḥammad

(Map of the Nineteenth Letter)

FIRST SIGN
Argues that Muḥammad has the highest personal qualities.

SECOND SIGN
Argues that Muḥammad's miracles are admitted by his enemies.

THIRD SIGN
Demonstrates two groups of wonders. First are the pre-prophetic era paranormal events, i.e. *irhāsāt* such as dying of the *majusi's* fire and drying up of Siwah Lake.
Second group is the wonders during his prophethood which are explored in the following signs.

FOURTH SIGN
Demonstrates how Muḥammad reported the unseen truths concerning the Godhead, the universe, and the hereafter, as well as his correct predictions about his Companions, his Family and his community.

FIFTH SIGN
Demonstrates examples of *Hadiths* concerning the matters of the Unseen.

SIXTH SIGN
Reports further specific future events such as the capture of Cyprus, conquest of Constantinople and some political events.

SEVENTH SIGN
Reports miracles that relate to the increase in food.

EIGHTH SIGN
Describes miracles which were manifested in connection with water

NINTH SIGN
Narrates incidents where trees obeyed Muḥammad's orders, and moving from their places to come to him.

TENTH SIGN
Corroborating the miracles concerning trees and reported in the form of 'consensus,' is the miracle of the *moaning of the pole*

ELEVENTH SIGN
Describes how rocks and mountains among lifeless creatures demonstrated prophetic miracles.

TWELFTH SIGN
Gives further three examples that are related to the Eleventh Sign.

THIRTEENTH SIGN
Reports incidents where the sick and the wounded being healed through Muḥammad's blessed breath.

FOURTEENTH SIGN
Demonstrates the wonders manifested as a result of his prayers.

FIFTEENTH SIGN
Demonstrates miracles where animals, the dead, the jinn, and the angels recognized Muḥammad and affirmed his prophethood.

SIXTEENTH SIGN
Elaborates pre-prophetic paranormal events (*irhāsāt*) which are already mentioned in the third sign. Here Nursi specially focuses on the mentioning of Muḥammad in the previous scriptures such as the Torah, the Bible, the Psalms of David.

SEVENTEENTH SIGN
Muḥammad's own self. That is, the elevated moral virtues brought together in his person, which as friend and foe agreed was in all respects of the very highest degree.

EIGHTEENTH SIGN
This is the All-Wise Qur'an, which comprises hundreds of evidences of Muḥammad's prophethood, and forty aspects of whose own miraculousness have been proven. The Twenty-Fifth Word (See Appendix 7) has explained concisely and proved those forty aspects in its approximately one hundred and fifty pages.

NINETEENTH SIGN
Further describes the correctness, truthfulness and integrity of Muḥammad.

Source: Risale-i Nur Collection and eRisale.com

Appendix 10: Outline of Kalām Cosmological Arguments

Ibn Sina	Al-Fārābī
1.Definitions: a. Contingent being: a being composed of essence and existence, which therefore requires an existential cause. b. Necessary being: a being not composed of essence and existence, which therefore does not require an existential cause. 2. Every being is either contingent or necessary. 3. If it is necessary, then a necessary being exists. 4.If it is contingent, then a necessary being exists. a. A contingent being requires an existential cause. b. If this cause is also a contingent being, then an existential causal series is formed. c. An existential causal series cannot be infinite. i. An infinite series has no first cause. ii. Therefore, there would be no cause of existence. iii. Therefore, contingent beings could not exist. iv. But this is absurd. d. Therefore, the existential causal series must terminate in a necessary being. 5. Therefore, a necessary being exists	1. Definitions: a. Every being has either a reason for its existence or no reason for its existence. b. A being which has a reason for its existence is contingent, both before it exists and after it exists. i. Because its actually coming to exist does not remove the contingent nature of its existence. c. A being which has no reason for its existence is necessary. 2. Every being is either contingent or necessary. 3. If it is necessary, then a necessary being exists. 4. If it is contingent, then a necessary being exists because: a. A contingent being cannot come into existence without a reason. b. If this reason is also contingent, then there is a series of contingent beings linked together. c. Such series cannot be infinite i. Because then there would be no being at all a. Because the being in question could come into existence only if it were preceded by an infinite succession of beings, which is absurd. d. Therefore, the series terminate in a necessary being. 5. Therefore, a necessary being exits.

Al-Ghazzālī	Ibn Rushd
1. Everything that begins to exist requires a cause for its existence. 2. The world began to exit. a. There are temporal phenomena in the world. b. These are preceded by other temporal phenomena. c. The series of temporal phenomena cannot regress infinitely. i. An actually existing infinite series involves various absurdities. d. Therefore, the series of temporal phenomena must have had a beginning. 3. Therefore, the world has a cause for its origin: its Creator	1. Possible beings must be caused. 2. There cannot be an infinite series of possible beings each caused by another because: a. In an infinite series there is no cause. b. So the possible being would be uncaused. c. But this contradicts (1): *Possible beings must be caused.* 3. Therefore, the series must end in a necessary cause, which is either caused or uncaused. 4. There cannot be an infinite series of caused necessary causes because: a. In an infinite regress there is no cause. b. So caused necessary causes would not be caused. c. But this is self-contradictory. 5. Therefore, the series must end in an uncaused necessary cause, which is the necessary being.

Appendix 11: Glossary

TERM	MEANING
'Alīm	All-Knowing
Abū Naṣr	Al-Fārābā or Alpharabius
Abū Sufyān	the leader of the Quraysh of Mecca, the most powerful tribe of pre-Islamic Arabia. He was a staunch opponent of prophet Muhammad, until later accepting Islam.
Abū Ṭālib	uncle of prophet Muhammad and father of the Fourth Caliph Ali.
aḥādith	various reports describing the words, actions, or habits of the prophet Muhammad.
Aḥmad	Another name of Prophet Muḥammad
Aḥzāb	the clans, the coalition, the combined forces, the parties
al-amīn	One of prophet Muhammad's nicknames, meaning the trustworthy
Al-Fārābī	renowned philosopher and jurist who wrote in the fields of political philosophy, metaphysics, ethics and logic. (died in 951 AD)
Al-Ghazzālī	medieval Muslim theologian, jurist, philosopher, and mystic. (died in 1111 AD)
Al-Lāt	Goddess of war, combat and fertility worshipped in pre-Islamic era
al Maqāṣid al-falāsifa	The Aims of the Philosophers, book written by Al-Ghazzālī.
al-Mathnawī al-'Arabī al-Nūriyah	One of Nursi's books, literally means 'The Seedbed of the Light'
al-mubdī	The originator
al-Rāzī	Muslim theologian and scholar, author of one of the most authoritative commentaries on the Qur'ān
al-Uzzā	Goddess of might, protection and love worshipped in pre-Islamic era
al-wājib al-wujūd	The necessary being

TERM	MEANING
al-ʿIshārāt al-I'jāz	One of Nursi's books, literally means 'The Signs of Miracoulesness'
Allāh	God in Islam
amānah	Divine trust
anā	ego, self or human 'I'
āsār	work
Ash'arite	Ashʿarism or Ashʿari theology is an early theological school of Sunni Islam, based on clerical authority and rejection of cause and effect reasoning.
ashq-ı ilāhi	Divine Love
āyāt	evidence, sign, or miracle
Ayāt al-Kübra	One of Nursi's books, literally means 'The Great Sign'
aʿwjadathu al-asbāb	Causes create this
balāghah	eloquence
barāhin	evidences
bayān	exposition
Bukhārī	author of the hadith collection known as Sahih al-Bukhari, regarded by Sunni Muslims as one of the most authentic (sahih) hadith collections
burhān	decisive proof
dalīl al-ʿināyah	divine providence
Dhāt	God's self
Divān-ı Harb-i Örfî	One of Nursi's books, literally means 'The Court Marshall'
fāil	doer
falāsifūn	philosophers
faṭānah	sagacity
Fāṭir-i Ḥakīm	The Wise Maker
Fattāḥ	He who opens all things
fiṭrah	creation, nature, natural disposition, innate character, and innate and unchanging natural predisposition
fiṭrat-i zī shuʿūr	primordial nature of living things
fıṭrat-ı bashar	human nature
Ghafūr	forgiving
Ghanī	wealthy
hadīth	one of various reports describing the words, actions, or habits of the prophet Muhammad.

TERM	MEANING
ḥads	intuition
Ḥalīm	forbearing
Hāmed	The praised one
Haqīqah	truth
Ḥarām	unlawful
ḥarf	letter
ḥiss-i sāiqah	sense of direction
ḥiss-i shāiqah	sense of eagerness
ḥurūf	letters
Hutuvat-i Sitte	One of Nursi's books, literally means 'The Six Steps'
i'jāz	inimitability of the Qur'an
ibdā	create
Iblīs	Devil
ījāz	brevity and conciseness
ijmā	consensus
ikhbār-i ghaybī	reporting the unseen
ilhām	inspiration
imāms	Islamic leaders
Incoherence of Incoherence	book by Andalusian Muslim polymath and philosopher Ibn-Rushd is an Islamic philosophical book in which the author defends the use of Aristotelian philosophy within Islamic thought.
Injīl	Bible
injizāb	attraction
insān-i kāmil	perfect human being
inshā	build
iqtaẓathu al-ṭabīʿah	nature requires this
irāda	free will
irhāṣāt	miraculous events prior to prophet Muhammad's birth
ishtiyāq	longing
ism al-ʿāẓām	the greatest name of God
iṣmah	purity
Isrā wa al-Mi'rāj	The night journey and the ascension of Prophet Muhammad
Isra'illiyāt	the body of narratives originating from Jewish and Christian traditions

TERM	MEANING
istimdāt	ask for help
istināḍ	stand
Jabrī	a school of thought which deny free will in man, fatalist
jāhiliyyah	Pre-Islamic age of ignorance
jāmiʿiyyah	community
jihād	striving in the way of God
juz'ī ikhtiyārī	human free will
juz'ī irāda	human free will
Ka'bah	The cube shaped building at the center of Islam's most sacred mosque, that is Al-Masjid Al-Ḥarām (The Sacred Mosque), in Mecca, in Saudi Arabia. It is the most sacred site in Islam and considered by Muslims to be the *bayt Allāh*, the "House of God"
kāfir	disbeliever
kahānah	oracle
kalām	Islamic scholastic theology
Khadījah	the first wife and follower of Prophet Muhammad. She is commonly regarded by Muslims as the 'Mother of the Believers.' (555–620)
Khāliq-i kulli shay	Creator of all things
Khariji	members of a group that appeared in the first century of Islam during the First Fitna, the crisis of leadership after the death of Prophet Muhammad.
kitāb-ı kabīr-i kāināt	The great book of the universe
kitāb-ı kāināt	Book of the universe
lafẓ	speech
latīfe-i Rabbaniye	subtle faculties
Lemaāt	One of Nursi's books, literally means Gleams
ma'nā-i ḥarfī	other-indicative meaning
mabādi	principles
madāris	a college or school for Islamic instruction
Madrasat uz-Zahrā	The name of Nursi's project university, literally means 'The School of Brilliance'
majūsis	Zoroastrians. The followers of Zoroastrianism, the ancient pre-Islamic religion of Iran that survives there in isolated areas and, more prosperously, in India, where the descendants of Zoroastrian Iranian (Persian) immigrants are known as Parsis, or Parsees.

TERM	MEANING
Manāt	one of the three chief goddesses of Mecca, Goddess of fate.
maqāṣid-i ʿarbaʾ	four purposes
Maria al-Qibṭiyya	One of the wives of Prophet Muhammad, Maria the Copt, was an Egyptian Coptic who was gifted to the prophet in 628 as a slave by Muqawqis the Copt, the Christian ruler of Egypt at the time.
Masīḥ al-Dajjāl	the false messiah, liar, the deceiver, an evil figure in Islamic eschatology. He is to appear, pretending to be al-Masih, before Yawm al-Qiyamah (Day of Judgement)
Māturidī	a Sunni Hanafi jurist, theologian, and scriptural exegete from ninth-century Samarkand who became the eponymous codifier of one of the principal orthodox schools of Sunni theology, the Maturidi school.
Mawdūdī	Indian Muslim philosopher, jurist, journalist and imam. (1903–79)
mayalān	tendency
Mi'yār al-ʿilm	One of Al-Ghazzālī's books on Islamic logic
Muḥākamāt	One of Nursi's books, literally means Reasoning
Muḥyiddin ibn Ārābī	Andalusian Sunni scholar of Islam, mystic, poet, and philosopher. He is renowned among practitioners of Sufism as Shaikh Al-Akbar "the greatest master" and also as a saint. (1165–1240)
munāfiq	Hypocrite, a person decried in the Qur'an as outward Muslim who is secretly unsympathetic to the cause of Muslims and actively seeks to undermine the Muslim community.
Munāẓarāt	One of Nursi's books, literally means Debates
musabbib al-asbāb	The cause of the causes
mutakallimūn	Kalām scholars, Islamic philosophers
mʿanā-i ismī	the significative or self-referential meaning of things
nabī	prophet
naẓm	order
Nizām al-Mulk	scholar and vizier of the Seljuq Empire.
nubuwwah	prophethood
Nūr	Light
Nutuk	One of Nursi's books, literally means Speech
qāḍī	Judge in the Islamic court

TERM	MEANING
qiyāmah	Resurrection
Raḥmān	the Entirely Merciful God
rasūl	Prophet with Holly Scripture
Reşhalar	One of Nursi's small books
ribā	Usury or unjust, exploitative gains made in trade or business under Islamic law.
Risālat al-Kindī	Book by Al-Kindī, literally means Al-Kindī Letters
Rūm	Roman
ruyā-i ṣādiqah	Genuine dreams
Salām	Peace
Şāmiye	Of Damascus
Ṣāni al-Raḥmān	Compassionate Maker
Sawdā	The second wife of prophet Muḥammad
shu'ūn	Works and acts
ṣidq	Truthfulness
Sunūḥāt	One of Nursi's small books, literally means Inspirations
tablīgh	a call toward one's religion by one nation to another
Tafsīr	exegesis
Tahāfut	Incoherence, a book by al-Gazzālī
tanjīm	astrology
taqdir Ilāhi	Divine providence
tashakkala bi nafsihi	It is happening by itself
tawḥīd	Unity and Oneness of God
Tawrāt	Torah
Uḥud	A mountain near Medina where a battle between the early Muslims and their Quraysh Meccan enemies in 624 AD
uslūb	style
Wāhid	One
waḥy	revelation
Wājib al-Wujūd	Necessarily Existent
Walī	The Protecting Friend
wijdān	conscience
Zabūr	the holy book of prophet Dawud

TERM	MEANING
Zakāt	the compulsory giving of a set proportion of one's wealth to charity.
Zaynab bint Jaḥsh	One of Prophet Muḥammad's wives
zinā	unlawful sexual intercourse
ʿ*Ādil-i Muṭlaq*	Absolute Just
ʿAqā*id*	Plural of ʿaqīdah
ʿaqī*dah*	creed
ʿibā*dah*	Worship, service or servitude
ʿulamā	scholars

Bibliography

Abu-Rabi, Ibrahim M. *Islam at the Crossroads: On the Life and Thought of Bediuzzaman Said Nursi*. Albany, NY: State University of New York Press, 2003.

Adamson, Peter, and Richard C. Taylor. *The Cambridge Companion to Arabic Philosophy*. Cambridge: Cambridge University Press, 2005.

Al-Ghazali, and Sabih Ahmad Kamali. *Al-Ghazali's Tahafut Al-Falasifah: (Incoherence of the Philosophers)*. Lahore: Pakistan Philosophical Congress, 1958.

Alexandre du, Pont, Gautier de CompiËgne, Yvan G. Lepage, and Robert Burchard Constantijn Huygens. *Le Roman De Mahomet* [in Old French]. Paris: Klincksieck, 1977.

Alston, William P. *Perceiving God: The Epistemology of Religious Experience*. Ithaca, NY: Cornell University Press, 1991.

Anselm. *Proslogion* [in Spanish]. La Plata: Universidad Nacional de La Plata, Facultad de Humanidades y Ciencias de la EducaciÛn, Instituto de FilosofÌa, 1950.

Aquinas, Thomas. *Summa Contra Gentiles* [in Latin]. Romae: Apud Sedem Commissionis Leoninae, 1934.

———. *Summa Theologiae: Latin Text and English Translation, Introductions, Notes, Appendices, and Glossaries*. New York: McGraw-Hill, 1964.

———. *Summa Theologica*. New York: Benziger, 1947.

Aristotle. *The Metaphysics* [in Greek and English.]. Translated by Hugh Tredennick and G. Cyril Armstrong. London: Heinemann, 1933.

Ashqar, Umar Sulayman, and Nasiruddin Khattab. *Belief in Allah: In the Light of the Qur'an and Sunnah* [English with some Arabic.]. Riyadh: International Islamic Publishing House, 2003.

Atiyeh, George N. *Al-Kindi: The Philosopher of the Arabs*. Islamabad: Islamic Research Instiute, 1967.

Augustine. *On the Trinity*. Edited by Gareth B. Matthews. Cambridge Cambridge University Press, 2002.

Badıllı, Abdulkadir. *Bediüzzaman Said-I Nursi, Mufassal Tarihçe-I Hayatı* [in Turkish]. 2nd ed. İstanbul: Timaş Yayınları, 1998.

Ball, W. W. Rouse. *A Short Account of the History of Mathematics*. New York: Main Street, 2001.

Ball, Warwick. *Rome in the East: The Transformation of an Empire*. London: Routledge, 2000.

Bamberger, Fritz. *Julius Guttmann, Philosopher of Judaism*. London: Doubleday, 1960.

Behe, Michael J. *Darwin's Black Box: The Biochemical Challenge to Evolution.* New York: Free, 1996.

Birnbaum, Philip. *A Book of Jewish Concepts.* New York: Hebrew, 1964.

Blenkinsopp, Joseph. *Treasures Old and New: Essays in the Theology of the Pentateuch.* Grand Rapids: Eerdmans, 2004.

Brockopp, Jonathan E. *The Cambridge Companion to Muhammad.* New York: Cambridge University Press, 2010.

Brown, Raymond Edward. *The Death of the Messiah: From Gethsemane to the Grave: A Commentary on the Passion Narratives in the Four Gospels. Vol. 1.* New York: Doubleday, 1994.

Bucaille, Maurice. *The Bible, the Quran and Science: The Holy Scriptures Examined in the Light of Modern Knowledge.* Indianapolis: American Trust, 1978.

Buenting, Joel. *The Problem of Hell a Philosophical Anthology.* Farnham, UK: Ashgate, 2010.

Bukhari, Muhammad ibn Isma il, and Muhammad Muhsin Khan. *Sahih Al-Bukhari: The Translation of the Meanings of Sahih Al-Bukhari: Arabic-English.* Riyadh-Saudi Arabia: Darussalam Pub. & Distr., 1997.

Camus, Albert. *The Stranger.* Translated by Matthew Ward. New York: Vintage International, 1989.

Cartledge, Paul. *Democritus.* New York: Routledge, 1999.

Cicero, Marcus Tullius. *De Natura Deorum* [in Latin]. Edited by Arthur Stanley Pease. Cambridge: Harvard University Press, 1955.

———. *The Nature of the Gods; and, on Divination.* Amherst, NY: Prometheus, 1997.

Clark, Ralph W. "The Evidential Value of Religious Experiences." *International Journal for Philosophy of Religion* 16, no. 3 (1984) 189–202.

Coggins, R. J. *Introducing the Old Testament.* Oxford: Oxford University Press, 2001.

Copleston, Frederick Charles. *Aquinas.* London: Penguin, 1961.

Craig, William Lane. *The Cosmological Argument from Plato to Leibniz.* New York: Barnes & Noble, 1980.

———. *The Kalam Cosmological Argument.* New York: Barnes & Noble, 1979.

Craig, William Lane, Antony Flew, and Stan W. Wallace. *Does God Exist? The Craig-Flew Debate.* Aldershot, UK: Ashgate, 2003.

Crone, Patricia, and M. A. Cook. *Hagarism: The Making of the Islamic World.* Cambridge: Cambridge University Press, 1977.

Darwin, Charles. *On the Origin of Species: A Facsimile of the First Edition.* Cambridge: Harvard University Press, 1964.

———. *On the Origin of Species by Means of Natural Selection; or, the Preservation of Favoured Races in the Struggle for Life.* London: Watts, 1950.

Davis, Stephen T. *God, Reason and Theistic Proofs.* Edinburgh: Edinburgh University Press, 1997.

Dawe, Alan H. *The God Franchise: A Theory of Everything.* Auckland, NZ: Life Magic, 2012.

Dawkins, Richard. *The Blind Watchmaker.* Harlow, UK: Longman Scientific & Technical, 1986.

———. *Climbing Mount Improbable.* New York: Norton, 1996.

———. *The God Delusion.* Boston: Houghton Mifflin, 2006.

———. *The Selfish Gene.* Oxford: Oxford University Press, 1989.

Dennett, Daniel Clement. *Breaking the Spell: Religion as a Natural Phenomenon*. New York: Penguin, 2007.
———. *Consciousness Explained*. Boston: Little, Brown and Co., 1991.
———. *Darwin's Dangerous Idea: Evolution and the Meanings of Life*. New York: Simon & Schuster, 1995.
Dostoyevsky, Fyodor. *The Brothers Karamazov*. Translated by Constance Garnett. New York: Modern Library, 1996.
El-Awa, Salwa M. S. *Textual Relations in the Quran: Relevance, Coherence and Structure*. London: Routledge, 2006.
Elliott, Calvin. *Usury; a Scriptural, Ethical and Economic View*. Millersburg, OH: Anti-Usury League, 1902.
Everitt, Nicholas. *The Non-Existence of God*. London: Routledge, 2004.
Fakhry, Majid. *A History of Islamic Philosophy*. New York: Columbia University Press, 1970.
Fellows, Otis. *From Voltaire to La Nouvelle Critique: Problems and Personalities*. Geneva: Droz, 1970.
Flew, Antony. *God & Philosophy*. New York: Harcourt, Brace & World, 1966.
Freud, Sigmund. *The Ego and the Id*. New York: Norton, 1961.
———. *The Future of an Illusion*. New York: Liveright, 1928.
Gale, Barry G. *Evolution without Evidence: Charles Darwin and the Origin of Species*. Albuquerque: University of New Mexico Press, 1982.
Gilson, Etienne. *The Christian Philosophy of St. Thomas Aquinas. With a Catalog of St. Thomas's Works*. New York: Random House, 1956.
Greenberger, Robert. *Suicide Bombers*. New York: Rosen, 2007.
Gülen, Fethullah. *Prophet Muhammad: Aspects of His Life*. 2 vols. Fairfax, VA: Fountain, 2000.
———. "Terror and Suicide Attacks." Lanham, MD: Tughra, 2008.
Gutting, Gary. *Religious Belief and Religious Skepticism*. Notre Dame, IN: University of Notre Dame Press, 1982.
Haeckel, Ernst. *The Evolution of Man: A Popular Exposition of the Principal Points of Human Ontogeny and Phylogeny. From the German of Ernst Haeckel*. New York: Appleton, 1897.
Hall, George M. *The Ingenious Mind of Nature: Deciphering the Patterns of Man, Society, and the Universe*. New York: Plenum, 1997.
Hammond, Robert. *The Philosophy of Alfarabi and Its Influence on Medieval Thought*. New York: Hobson, 1947.
Hanioglu, M. Sükrü. "Bir siyasal düşünür olarak Doktor Abdullah Cevdet ve dönemi." [Turkish]. PhD diss., İstanbul Üniversitesi, 1981.
Bir Siyasi Dusunur Olarak Dr Abdullah Cevded Ve Donemi [in Turkish]. Istanbul: ?, ????.
Harris, Sam. *The Moral Landscape*. London: Bantam, 2010.
Haught, James A. *2000 Years of Disbelief: Famous People with the Courage to Doubt*. Amherst, NY: Prometheus, 1996.
Haylamaz, Reşit. *GöNüL Tahtımızın EşSiz Sultani: Efendimiz (Sallallahu Aleyhi Ve Sellem)*. [in Translated from Turkish.]. Istanbul: Muştu, 2008.
Hick, John, ed. *The Existence of God*. New York: Macmillan, 1964.
Hitchens, Christopher. *God Is Not Great: How Religion Poisons Everything*. New York: Twelve, 2007.

Holland, R. F. "The Miraculous." *American Philosophical Quarterly* 2, no. 1 (1965) 43–51.

Hume, David. *Dialogues Concerning Natural Religion*. Edited by Norman Kemp Smith. Indianapolis: Bobbs-Merrill, 1947.

———. *Enquiries Concerning Human Understanding, and Concerning the Principles of Morals*. Edited by Lewis Amherst Selby-Bigge and P. H. Nidditch. Oxford: Clarendon, 1975.

Husik, Isaac. *A History of Mediaeval Jewish Philosophy*. New York: Macmillan, 1916.

James, William. *The Varieties of Religious Experience: A Study in Human Nature*. New York: Modern Library, 1994.

Kant, Immanuel. *Critique of Practical Reason*. New York: Liberal Arts, 1956.

———. *Critique of Pure Reason*. Translated by Norman Kemp Smith. London: Macmillan, 1956.

———. *The Critique of Pure Reason; The Critique of Practical Reason, and Other Ethical Treatises; The Critique of Judgement*. Translated by J. M. D. Meiklejohn, Thomas Kingsmill Abbott, W. Hastie, James Creed Meredith. Chicago: Encyclopedia Britannica, 1990.

Kindi, Ya qub Ibn-Ishaq al, and Alfred L. Ivry. *Al-Kindi's Metaphysics: A Translation of Ya`Qub Ibn-Ishaq Al-Kindi's Treatise "On First Philosophy" (Fi Al-Falsafah Al-Ula)* [in Arabic]. Albany, NY: State University of New York Press, 1974.

Klein, David Ballin. *A History of Scientific Psychology: Its Origins and Philosophical Backgrounds*. New York: Basic, 1970.

Kropotkin, Petr Alekseevich. *Mutual Aid: A Factor of Evolution*. Mineola, NY: Dover, 2006.

Küng, Hans. *Does God Exist? An Answer for Today*. Garden City, NY: Doubleday, 1980.

Kurtz, Paul. "Darwin Re-Crucified: Why Are So Many Afraid of Naturalism?" *Free Inquiry* 18.2 (1998) 15–17.

Kvanvig, Jonathan L. *The Problem of Hell*. New York: Oxford University Press, 1993.

Lamarck, Jean Baptiste Pierre Antoine de Monet. *Zoological Philosophy: An Exposition with Regard to the Natural History of Animals*. Translated by Hugh Samuel Roger Elliott. New York: Hafner, 1963.

Leucippus, Democritus, and C. C. W. Taylor. *The Atomists, Leucippus and Democritus: Fragments: A Text and Translation with a Commentary* [in Greek text with English translation and commentary]. Toronto: University of Toronto Press, 1999.

Lewis, Wade V. *One Planet, Many Worlds*. Boston: Christopher, 1949.

Lindberg, David C., and Ronald L. Numbers. *When Science & Christianity Meet*. Chicago: University of Chicago Press, 2003.

Lings, Martin. *Muhammad: His Life Based on the Earliest Sources*. New York: Inner Traditions International, 1983.

Mackie, J. L. *The Miracle of Theism: Arguments for and against the Existence of God*. Oxford: Clarendon, 1982.

Maimonides, Moses. *Maimonides, the Guide of the Perplexed*. London: East and West Library, 1952.

Martin, Michael. *Atheism: A Philosophical Justification*. Philadelphia: Temple University Press, 1990.

Matson, Wallace I. *The Existence of God*. Ithaca, NY: Cornell University Press, 1965.

Maudoodi, Syed Abul Ala, and Zafar Ishaq Ansari. *Towards Understanding the Quran*. Leicester, UK: Islamic Foundation, 1988.

McGrath, Alister E. *Christian Theology: An Introduction*. Oxford: Blackwell, 1994.
Mill, John Stuart. *Nature, the Utility of Religion, and Theism*. London: Longmans, Green, Reader, and Dyer, 1874.
———. *A System of Logic, Ratiocinative and Inductive: Being a Connected View of the Principles of Evidence and the Methods of Scientific Investigation*. London: Longman, Green, 1930.
Miller, Kenneth R. *Only a Theory: Evolution and the Battle for America's Soul*. New York: Viking Penguin, 2008.
Morewedge, Parviz, and Avicenna. *The Metaphysica of Avicenna (Ibn Sìna): A Critical Translation-Commentary and Analysis of the Fundamental Arguments in Avicenna's Metaphysica in the Danish Nama-I 'Alai (the Book of Scientific Knowledge)*. New York: Columbia University Press, 1973.
Mürsel, Safa. *Bediüzzaman Said Nursi Ve Devlet Felsefesi* [in Turkish]. Istanbul: Yeni Asya Yayinlari, 1976.
Nasr, Seyyed Hossein. *An Introduction to Islamic Cosmological Doctrines: Conceptions of Nature and Methods Used for Its Study by the Ikhwan Al-Safa, Al-Biruni, and Ibn Sina*. Cambridge: Belknap Press of Harvard University Press, 1964.
Newton, Isaac. *Newton's Philosophy of Nature: Selections from His Writings*. New York: Hafner, 1953.
Nietzsche, Friedrich Wilhelm, Walter Arnold Kaufmann, and R. J. Hollingdale. *The Will to Power*. New York: Vintage, 1968.
Nietzsche, Friedrich Wilhelm, Walter Arnold Kaufmann, and Friedrich Wilhelm Nietzsche. *On the Genealogy of Morals*. New York: Vintage, 1967.
Nirenstein, Samuel. *The Problem of the Existence of God in Maimonides Alanus and Averroes*. Philadelphia: JPS, 1924.
Nursi, Said. *Al-Mathnawi Al-Nuri* [in Turkish]. Istanbul: Nesil, 2004.
———. *The Flashes* [in Turkish]. İstanbul: Nesil 2004.
———. *The Letters* [in Turkish]. İstanbul: Nesil, 2004.
———. *The Rays* [in Turkish]. İstanbul: Nesil, 2004.
———. *Risale-i Nur Külliyati 1* [in Turkish]. Istanbul: Nesil, 1994.
———. *Risale-i Nur Külliyati 2* [in Turkish]. Istanbul: Nesil, 2004.
———. *The Words* [in Turkish]. Istanbul: Nesil, 2005.
O'Callaghan, Jeremiah. *Usury, or Interest: Proved to Be Repugnanat to the Divine and Ecclesiastical Laws, and Destructive to Civil Society*. New York: published by the author, 1824.
O'Grady, Patricia F. *Thales of Miletus: The Beginnings of Western Science and Philosophy*. Aldershot, UK: Ashgate, 2002.
O'Leary, De Lacy. *Arabia before Muhammad*. London: Dutton, 1927.
Packard, A. S. *Lamarck, the Founder of Evolution: His Life and Work*. New York: Longman, Green, and co., 1901.
Paley, William. *Natural Theology, or, Evidences of the Existence and Attributes of the Deity Collected from the Appearances of Nature*. Albany, NY: Printed for Daniel & Samuel Whiting, 1803.
———. *Natural Theology; Selections*. Indianapolis: Bobbs-Merrill, 1963.
Passmore, John Arthur. *Hume's Intentions*. Cambridge: Cambridge University Press, 1952.
Peterson, Michael L. *Reason and Religious Belief: An Introduction to the Philosophy of Religion*. New York: Oxford University Press, 1991.

Plantinga, Alvin, and James F. Sennett. *The Analytic Theist: An Alvin Plantinga Reader.* Grand Rapids: Eerdmans, 1998.

Plato. *The Laws.* Edited by Taylor A. E. London; New York: Dutton, 1960.

Prideaux, Humphrey. *The True Nature of Imposture Fully Displayed in the Life of Mahomet with a Discourse Annexed for the Vindicating of Christianity from This Charge.* London: Printed for William Rogers, 1697.

Quine, W. V. *Ontological Relativity, and Other Essays.* New York: Columbia University Press, 1969.

———. *Theories and Things.* Cambridge: Harvard University Press, 1981.

Ratzsch, Del. "Teleological Arguments for God's Existence." In *Stanford Encyclopedia of Philosophy* (1997). https://stanford.library.sydney.edu.au/archives/sum2007/entries/teleological-arguments/.

Riedl, John O. *Maimonides and Scholasticism.* Baltimore, MD: n.p., 1936.

Ross, W. D. *Aristotle.* London: Methuen, 1949.

Rushdie, Salman. *The Satanic Verses.* New York: Viking, 1989.

Russell, Bertrand. *A History of Western Philosophy.* New York: Simon and Schuster, 1972.

Sa`adia ben, Joseph, and Samuel Rosenblatt. *The Book of Beliefs and Opinions.* New Haven: Yale University Press, 1948.

Şahiner, Necmeddin. *Bilinmeyen Taraflariyla Bediüzzaman Said Nursi: Kronolojik Hayati* [in Turkish]. Istanbul: Nesil, 1997.

Saritoprak, Z. "Said Nursi on Muslim-Christian Relations Leading to World Peace." *Islam and Christian-Muslim Relations* 19, no. 1 (2008) 25–37.

Sartre, Jean-Paul. *Existentialism and Humanism.* London: Methuen, 2007.

Sartre, Jean-Paul, and Robert Denoon Cumming. *The Philosophy of Jean-Paul Sartre.* New York: Random House, 1965.

Schopenhauer, Arthur. *The World as Will and Representation.* New York: Dover, 1966.

Simmons, Geoffrey S. *What Darwin Didn't Know.* Eugene, OR: Harvest House, 2004.

Simpson, J. A., E. S. C. Weiner, eds. *The Oxford English Dictionary.* Oxford: Clarendon, 1989.

Singer, Charles Joseph. *A Short History of Science to the Nineteenth Century.* Oxford: Clarendon, 1941.

Spetner, Lee M. *Not by Chance! Shattering the Modern Theory of Evolution.* Brooklyn, NY: Judaica, 1997.

Spinoza, Benedictus de, and A. G. Wernham. *The Political Works: The Tractatus Theologico-Politicus in Part, and the Tracatatus Politicus in Full.* Oxford: Clarendon, 1958.

Stewart, Jon. *Kierkegaard and Existentialism.* Farnham, UK: Ashgate, 2011.

Strauss, Leo. *Philosophy and Law: Essays toward the Understanding of Maimonides and His Predecessors.* Philadelphia: Jewish Publication Society, 1987.

Swinburne, Richard. *The Existence of God.* Oxford: Clarendon, 1979.

———. *Miracles.* London: Macmillan, 1989.

———. *Simplicity as Evidence of Truth.* Milwaukee: Marquette University Press, 1997.

Theophanes, Cyril A. Mango, Roger Scott, and Geoffrey Greatrex. *The Chronicle of Theophanes Confessor: Byzantine and near Eastern History, Ad 284–813* Oxford: Clarendon, 1997.

Thielicke, Helmut. *Nihilism; Its Origin and Nature, with a Christian Answer.* New York: Schocken, 1969.

Tolstoy, Leo. *Itiraflarim* [in Turkish]. Istanbul: Lacivert Yayinlari, 2008.
Tolstoy, Leo. *A Confession and Other Religious Writings*. Translated by and Jane Kentish. Harmondsworth, UK: Viking Penguin, 1987.
Turgenev, Ivan Sergeevich. *Fathers and Sons*. New York: Modern Library, 1950.
Turner, Colin, and Hasan Horkuc. *Said Nursi*. London: I. B. Tauris 2009.
Vahide, Şükran. *Bediüzzaman Said Nursi: The Author of the Risale-I Nur*. Cağaloğlu, Istanbul: Sözler, 2000.
Vahide, Şükran, and Ibrahim M. Abu-Rabi, eds. *Islam in Modern Turkey an Intellectual Biography of Bediuzzaman Said Nursi*. Ithica, NY: State University of New York Press, 2005.
Voltaire. *A Philosophical Dictionary*. Paris: DuMont, 1901.
Wādi'ī, Muqbil ibn Hadi. *Rijal Al-Hakim Fi Al-Mustadrak* [in Arabic]. al-Qahirah: Dar al-Haramayn, 1998.
Wagner, Walter H. *Opening the Qur'an: Introducing Islam's Holy Book*. Notre Dame, IN: University of Notre Dame Press, 2008.
Wansbrough, John E. *Quranic Studies: Sources and Methods of Scriptural Interpretation*. Oxford: Oxford University Press, 1977.
Webster, Donald Everett. *The Turkey of Ataturk: Social Process in the Turkish Reformation*. 1939.
Wolfson, Harry Austryn. "Notes on Proofs of the Existence of God in Jewish Philosophy." *Hebrew Union College Annual I*, 575–96. Cincinnati: 1924.
Xenophon. *The Memorable Thoughts of Socrates*. Translated by Morris B. Kaplan. New York: Kaplan, 2009.
Yahya, Harun. *Atlas of Creation*. Kuala Lumpur: Malaysia Saba Islamic Media, 2011.
Yıldırım, Suat. *Kur'an-I Hakim Ve Meali* [in Turkish]. Istanbul: 1998.

Index

Abbasids, 13
Abdullah al-Ansari, 109
Abraham, 5, 100, 105, 114, 132, 146, 162, 204, 223, 230
Abraham ibn Daud, 29
Abrahamic religions, xiv, 1, 42, 112, 198, 212
Abū Dawūd, 106, 206
Abu Tālib, 108–9, 113, 236
Abunaser, 18
Adam, 104, 111, 125, 140, 147, 152, 154, 160, 168, 204, 230
Adelphus, 120
adultery, 109, 174, 225
Africa, 177
Afyon, 52, 202
agnosticism, 31
Ahmadzay, 176
Aims, 236
Aisha, 101, 106, 121, 221
Alexandre du Pont, 120, 243
Ali Ünal, xi
Allah, 2–7, 22–24, 56, 65, 67, 70, 105–7, 113, 123, 128, 132–33, 135, 137–38, 140–41, 143, 146–47, 151–55, 160–61, 168, 176–77, 180, 187, 192, 209, 215–16, 218, 221, 223–25, 227, 230–31, 237, 239, 243, 245
Alpharabius, 18, 236
al-'Alīm, 67, 145–47, 154, 215, 236
Al-Andalus, 13
al-Fārābī, xi, xiv, 5, 7, 13, 14, 16, 18–25, 31, 63, 132, 208–9, 211, 234, 236
al-Ghazzālī, xiv, 5, 7, 13, 16, 21–22, 24–25, 27, 56, 63, 96, 211, 235–36, 240
al-' Ishārāt al-I'jāz, 48, 53, 62, 135–36, 144, 237
al-Kindī, xiv, 13, 17–18, 22, 24, 119–21, 209, 241
al-Mathnawī, 49, 59, 68, 70, 96, 108, 132, 135, 149, 169–72, 202, 206, 210, 213–14, 236, 247
al-sabab al-awwal, 19–20
American Independence Movement, 36
anā, xvi, 43, 54–55, 57, 70, 207, 237
analytic, 11, 85, 248
Anatolia, 43–44, 46, 49, 59, 140, 202
Ancient Greek, xii, xv, 1–3, 5, 15, 18, 33, 48, 64–65, 70, 72, 164, 201, 208
Ankara, 61
apex, 2
Aphrodite, 2
Arabs, 5, 13, 17, 109, 113, 120, 161, 243
Arabian Peninsula, 5–6, 108, 134
Aramaic, 4
Archbishop of Canterbury, 8
ARE, 99–100, 103, 115–19, 129, 205
arguments from contingency, 15, 19, 31, 210
arguments from miracles, xv, 1, 12, 40, 115, 119, 132, 155–56, 159, 203, 211
arguments from religious experience, xv, xvi
Aristotelian, 15, 17, 20, 24, 26, 29, 238

Aristotle, xiii, 2–3, 13–15, 17, 20–23, 28–31, 33–34, 72, 83, 91, 208–9, 243, 248
Ash'arite, 21, 23, 211, 237
Ashqar, 2–3, 6, 65, 70, 243
assumptions, xvi, 11, 83, 90, 154
astrology, 109, 241
Atheism, i, iii, iv, vii, xii, xiv, xv, xvi, 1–44, 46, 48, 50, 52, 54, 58, 60–62, 66, 68, 70–72, 74, 76, 78–80, 82, 84, 86, 88, 90, 92, 94, 96, 100, 102, 104, 106, 108, 110, 112, 114, 116, 118, 120, 122, 124, 126, 128, 130, 132, 134, 136, 138, 140, 142, 144, 146, 148, 150, 152, 154, 156, 158, 160, 162, 166, 168, 170, 172, 174–176, 178–180, 182, 184, 186, 188, 190, 192, 194–198, 201–2, 204, 206–8, 210, 212, 246
Athene, 2
Augustine, 3, 29, 243
Austria, 170
Averroes, xiv, 16, 22, 247
Avicenna, xiv, 16, 20, 247
a' wjadathu al-asbāb, xvi, 20, 237
Ayāt al Kübra, 237
Ayer, xiii

Bertrand Russell, xii, 8, 202
bedrock, xv, 155
book of universe, xvi, 43, 53, 59
blessed, 3, 110, 113, 124, 147, 201, 233
Boyle, 4
Berkeley, xiii, 4, 14
Bestower of Faith, 6
Baghdad, 13, 21
Bonaventura, 14
Book X of the *Laws*, 14
Bediüzzaman, 213, 243
Balkan Journey, 47
British, 47, 62, 131, 151
Behe, 71, 75–76, 96, 244
Bacon, xiii, 71, 83–84
Bukhārī, 101, 108–9, 111, 155, 206, 244
Battle of Trenches, 109
Brahman, 116, 119
Battle of *Uḥud*, 230
bayān, 135, 138, 237
Blaise Pascal, 198

Critique of Pure Reason, 11
Christian, xii, xiv, xv, 3, 5, 24, 29–30, 39–40, 48, 61, 83, 91, 113, 115, 119–21, 162, 175, 181, 185, 195, 211–12, 238, 240, 245, 247–48
cosmological argument, xiv, 9, 12–15, 17, 19, 22, 25–33, 55, 64, 165, 211, 244
Craig, xiv, 9, 12, 15, 17, 22, 26–31, 34, 164–67, 173, 177, 198, 211, 244
Creator, xiv, xvi, 1, 6–7, 14, 17, 25, 36, 40–41, 53–54, 56–58, 71, 73–74, 80–84, 89–90, 94–96, 145, 149–50, 167, 169–70, 192–93, 197, 209–10, 216, 218, 235, 239
chance, 65–66, 72–75, 93, 95–96, 180, 196, 202, 248
counterarguments, xv, 129–30
Chapter, xv, xvi, 1, 3, 8, 13, 15, 30, 38, 41, 43, 53, 62, 86, 91, 95, 97–99, 107, 114–15, 123–24, 129–30, 132, 134–35, 137, 140, 144, 146, 145, 153, 159, 163–64, 167, 169, 175, 181, 193, 198, 201, 203, 205–7, 211
criticisms, xv, xvi, 1, 8, 21, 63, 68, 91, 93, 99, 115, 117, 119, 121, 130, 132, 134, 148
causes as creator, xvi
conscience, vii, xvi, 1, 42, 59, 132, 144, 164–65, 167, 169–71, 173, 175, 177, 179, 181, 183, 185, 187, 189–91, 193, 195–99, 201, 206, 241
Concept of God, 1–2, 4–5, 11, 24, 165, 199
celestial, 2,19, 80
Christ, 3, 154
creation, xvi, 2, 17–18, 22–26, 39, 49, 53–58, 64, 71–72, 75, 77, 81–82, 91, 93, 96, 107, 142, 145, 147, 167–68, 183–84, 186–87, 193, 202, 209–10, 217, 237, 249
consciousness, 2, 38, 78, 86, 125, 136, 158, 169, 190, 245

causality, 4, 12, 25–26, 32–33, 38, 41, 56
Cartesian philosophy, 8
cosmos, 12, 24, 55, 64, 132–33, 142, 168, 201–2, 208
caliph, 13, 16, 62, 236
Callippus, 15
Cordoba, 22
Cleanthes, 32–33, 35, 60, 66, 68
Constitutional Revolution, 45
Court Martial, 46
Nutuk, 46, 240
Colonies, 47, 131
Comte, 49–50, 59, 202
Caliphate, 50
Cicero, 14, 65–66, 244
complexity, 75
catapult,
conflict, 25, 39, 46, 48, 69, 78, 96, 140, 150–51, 167, 175, 177, 181
clockwork universe theory, 84
Climbing Mount Improbable, 94, 244
cranes, 95
Cyprus, 108, 232
Constantinople, 5, 232
confederates,
Crusades, 120
comprehensiveness, 133, 138–39, 163, 205–6, 228–29
Coincidence, 75, 88, 158
Calamities, 68, 182, 184, 199
contrast, 5, 16, 20, 40, 54, 69, 94, 111, 117, 149–50, 187
Camus, 196–97, 244

David Hume, xiii, 8, 32, 182
determine, xv, xvi, 190
defense, 21, 25, 39, 42, 46, 64, 83, 93, 96, 108, 126, 133, 150, 166, 176, 189, 200, 204, 211–12
disbelief, xvi, 16, 95, 133, 188, 190, 208, 245
design argument, xvi, 33–37, 42, 64–65, 68, 72, 95, 99, 132, 169, 177, 201–3
Darwin, 37, 42, 49, 71, 75–76, 78–80, 84, 91–94, 96, 169, 202, 244–246, 248
Darwinian, xvi, 91–93, 96, 112, 169
deity, xvi, 5–6, 34–35, 40, 60, 64–65, 68, 82–84, 132, 155–56, 164, 169, 171, 173, 180, 193, 196, 203, 206–7, 210–11, 247
divine existence, 2
demiurge, 2, 64, 72
Deism, 4
Descartes, xiii, 4, 8, 10–11, 14, 41
Dialogues Concerning Natural Religion, 32–33, 35, 65, 68–70, 96, 246
Demea, 32–33, 60
Dostoyevsky, 39–40, 178, 196–97, 245
Divān-ı Harb-i Örfî, 46, 237
Damascus, 13, 46–47, 161, 210, 213, 241
Damascus Sermon, 46, 47, 210, 213
Doctrine, xiv, 5, 16, 21, 48, 59, 100, 153, 189
Denizli, 51–52, 202
DNA, 75
Darwin's Black Box, 75–76, 244
Democritus, 71–72, 83, 244, 246
The Descent of Man, 92
Dennett, 95, 169, 175, 190, 202, 245
Deuteronomy, 114
Davis, 99, 102–3, 116–17, 119, 244
Dharmakaya, 116
Divine names of God, 145
Dilemma, 164, 166, 173, 181–82, 186, 188
deterrent, 185–186
Determinism, 16, 189–91, 199
Deeper Blue, 190

Existence, xiii, xv, xvi, 1–2, 4, 8–15, 17, 19–21, 23–36, 38–42, 50, 53–56, 58–59, 64–65, 67–68, 70–75, 83–89, 91–100, 102, 107, 112, 115–19, 124–25, 129–33, 148, 152, 155–59, 162–73, 179–89, 192–93, 196–203, 203–10, 212, 234–35, 245–49
eternal, xiv, 3, 5, 22, 28, 34, 39, 67, 72, 82–83, 108, 126, 175, 184, 188, 192, 197, 217–18
extension, 1
emotions, 2, 4, 151, 170, 190
enmity, 2, 47
Enlightenment, 4, 50, 80, 83, 194

Empiricist, 4
Everitt, 8–12, 91, 93–94, 100, 133, 157–59, 167–68, 173, 245
Eudoxus, 15
ex nihilo, 17, 91, 167
essence/existence distinction, 20
Epicurus, 35–36, 71, 182
Epicurean Problem, 36
evil, xv, 35–36, 39, 42, 68, 104, 110, 120, 151, 164, 167, 175–78, 182–85, 187–88, 193, 196–97, 199, 224, 240
Epistles of Light, xi, 44, 200
exegesis, 48, 50, 241
Eskişehir, 51, 202
Evolution, 37, 42, 66, 70, 72, 75–76, 78–79, 91–96, 169, 244–48
Egyptian, 150, 162, 240
Embrico of Mainz, 120
eloquence, 48, 133–34, 159, 161, 163, 205, 208, 228, 237
exposition, vii, viii, 18, 53, 92, 134–35, 138, 159, 206, 228, 229, 232, 237, 245–46
The Euthyphro Dilemma, 181–82
Euthyphro, 164, 181–82

fıṭrat-ı bashar, xvi, 237
First Cause, 12, 19–21, 24, 28, 30, 72, 83
Freud, 4, 116–17, 168–69, 204, 245
Father, 5, 13, 83, 100, 114, 116, 153, 181, 191, 227, 236
Flew, 8, 91, 133, 159, 166, 168, 173, 244–45
falsafa, 13, 15, 17–18, 20, 22, 60, 70
Fakr al-din al-Rāzī, 24
Five Ways of Thomas Aquinas, 29
Fine Tuning of the Universe, 34
French Revolution, 36
Free Will, 16, 25, 39, 128, 164, 189–92, 199, 209, 238–39
Fathers and Sons, 40, 249
al-Fard, 67, 155
fallacy, 78, 95
Family of Imran, 106, 187
FGM, 175, 178
Fethullah Gülen, 177, 245

Gottfried Leibniz, xiii
George Berkeley, xiii, 4
Voltaire, xiii, 71, 84, 156, 159, 245, 249
God, iv, vii, xii, xiv, xv, xvi, 1–17, 19–26, 28–42, 50–51, 53–60, 64–71, 74, 76, 78–80, 82–85, 87, 91–108, 111–19, 122, 124–25, 127–33, 136–37, 140, 145–48, 150–60, 163–75, 178–201, 203–12, 215–19, 224, 237–39, 241, 243–49
Gibraltar, 13
Guttman, 26
Gilson, 30–31, 245
German, xiii, 37, 110, 160, 170, 191, 245
Gladstone, 47, 62, 131
Green Crescent Society, 49
al-Ghafur, 67, 147, 187, 217
al-Ghani, 67, 150, 184, 217
Gospels, 91, 98, 101, 132, 152, 180, 244
Gabriel, 101, 116, 118, 130, 230
Genesis , 91, 114
Gutting, 118–119, 245
Gautier de Compiegne, 99, 120
Guibert of Nogent, 120
Gülen, 110, 122, 177, 245

holy, xiv, 5, 16, 91, 98, 100–102, 113–14, 123, 155, 159–60, 168, 177, 180, 189, 209, 241, 244, 249
hatred, 2, 143
Holy Spirit, 5
Hajj, 5
ḥashr, 6–7, 53, 145, 178–79, 204, 206
Hartshorne, 8, 10, 211
heretics, 21
Husik, 26–27, 29, 246
Haeckel, 37, 245
Hitchens, 39, 112, 175–78, 190, 245
Hunt, 39, 94
Hutuvat-i Sitte, 49, 213, 238
Horkuç, 58, 249
al-Haiy, 67
ḥadīth, 16, 53, 60, 105, 121, 126, 154–55, 237
harmony, 69, 71, 82, 88, 144, 146, 205, 215–16, 229
human primordial nature, 164, 169
Hamas, 176
Heisenberg, 191

Islam, iv, vii, xv, 2, 4–6, 13–14, 16–18, 21, 24, 43–44, 46, 48–51, 57, 61, 63, 67, 70, 106–7, 109, 119–21, 123, 128–29, 131, 133, 141, 145, 154, 161–62, 168, 176, 181, 184–85, 191, 204, 215–219, 225–27, 230–31, 236–37, 239–40, 243, 248–49
Islamic, iv, xiv, 3, 5–6, 13, 15–16, 18, 20–22, 24–26, 29, 46–52, 54, 57, 60–62, 96, 98–99, 106, 109, 130, 132, 142, 153, 167, 177, 181–82, 185, 188, 200–201, 204, 211, 222, 231, 236, 238–41, 243–47, 249
Ibn Sina, xiv, 5, 8, 13–14, 16, 20–25, 31, 208–9, 211, 234
Ibn Rushd, xiv, 5, 13, 16, 22–25, 235
identify, xv
iqtaẓathu al-ṭabīʿ ah, xvi, 202, 238
idea, xiii, xvi, 2, 11, 16, 36, 42, 45, 57, 64–65, 69–70, 74, 77–78, 80–84, 88–89, 92, 96, 117, 120, 157, 167, 169, 190, 194, 198, 201–2, 245
Incoherence of Incoherence, 23, 25, 238
Incorporeal, 3, 19, 28
intelligence, 3, 7, 14–15, 25, 35, 38, 42, 58, 60, 65–66, 70, 78–79, 81, 88, 95, 104, 128, 138, 152, 165, 167, 171, 173, 179, 186, 190, 193, 198, 207
Ishmael, 5, 132, 223
idols, 5–6, 110, 130
Ibn Tufayl, 13, 16, 193
Iberian Peninsula, 13
Ibn Bajja, 16
Indian, 17, 151, 240
'*ibda*', 17, 56–57, 238
The Intentions of Philosophers, 21
Isogage of Prophecy, 23
Ibn Maymūn, 27
Ivan Fyodorovitch, 178
Ivan Turgenev, 40
Ittihad-i Muhammedi Cemiyeti, 46
Isra'illiyāt, 48, 238
Impossibility, 11, 25, 72–74, 76, 78–81, 95
Intelligent Design, 76
Isaiah, 101–2, 114
Israel, 113, 124, 153
irhāṣāt, 129, 232–33, 239
IBM, 190

John Locke, xiii, 4, 164
Jewish, xiv, xv, 2–3, 23–24, 26–27, 29–30, 39, 113, 160–62, 170, 212, 230, 238, 244, 246, 248–49
jihād, xvi, 239
Jesus, 4–6, 102, 105–6, 118, 132–33, 153–56, 158, 180, 196, 204, 211, 223, 230
jāhiliyyah, 5, 109, 239
justice, 7, 39, 50, 53, 114–15, 141, 145, 160, 178–80, 184–86, 188, 199
Jonathan Kvanvig, 185
Joel Buenting, 39, 244
Jethro, 100
Jonah, 104, 107, 223–24
John, xiii, 4, 36, 83, 113, 119, 157, 164, 182
Justice, 7, 39, 50, 53, 114–15, 141, 145, 160, 178–80, 184–86, 188, 199

Kant, xii, 4, 8, 10–11, 38, 66, 164–65, 168, 198, 246
kalām, xiv, 12–13, 17, 20–22, 24–27, 41, 58–59, 62, 148, 155, 181, 184, 209–11, 235, 239, 244
kalām cosmological argument, xiv, 13, 22, 26, 211, 244
kitāb-ı kāināt, xvi, 54, 239
knowledge, ix, 1–4, 7, 9, 20, 22, 24–25, 34, 44–45, 48–49, 54–55, 58–59, 61–61, 65, 69, 73, 78–79, 99, 103, 112, 120, 131, 134, 139, 142, 145–47, 154, 171–72, 192, 195, 200–202, 208–10, 215, 218, 226, 228, 244, 247
Kepler, 4, 191
Ka'bah, 5–6, 162, 239
kāfir, 15–16, 239
Khariji, 16, 239
Kurdistan, 43
Kostroma, 49
Kemalist, 50–51, 59, 62
Kurtz, 80, 84, 246
King Uzziah, 101

Khadījah, 122, 230
The Brothers Karamazov, 40, 178, 196–97, 245
Kasparov, 190

literature, xv, 2, 22, 24, 48, 106, 129–30
love, 2–3, 15, 47, 126, 131, 171–72, 178, 186, 194, 197, 236–37
laws of physics, 4, 84
Locke, xiii, 4, 14, 164
lost island, 9
Leibniz, xiii, 12, 14–15, 17, 22, 26–31, 244
Latin, xi, 18, 30–31, 39, 50, 52, 61, 120–121, 160, 213, 243–44
logic, 14, 60, 78, 81, 130, 157, 189, 193, 198, 202, 211, 236, 240, 247
Leninist, 176
Loren Eiseley, 196

Meditations, xiii, 10
Mackie, xiii, xiv, 32–35, 91–93, 133, 159, 173, 246
Muslim, xiv, xv, 7, 13–17, 20, 23–24, 26, 30, 39, 46, 61–63, 106–8, 115, 120–22, 144, 148, 152, 154, 169, 176, 206, 208–9, 211, 230, 236, 238, 240, 248
monotheism, xiv, 1–2, 132, 154, 161
moral, xiv, xv, 1, 11–12, 35, 38–40, 42, 100, 103–4, 110, 134, 144–45, 149–50, 155, 160, 164–69, 173–75, 178, 180–82, 185, 190, 194, 196–99, 201, 208, 211–12, 233, 245
moral obligation, xiv
Maimonides, xiv, 2–3, 14, 23, 27–29, 31, 246–48
meaning of life, xv, 39, 55, 70, 187, 200
moral arguments, xv, 42, 100, 164, 198, 201, 208
morality, vii, xv, xvi, 1, 4, 38–40, 42, 86, 149, 164–65, 167–69, 171, 173, 175, 177–79, 181, 183, 185, 187–91, 193, 195–97, 199
moral authority, 1, 174–75
ma'nà-i ismī, xvi
Marty, 3
ma'nà-i ḥarfī, xvi, 54, 239
Mecca, 5, 101, 110, 140–41, 146, 161–62, 221, 230–31, 236, 239–40
Muḥammad, 21, 125, 135, 141, 161, 222–23, 231, 233, 236–40, 244–47
Merciful, 6, 107, 126, 138, 148, 217, 241
Mary, 6, 102, 105–6, 119, 154
Malcolm, 8, 10
Monk Gaunilo, 8–9
maximal excellence, 11
Majid Fakhry, 13
mutakallimūn, xiv, 13, 15, 20, 132, 148, 240
motion, 14–15, 17–18, 23, 27–31, 33, 66, 126, 189
medieval, xiii, 15, 19, 21, 23, 26, 29, 236, 245
Muḥyiddin ibn Ārābī, 16, 240
Mu'tazili, 16, 25
Murji'ah, 16
Metaphysics, 14, 17–20, 33, 236, 243, 246
Mill, 35–36, 157, 182, 247
Moral Nihilism, 39, 194
magnum opus, xi, 44, 49
Mullah Fethullah, 44
Madrasat uz-Zahrā, 47, 239
Munāẓarāt, 45–46, 48, 213, 240
Muḥammadan Union for Muslim Unity, 46
Mount Ararat, 48
musabbib al-asbāb, 240
Miller, 76, 247
mousetrap, 76
Mackie, xii, xiv, 32, 35, 91, 93, 133, 159, 173, 246
Moses, 27, 41, 100, 102, 104–5, 114, 132, 153–55, 158, 162, 180, 204, 223, 230, 246
Muslim, xiv, xv, 7, 13–17, 20, 23–24, 26, 30, 39, 46, 61–63, 106–8, 115, 120–22, 144, 148, 152, 154, 169, 176, 206, 208–9, 211, 230, 236, 238, 240, 248
Mecca, 5, 101, 110, 140–41, 146, 161–62, 221, 230–31, 236, 239–40

Miracles, viii, xv, 1, 12, 40–42, 86, 99, 108–9, 111, 115, 119, 123–24, 127–128, 130, 132–33, 155–59, 163, 203, 205, 211, 232–33, 248
moaning of the trunk, 111
Monk Bakhira, 113
majūsis, 130, 239
Marxist, 176

Nursi, iii, iv, vii, viii, xi, xiv, xv, xvi, 1, 7, 14, 24–25, 43–64, 66–83, 85–91, 94–97, 99, 102, 107–19, 121–52, 154–155, 158–64, 167–76, 179–84, 186–89, 191–94, 196–213, 228–29, 232–33, 236–41, 243, 247–49
necessary being, xiv, 20–21, 24, 28–29, 210, 234–36
Nursian, xv, xvi, 54, 58, 63, 69, 74, 91, 95–96, 98–99, 117–18, 129, 167–68, 186, 193, 201, 203, 205, 209, 211–12
nubuwwah, vii, xvi, 7, 53, 59, 98, 145, 200, 203–4, 209–10, 240
Nesil Publication, xi
necessarily loving, 2
Newton, 4, 189–191, 247
Natural Religion, 4, 32–33, 35, 60, 65–66, 68–70, 96, 246
Nietzsche, 4, 40, 49, 195–96, 247
Neo-Platonic, 15, 21–22
necessary/possible distinction, 20
Necessary Being, xiv, 20–21, 24, 28–29, 210, 234–36
Nizām al- Mulk Madrasah, 21
Natural Theology, 14, 33–34, 66, 132, 247
nihil, 39
nothingness, 39–40, 91, 195–96
Nokta, 59
natural selection, 66, 70, 72, 78–79, 92–95
Night Journey and Descent, 101
nabī, 105, 240
Negus of Abyssinia, 109
Newton's Laws of Motion, 4, 189

Ottoman Empire, xi, xv, 43–46, 49–50, 62, 210, 213
Omnipresent, xiv, 3
Omnipotent, xiv, 3, 10–11, 35–37, 39, 116, 156, 184
Omniscient ,xiv, 3, 35, 37
origin of the universe, xv
objectives, xv
Outline, viii, xv, 99, 228, 234–35
ontological arguments, xv, 1, 8, 12
other-indicative, xvi, 55, 70, 149, 207–8, 239
On First Philosophy, 17–18, 246
Origin of Species, 37, 79, 92, 96, 244–45
organisms, 37, 68, 73–78, 94, 146, 202
Ockham's Razor, 89–90, 95
omens, 109

Plato, xiii, 2–3, 8, 12, 14–15, 17, 21–23, 26–31, 33, 36, 60, 64–65, 72, 78, 164, 181, 200, 208–9, 244, 248
philosophers, xiii, xiv, xv, 1, 5, 7–8, 12–15, 18, 20–22, 25–26, 29, 32, 34, 37, 41–42, 58–59, 62–63, 65, 71, 80, 83, 91, 96, 99, 110, 115, 119, 142, 152, 157–59, 194–96, 200–201, 208–11, 229, 236–37, 240, 243
pagan, xv, 5, 230
problem of evil and suffering, xv, 35, 36
problem of Hell, xv, 39, 164, 184–85, 244, 246
prophethood, vii, xvi, 7, 50–51, 53, 59, 98–99, 101, 103–5, 107–9, 111–113, 115, 117–21, 123–25, 127, 129–30, 132–33, 141, 145, 153, 155, 200, 203–5, 209–11, 232–33, 240
proof, iv, xvi, 9, 20–21, 23, 25–26, 28, 30–31, 42, 59, 63, 65, 87–90, 96, 98–99, 115–16, 118–19, 122, 132, 138, 152, 164–66, 169, 212, 228, 237
power, 1–2, 7, 29, 40, 57, 64, 66, 69, 71, 79, 81, 83, 85, 94, 102, 110, 114, 117, 121, 125, 127, 145, 150, 152, 161, 170, 191, 202, 206–7, 213, 216, 224, 236, 247

philosophy, xiii, xiv, xvi, 1, 3–4, 7–8, 13–22, 24–27, 29–30, 36, 38–39, 42, 48, 50, 52, 54–55, 58–63, 65–66, 70, 72, 74, 80, 83, 85–86, 92, 95, 97, 131–33, 148–51, 155–56, 159, 164–65, 167, 173, 181, 184–85, 195–96, 200–202, 205, 207–10, 229, 236, 238, 243–49
planetary movements, 2, 14
Prometheus, 2, 244–45
perfection, 2, 6, 10–11, 58, 104, 106, 168, 194
Plotinus, 2, 17
pagan, xv, 5, 230
process, 2, 50, 52, 68, 77, 79, 92, 96, 167, 169, 249
Plantinga, 8–9, 11–12, 85, 96, 211, 248
Proslogion, 8, 243
Psalms, 8, 102, 112, 223, 233
perfect island, 9, 41
predicate, 10–11
possible worlds, 10–11
posteriori, 12, 33, 35, 68
pagans, 12
pantheists, 12
Prophet Muḥammad, 141, 161, 222, 231, 233, 236–40, 245
peripatetic, 17
Principles of the Opinions, 19
Prime Motor, 28
Philo, 32–33, 35, 60, 66, 68
Passmore, 32, 247
Pope, 36
poor design, 37
Plantinga, 8–9, 11–12, 85, 96, 211, 248
Persian, 108, 140–41, 160
pharaoh, 100, 150
PKK, 176

Qur'an, vii, xi, xvi, 5–7, 16, 22–25, 46–51, 53–56, 59–60, 62, 69–70, 91, 98, 101, 103–7, 110, 112–13, 121, 123–24, 128, 130–55, 159–63, 168, 176–77, 180, 185–88, 192, 200–206, 209–12, 223–25, 233, 236, 238, 240, 243, 249
Qur'anic, 16, 22–25, 48–50, 53–54, 60, 107, 123, 137, 145, 147–48, 150–52, 159, 200, 209–10, 229
Qadī Iyāz, 106

Risale-i Nur, vii, xi, xv, 4, 7, 44, 49–50, 52–54, 57, 60–62, 72, 85, 94–96, 121, 130, 132–33, 135, 148, 168, 174, 193, 199–205, 208, 210–11, 213–14, 233, 247, 249
Roger Bacon, xiii
René Descartes, xiii, 4, 8, 10
Richard Swinburne, xiii, 102, 211
religion, iv, 1, 4–6, 26, 29, 32–33, 35–36, 39, 44, 48, 50–51, 55, 57, 60, 65–66, 68–70, 84, 96, 106, 115, 122, 128, 149, 151–53, 161–62, 164–65, 174–78, 181, 184, 190, 239, 241, 244–47
refute, xv, xvi, 8, 33, 37, 41, 80, 94, 96, 113, 120, 132, 159, 161–63, 167, 177, 202, 205
religious experience, xv, xvi, 12, 40, 42, 99–102, 115–17, 119, 124, 129, 203–3, 211, 243, 246
Republic of Turkey, 43, 50, 213
Risale-i Nur Külliyatı, xi, xv, 229
ruler, 1, 13, 60, 67, 69, 86, 88, 95, 110, 125, 179–80, 219, 222, 225, 231, 240
righteous, 3, 13, 16, 42, 105, 107, 128, 152, 174, 179–80, 186, 188, 217, 223
reason, xiii, 3–4, 7, 11–12, 19–20, 25, 32, 38–42, 45, 59, 66, 74, 81, 95, 99, 103, 112, 116–17, 119, 122–24, 126, 128, 133, 142, 156, 158, 165, 194, 197–198, 201–2, 204, 210–11, 234, 244, 246–47
revelations, vii, 3–4, 58, 98, 100, 131–33, 135, 137, 139, 141, 143, 145, 147, 149, 151–53, 155, 157, 159, 161, 163, 168, 203, 205, 210
resurrection, 7, 22, 50, 51, 53, 55, 67, 95, 106, 141, 145, 154, 160, 168, 178–80, 182, 195, 197, 204, 206, 241
Russell, xiii, 8, 202, 248

Ross, 15, 248
Republic, xi, xv, 23, 43, 50, 59, 61–62, 200, 210, 213
Riedl, 29, 248
Roman Catholic Church, 29
Rashdall, 38
Reality, 4, 8–10, 15, 38, 48, 85, 102–3, 119, 128, 138, 149, 181, 183, 209
Rhetoric, 14, 148
Russian, 48
Republican People's Party, 52, 61
Reşhalar, 59
Revelation, xvi, 4, 17, 25, 63, 84, 98, 102, 132–34, 140, 144–45, 153, 155, 160–61, 163, 193, 201, 203, 205, 209–11, 230, 241
rasūl, 105, 241
Roman, 29, 108, 120, 140–41, 241, 243
Ramon Marti, 120
Resurrection, 7, 22, 50–51, 53, 55, 67, 95, 106, 141, 145, 154, 160, 168, 178–80, 182, 195, 197, 204, 206, 241
Repentance, 138, 176, 186–87, 218

Saïd Nursi, 44–53, 55, 57–59, 61, 63, 131, 149, 164, 179, 201, 209, 212, 243, 247–249
Socrates, xiii, 3, 15, 64, 181, 208, 249
St Anselm, xiii, 3, 8–10, 41, 211
Saadia, xiv, 14, 26–27, 29
Sustainer, xiv, 7, 136, 145, 169, 197, 218
skeptics, xv, 39, 41, 103, 121, 124, 132, 163, 194, 204
self, xvi, 9–10, 14, 18, 20, 39, 43–44, 54–58, 75, 77, 80, 96, 101, 122, 128, 149, 155, 10, 186, 191, 193, 197, 207–8, 210, 217, 233, 235, 237, 240
self-referential, xvi, 43, 54–55, 149, 207–8, 240
self-creation, xvi, 77, 96, 210
scriptures, xvi, 42, 112, 113, 115, 131–32, 152, 155, 159–161, 173, 180, 193, 201, 203, 205–6, 233, 244
support, ix, xvi, 46–47, 76, 78, 87, 99, 111, 118, 148, 150–51, 155, 158
significance, 1, 41
source, xiv, 1–2, 4, 7, 16, 25, 29–31, 39–40, 73, 80, 121, 130, 139, 169–70, 172, 174–75, 177, 184, 196, 198, 216, 218, 220, 222, 229, 233
Supreme Being, 1–2, 38, 119, 132, 165
source of the universe, 2
sublime, 3, 151
Spinoza, 4, 14, 156, 248
Son, 5–6, 16, 24, 105, 108, 122, 125, 154
Sūrat al-'Ikhlās, 5
Sūrat al-Ḥashr, 6, 53
Sovereign, 6
Sūrat al-Nisā, 6
shunicorn, 10, 41
synthetic, 11, 179
Spain, 13, 16, 22, 24
Scotus, 14
Suarez, 14
self-moved, 14
Sunni schools, 16
Shi' a school, 16
Seville, 23
Strauss, 27, 248
Saint Augustine, 29
Summa Theologiæ, 29–31, 65, 243
Summa Contra Gentiles, 30, 243
Scottish, 32
summum bonum, 38, 165, 198
Siirt, 44
Sultan Abdulhamid II, 45
Second Constitution, 45
Surat al 'Alaq, 53
al-Samed, 67
skyhook, 94–95
soothsaying, 109, 163
Sawdā bint Zam'a, 121
suhuf, 132
style, 59–60, 62, 109, 135–37, 143, 163, 228–29, 241
Speech, 15, 19, 46, 106, 137, 206, 211, 239–40
Satan, 104, 143
Sartre, 173, 196–97, 248

Turkey, xi, xvi, 21, 43–44, 46, 50–52, 61–62, 131, 211, 213, 249
Turkish Republic, xi, 43, 50, 62, 210

Thomas Aquinas, xiii, 3, 8, 23, 29–30, 211, 245
theism, i, iii, iv, xiii, xiv, xv, xvi, 1–46, 48, 50, 52, 54, 56, 58, 60, 62, 64, 66, 68, 70, 72, 74, 76, 78, 80, 82, 84–86, 88, 90–94, 96, 100, 102, 104, 106, 108, 110, 112, 114–16, 118–20, 122, 124, 126, 128, 130, 132–34, 136, 138, 140, 142, 144, 146, 148, 150, 152, 154–56, 158–60, 162, 166, 168, 170, 172, 174, 176, 178, 180, 182, 184, 186, 188, 190, 192, 194, 196, 198, 200–204, 206–8, 210–12, 246–47
theologians, xiv, xv, 5, 13, 15, 39–40, 95–96, 115, 155, 183, 205
transcendent, 165, 194
timeless, 2
tyranny, 2
Tertullian, 3
theistic arguments, xv, 1, 12, 26, 33, 55, 173
teleological arguments, xv, 1, 64, 68, 83, 96, 248
theological non-cognitivism, xv, 192
tashakkala bi nafsihi, xvi, 77, 202, 241
Trinity, 3, 5, 29, 243
tawḥīd, 3, 5–7, 53, 145, 160, 204, 209, 212, 241
temporal regress, 15
telos, 33, 64
The Nature and Utility of Religion, 36, 247
Taylor, 18–21, 40, 72, 243, 246, 248
Thirty-First of March Incident, 46
The Words, 48–49, 51, 55, 57–59, 66, 69–70, 74, 85–86, 96, 114, 125, 128, 132–33, 135, 142, 149, 152, 160–61, 168, 172, 181, 191, 193, 202, 207, 213–14, 228, 236–237, 247
The Letters, 49, 51, 53, 60, 62, 107–8, 110–15, 122, 140, 149, 155, 159, 167, 175, 178, 183, 194, 198, 202, 208, 213–14, 247
The Flashes, 49, 51, 56–57, 60, 62, 68, 76, 83, 85, 96, 148, 170, 202, 213–14, 247
The Rays, 7, 46, 49, 51, 57, 61, 74–75. 85, 91, 96, 170–71, 174, 186–88, 202, 213–14, 247
Turner, ix, 53, 58, 149, 249
Tabiat Risalesi, 57, 202
Truthfulness, 4, 47, 103, 112, 130, 132–33, 138, 142, 152, 233, 241
Trustworthiness, 103–5, 130
tradition, xiii, xiv, 14, 16–18, 24–25, 29, 54, 83, 91, 105, 120, 130, 176–77, 201
Tirmidhī, 106
transformation, 99, 109–11, 130–32, 141, 243
Tolan, 119–20
Tamil Tigers, 176
Tribulations, 182, 184, 199

universe, xiv, xv, xvi, 1–2, 4, 14–15, 17, 19–20, 24–25, 27–28, 30, 32–34, 40–43, 53–59, 64–65, 68–72, 74, 80–84, 86–88, 91, 93–95, 99, 107, 112, 116, 125, 129, 132, 137, 142, 145, 147–49, 156, 158, 167–71, 180, 187, 189–91, 193, 196–97, 199–203, 205, 207–9, 219, 232, 239, 245
unmoved mover, 2, 14
uncreated matter, 2
al-Uzzā, 5, 236
unicorn, 9–10
Umayyads, 13
Uncaused Cause, 4, 25, 41
Urfa, 62
Ultimate Boeing 747 Gambit, 95
Usury, 143–44, 241, 245, 247
USSR, 150–51, 174, 178
Uncertainty Principle, 191
USA, 197

Vahide, 43–51, 61, 131, 249
Volga, 49
Voltaire, xiii, 71, 84, 156, 159, 245, 249
Virgin Mary, 102, 119
The Victory, 107

veridical, 99, 103, 119
Vedantic, 119

Wittgenstein, xiii
worship, 53, 143, 150, 167, 215, 224, 242
waḥy, vii, xvi, 98, 131–32, 201, 203, 205, 209–11, 241
wijdān, xvi, 132, 164, 169–70, 172, 201, 206, 210, 241
weaknesses, 2, 96
Wolfson, 26, 249
William Paley, 34, 66, 201
watchmaker analogy, 34
Wise, 10, 37, 54, 59–60, 67, 72, 135–136, 146–47, 151–52, 156, 160, 217, 223, 229, 233, 237
World War I, 46–47, 49, 212
Warsaw, 49
al-*Wāhid*, 67, 219
Welsh, 83
William Williams, 83
water-bags, 109
word-order, 48, 135, 228

Young Turks, 45–46

Zeus, 2, 116
Zeno, 3
Zamakshari, 49
Zaynab bint Jaḥsh, 122, 242
Zakāt, 143, 151, 242

www.ingramcontent.com/pod-product-compliance
Lightning Source LLC
Chambersburg PA
CBHW050342230426
43663CB00010B/1959
* 9 7 8 1 5 3 2 6 4 6 7 9 9 *